M000280955

WHO WILL GO

INTO THE SON TAY POW CAMP

TERRY BUCKLER SON TAY RAIDER

with Cliff Westbrook

FOREWORD BY COL ROGER DONLON, MEDAL OF HONOR

PALMETTO
PUBLISHING

Charleston, SC
www.PalmettoPublishing.com

WHO WILL GO

Copyright © 2020 by Who Will Go, LLC (Terry Buckler and Cliff Westbrook)

All rights reserved. No portion of this book may be reproduced, stored in a retrieval system, or transmitted in any form by any means–electronic, mechanical, photocopy, recording, or other–except for brief quotations in printed reviews, without prior permission of the author.

First Edition

Hardback ISBN: 978-1-64990-151-4
Paperback ISBN: 978-1-64990-150-7
eBook ISBN: 978-1-64990-149-1

Cover photos of Blueboy, Greenleaf, Redwine are Joint Contingency Task Group photos provided by LtCol Elliott "Bud" Sydnor, renovated by John Gargus.

Image 1: The model layout of the Son Tay POW camp, viewed from the southwest corner. The landing zone (LZ) is in the foreground

At the launch of the Son Tay Raid, Colonel Bull Simons said, "You are to let nothing—I repeat—*nothing* interfere with this operation. Our mission is to rescue prisoners, not to take prisoners." That is the core message of this book. This account of the operation is well sourced and documented. The authors illustrate how the brave men on the Son Tay Raid risked all. Scripture tells us, "There is no greater love than this: to lay down one's life for one's friend." Well done, Son Tay Raiders! And with one voice they said, "Let's go get 'em!"

Colonel James P. Fleming, US Air Force (retired)
Congressional Medal of Honor
Military Assistance Command, Vietnam—Studies and Observations Group

A great addition to the works on Special Operations conducted in Vietnam. Terry Buckler has provided a new and unique perspective on the November 1970 Son Tay Raid to rescue American POWs held in North Vietnam, told as only someone who was actually there could.

Rich Kolb
Editor of *Brutal Battles of Vietnam*
Former Publisher and Editor-in-Chief of VFW Magazine, 1989-2016

It is impossible to imagine what courage it took for young Terry Buckler to face the danger he describes in this well-written but far-too-humble memoir. It is unsung heroes like Buckler who keep America safe.

Jim Ferrell
Chairman and CEO, Ferrellgas

FOREWORD

THE SON TAY RAIDERS: fifty-six Special Forces Green Berets who volunteered for one of the most daring missions in military history! On November 21st, 1970—nearly fifty years ago—these brave soldiers struck deep inside North Vietnam with the goal of freeing fellow Americans, prisoners of war (POWs) who were tortured, beaten, and starved by their captors.

Many accounts of "the Raid" have been published, but the veterans who were actually there on the ground are not as well-known as they should be.

Who Will Go is the exciting first-hand account of the youngest Raider, Terry Buckler. From the secret planning, to the call for volunteers by Colonel Arthur "Bull" Simons (a legend in Special Forces), the author leads us on his first combat mission. Of the 500 men who volunteered, 109 were selected and only 56 actually participated in the Raid!

You will learn about the vigorous training demanded of Special Forces and the grueling preparations for the Raid in their secret locations. This candid saga can only be provided by someone who was actually there. Paired directly with the Commander of the Redwine Security Group throughout the Raid, Buckler was in the thick of the battle. It entailed furious firefights, eliminating many North Vietnamese enemy soldiers.

Studied by professionals and seldom surpassed in the annals of military history, the Son Tay Raid is a historic event that teaches us the all-important lesson of the value of *teamwork*. With underlying themes of family, faith, and the perennial fight for freedom, *Who Will Go* is far more than one man's autobiography—it is a testament to the fortitude of *all* the operators who risked their lives to send America's message to our POWs that we would do whatever it took to bring them home!

Those 27 minutes on the ground in North Vietnam would change the lives of POWs, giving them hope, strength, and the will to live. Those POWs and the Raid participants share their memories with you. The event also was a life-altering experience for Terry Buckler, the all-American farm boy from the heartland who hailed from a family with military heritage, the youthful sergeant who saw it his duty to give his utmost. He now had the character-building foundation of Special Forces. All this has contributed to his career success.

Who Will Go is an inspiring story. It leaves this reader with the question for America's future generations: when your time comes… who will go? As a friend and proud fellow Vietnam Veteran it is my privilege to write this Foreword.

Colonel Roger H. C. Donlon, US Army (retired)
Congressional Medal of Honor
Special Forces

WE'D LIKE TO EXPRESS OUR APPRECIATION...

...to our wives and our families for their support during this project. Marsha Buckler and Stephanie Westbrook. Hana & Nick, and Aaron & Gayle. Nick, Ben, Abby, and Matt.

...to all the POWs. They have given so much for this country.

...to those that contributed their recollections of the events around November 21st, 1970.

...to all those that participated in the success of the Raid from the Green Berets, to the aircrews, to the maintainers, to the planners, to the support teams, and to their families.

...to John Gargus (Colonel, USAF, retired) and to Earl Burress (Major, USAF, retired, Ph.D.) for their inexhaustible research over the years and their monumental contributions to historical integrity, relied upon by countless historians, including their technical review of this book. If any errors are found in this book, they are solely the responsibility of the authors—we should have listened more closely!

...to the military men and women that stand guard over the greatest nation in the world.

DEDICATION

to the memory of young Army Capt Dan Turner, Son Tay Raider,
Terry Buckler's mentor

also

to the memory of young Air Force Capt Ray Bean, POW 1972-1973,
Cliff Westbrook's cousin

also

to the men and women serving today in America's armed forces

also

to their families.

Sacrificial Living.

TABLE OF CONTENTS

PREFACE

THE SON TAY RAID, in the early morning hours of November 21st, 1970, ranks as one of the most daring missions in military history. I was one of the 56 Green Berets that participated in that assault on the Son Tay POW camp located 23 miles west of Hanoi, the capital of North Vietnam.

In military academies around the world, the Son Tay Raid is studied for its excellence in planning and execution.

I am writing this book for three reasons. First, I'm writing this for my children and for their children's children. Secondly, I believe that this is the first time the Son Tay Raid has been told from the viewpoint of an enlisted Raider. It will provide the thoughts and perspective of the youngest Son Tay Raider's first time in combat. The third reason is to record, for history, "Memorable Moments" as told by many other Raiders. You'll find their stories in Appendix 4. Many of the Raiders have graciously contributed to this book, and we are thankful to have, in that Appendix 4, a record of them speaking in their own words.

From the founding of our nation, men and women have given their all for the freedoms enshrined in our Constitution. The American military will always respond to the call—knowing the risks—to keep our country and its people free. When the men stepped forward for this particular mission—which Colonel Arthur "Bull" Simons described as "moderately hazardous"—they never questioned the risk. It was our duty and our honor to serve. The men on this mission freely volunteered to subordinate their lives to free fellow warriors who, against all standards of human decency, were being tortured and starved.

My mentor, Captain Dan Turner, whom I served with on the Raid, lived by Isaiah 6:8. These words, spoken 2,700 years ago, reveal the heart of the men who would later be known as the Son Tay Raiders.

I heard the voice of the Lord saying,

"Whom shall I send? And who will go for us?"

And I said,

"Here am I. Send me."

CHAPTER 1

0220 hours, November 21st, 1970, Just outside Hanoi, North Vietnam

"ALTERNATE PLAN GREEN!"

"I repeat: ALTERNATE PLAN GREEN! DO YOU COPY?"

It was a moment that I (and 55 other US Army Special Forces warriors—Green Berets) would never forget. We were locked and loaded aboard two USAF HH-53s and one HH-3 for a mission deep into enemy territory to rescue American POWs tortured and tormented by the North Vietnamese government.

For the past three hours, riding just above the jungle rising and falling with each hill and valley, I'd had the opportunity to review my 20 years on this earth. One of my childhood buddies was getting married tonight back in Clark, Missouri, beginning a new chapter of his life. But here I was, halfway around the world, armed to the teeth in a helicopter 100 feet above the LZ with an honest prospect that this might be the final chapter of mine.

Alternate Plan Green meant one thing to all of us Green Berets on our chopper: We knew we had 22 fewer men—a third of our force. There would be a lot less fire power as we hit the ground.

1

This plan was for the contingency that Greenleaf Support Group, comprised of those 22 men, would not make it to Son Tay. Whether it had mechanical problems or had been shot down, we had no way of knowing. What we did know was the mission, including all Alternate Plans. With or without those important 22 men of Greenleaf, we were going to execute the mission and would now have to perform their role as well as ours.

At that moment, the huge mounted machine gun in the door to our right fired off a few hundred rounds. For those of you not familiar with a "minigun," it fires 4,000 rounds of 5.62mm ammo per minute. It has an electrically driven rotary breech to feed the ammo belt at lightning speed. Now, my heart was already pounding, but the sound of that minigun firing two feet from me really spiked my adrenaline.

Image 2: The "Minigun"

This was the moment I had trained for since I joined the Green Berets. I couldn't let Captain Dan down or the other raiders.

We had been flying in the draft of an Air Force Special Operations C-130, call sign *Cherry 1*. Never before had a C-130 and helicopters flown a formation like this. The C-130 was flying a mere five knots above her stall speed in order to allow the helicopters to keep up, drafting like geese in a V-formation. The men flying *Cherry 1* were doing an unbelievable job of getting us to our destination. We had flown those three hours with no radio contact and no lights. We had the best Air Force pilots possible!

As we snaked along the hills and valleys just above the treetops of the most highly defended air space of North Vietnam, *Cherry 1* was leading us through the valley of the shadow of death. The Son Tay POW camp was located in the bend of the Song Con River. Colonel Bull Simons told us that if there was a security breach there was no E&E (Escape & Evasion) plan other than to back up to the river and fight it out: We would just stand our ground and make them pay for every inch of land to get to us. We staked our lives on our helicopters.

As I looked out the window of our chopper, it looked as if you could reach out and touch the trees. The quarter moon was just what the mission planners ordered. There wasn't a cloud in the sky. The moon was bright enough for our pilots to see the terrain, but not so bright that it would give us away as we were hurtling toward our objective.

All the men in our Redwine Security Group, except for myself, had experienced combat multiple times. Of the 56 raiders in all three groups (Redwine Security Group, Blueboy Assault Group, and Greenleaf Support Group), three others were also cherries with no combat experience. They were Sgt Keith Medenski, Sgt Marshall Thomas and Sgt Pat St.Clair. As I looked around our Redwine helicopter, the other raiders all looked relaxed. Several of them had their eyes closed, either sleeping or praying. Others were talking with one another, even laughing. We had rehearsed our mission over 170 times. Each of us knew our job and what we had to do.

Before we left, Colonel Simons—"the Bull"—had told us we had a 50/50 chance of not making it back. It's hard to get those words out of your mind when you're 20 years old, but each one of us knew the risk and could have backed out. It's too late now—we are about to step onto the soil of North Vietnam.

As planned, *Cherry 1* left us two minutes ago and started her climb. *Cherry 1*'s role now was to drop four Mk-24 parachute flares over the camp. And that she did. These flares have turned the black of night into the light of day for us raiders.

Apple 2 is the call sign of our helicopter. Captain Dan Turner is the Commander of the Redwine Security Group comprised of 15 men divided into four elements. (Also aboard are five more men that comprise the "Ground Force Command Group", including Lieutenant Colonel Bud Sydnor, the Ground Force Commander. They are attached to the Redwine Security Group.) Capt Dan turns to me and gives me a wink and says, "Kid are you ready for this, it's the real thing." I'm his RTO (Radio Telephone Operator), so I am required to be at his side at all times. I believe he saw the fear in my face and was trying to keep me calm. My heart is pounding like it's going to come out of my chest. This mission is what we trained for exclusively over the past three months. We are about to be tested in combat as our chopper is starting our landing.

I adjust my headset and the PRC-25 radio on my back, feel for my ammo pouches, check for my frag grenades and concussion grenades. I check that I had my safety off and that my CAR-15 "Colt Commando" machine gun is set to AUTO. I make sure I have the 30-round magazine well seated and I chamber a round. This is it. My first time in combat. This is no game. I'm not scared as much as I am excited.

I stand up and do a couple squats to get the blood flowing in my legs after sitting most of the three hours. I re-adjust my head set so I only have one ear covered and the other ear uncovered so I can hear Capt Dan. I re-check that my CAR-15 is set for rock & roll and my 30-round clip is in. I pull EJECT just to confirm I have a round in the barrel. The last thing I want is to have my weapon go "click" with my first shot when I step on the enemy's territory. I feel my web gear to re-confirm that I have my grenades and that all my ammo is secured in my ammo pouches. My PRC-25 radio is squared away on my back. I have over 70 pounds of gear, but with the adrenaline pumping through my body I move as if I don't have any extra weight.

As was rehearsed, all raiders are making the same checks to their equipment and each warrior is preparing to do what we came here for and that is to bring our POWs home. Mental checks. Say our prayers. Now it's time to do our job!

Then, just as we are settling to the rice paddies at Son Tay and we are about to burst out the tail of the chopper onto the battle-field, I hear in my headset the voice of SFC (Sgt 1st Class) Howell, LtCol Sydnor's RTO: "ALTERNATE PLAN GREEN!" "I repeat: ALTERNATE PLAN GREEN! DO YOU COPY?"

This is the first of the bad news I would hear tonight.

CHAPTER 2

May 1970, Washington, DC
The Secret Planning of the
Son Tay Raid

THE PLANNING OF THE raid was begun in May of 1970 when reconnaissance photos taken from an SR-71 Blackbird revealed that a POW camp existed near a town named Son Tay on the outskirts of Hanoi. The intelligence was presented to Brigadier General Donald Blackburn, the Pentagon's Special Assistant for Counterinsurgency and Special Activities. He formed a team of fifteen from his staff to conduct a feasibility study. Their findings convinced him a rescue was possible and he presented it to the Chairman of the Joint Chiefs of Staff, Admiral Thomas Moorer. The Son Tay Raid would become the first military operation in American history under the direct control of the Joint Chiefs of Staff.

The North Vietnamese government, in heinous violation of the Geneva Convention, was systematically torturing POWs in order to get classified information and to use them as pawns for propaganda. They would not allow the Red Cross to check on the health of the POWs, or even tell us the names of the POWs they held and where, or even simply tell us how many POWs they held.

Our Department of Defense estimated there were at least 335 POWs, as of May 1970, having been held for an average of five years. The POWs were being held in terrible conditions, starved, tortured, and deprived of medical care. These men were living in hell. They (and their families) needed to know that our country cared.

The mission was to free American POWs. Son Tay was the only camp where American POWs were known to be, other than those in downtown Hanoi from which the propaganda films were being released. Any raid on a POW facility in the heart of Hanoi had zero chance of success. When the Son Tay camp was identified, US intelligence estimated that it could have as many as 60 or 70 POWs. How many were American? There was no way of knowing. In Appendix 4 at the end of this book, some of these very POWs have graciously shared stories in their own words for this book.

CHAPTER 3

August 1970, Fort Bragg, NC
The Word on the Hill:
Bull was Looking for Men

IN EARLY AUGUST OF 1970, my company, Company D, 7th
Special Forces Group, was training at Nantahala National Forest
in the Smokey Mountains. In the Special Forces life, you're either
training, headed to a training location, or deployed, and at this
time, I was helping teach mountain climbing. I was sent on an er-
rand to Fort Bragg to pick up some supplies for our company, and
there at Fort Bragg, I heard from one of my buddies that there was
a notice posted at Smoke Bomb Hill by Colonel Simons (famously
known as the "Bull") looking for volunteers for a mission.

Now, Bull Simons was not just any "full bird" colonel. He was
a legend in Special Forces. Bull was the man movies are made of.
He made Rambo look like a punk kid! He was an alumnus of the
University of Missouri ROTC program. He was not a West Point
graduate—which, to most of us Green Berets, was a big plus.

His story begins in World War II, when he participated in several hazardous landings in the Pacific. His first mission was to

destroy a Japanese radio tower on an island in the Philippines. He was awarded his first Silver Star for his actions there.

Another of his missions was with the 6th Ranger Battalion commanded by Lieutenant Colonel Henry Mucci. The Bull was among the Rangers, Alamo Scouts, and Filipino guerrillas who rescued over 500 POWs held by the Japanese in the famous Cabanatuan POW Camp Raid. Most of these POWs were survivors of the Bataan Death March. Bull was awarded a second Silver Star in that operation.

Bull was so highly respected by all of Special Forces that, after his retirement, the US Special Operations Command (USSOCOM) commissioned a statue of Simons, next to the Special Forces Museum at Fort Bragg (you'll find a picture of his statue at the end of Appendix 4.) It is a continuing tribute to his memory and legacy in the special warfare community. USSOCOM yearly bestows The Bull Simons Award to the top special warfare professional who embodies "the true spirit, values, and skills of a Special Operations warrior." I was star struck by Colonel Simons.

While waiting for my supplies to be loaded onto the truck for my trip back to Nantahala, I thought I would go down to what we called The Little White House and see what the colonel had to say. When I walked into the theater, it was already packed with hundreds of career soldiers. Everyone was talking about what the mission might be. It was 1970 and Palestinian militants had hijacked planes bound for New York and London. They were demanding the release of activists held by Israel. Three of the planes had been forced to land at Dawson's Field, a former British air force base in a remote area of Jordan and the fourth had been diverted to Egypt. Most everyone thought it would be a mission to rescue those passengers.

This was the first time I had ever laid eyes on the man they called Bull. "Bull," as used by Special Forces with reference to Simons, was a name of great admiration and affection. He had earned the name in a physical training game called the "bull pit," where one soldier climbs down into a pit and other soldiers try to force him up out of the pit. He stood about six foot and weighed in around 200 lbs. He was a big, barrel-chested man and his face showed the years of experience he possessed. He walked on that stage chewing on a short cigar, a look for which he was famous. The auditorium went to dead silence when Bull began to speak. The Bull said he would be running a moderately-hazardous mission and was looking for volunteers.

["*Moderately Hazardous.*" *This stuck in my mind. Later, on November 20th, the night Bull told us in the theater at Takhli Royal Thai Air Force Base what our real mission was, I wondered what the Bull considered a* very *hazardous mission!*]

He told us there would be no TDY pay for this mission. This would reduce the number of volunteers. TDY stands for Temporary Duty and usually means extra money. Bull said, "If you're interested in volunteering, be back here at 1300 hrs today."

I returned that afternoon along with over 500 volunteers hoping to find out what the mission was. We were told that there would be a personal interview for each solider. Because of the large number, they divided up the volunteers. Sergeant Major Pylant and Sergeant Major Davis were running the interviewing process for my group, and I was the last person in the group. I had spent the afternoon waiting in the hall for them to call my name to be interviewed. At about 6pm, the two Sergeant Majors came walking out of the interviewing room. They walked by me, sitting there. I thought, *What's going on? They haven't interviewed me*!! I ran out the door and yelled for them to stop. I asked them why they hadn't called me into the room for my interview.

[Afterward I thought, *What did I just do!? Here I am—a buck sergeant—questioning not one, but two Sergeant Majors.* Anyone that ever enlisted in the Army knows that Sergeant Majors are gods.]

I must have caught them by surprise. They asked my name. They said they didn't have my 201 file. (That's a soldier's personnel file. It had apparently been misfiled.) I told them I needed to leave at noon the next day to get back to Nantahala. They said if I could be back in the morning with my 201 file, they would interview me first.

I called one of my roommates, E. J. Goodale, who worked at 7th Group HQ, and I knew he could get in after hours to find my 201 file. We went to HQ and, sure enough, E.J. got it for me.

The next morning, I was there bright and early ready for the interview, which lasted about ten minutes. They asked me if I had ever been in combat. Well, I knew they had my 201 file, so they knew I had no combat experience. They asked me if I knew how to weld. Now, growing up on a farm you learn a lot of different skills. One of our neighbors Sam Chism could weld anything we broke. Over the years on the farm I had watched Sam weld several things for my dad. I thought, *If Sam can weld, I can too.* So, I told them, "Yes, I can weld." They asked if I could scuba dive, to which I answered that I could not. (Years later, I did become certified to dive.)

After a few more questions, they told me that would be all. I left unhopeful thinking, "Well, at least they let me interview." I drove back to Nantahala with the supplies, trying to imagine what this mission was all about.

My job at Nantahala was to help four Master Sergeants train other Green Berets in mountain climbing, repelling and rope tying. As the lowest rank on the team—and the youngest—I was volunteered to climb up and down the side of mountain. It was fun working with the older sergeants.

A couple of days later, on August 19th, our colonel called me into his office at Nantahala and told me to pack my gear and report back to Fort Bragg. I had been selected for the mission. I was so excited.

The next couple of weeks at Ft Bragg were hectic. I was a member of the Advance Party that was going down early to get everything ready for the rest of us who were selected. We had to get our shots, ensure we had a Last Will and Testament, and fill out life insurance beneficiary forms along with all the other paperwork.

I had never filled out a Will before. This should have been an indication to me that this might be more than a "moderately hazardous" mission. It prompted me to write a letter to my mom and dad explaining why I had volunteered for this mission, just in case I didn't make it back. I gave it to a buddy of mine and told him to mail it if the time ever came.

We were told to tell our families we were going on a training mission that might last a few months. We were not to say where we were going. Special Forces guys are always training, so this would not be very surprising to the families. We (there were 25 of us) loaded our trusty duffel bags and headed out (destination undisclosed) on two C-123s on Wednesday, September 2nd, 1970.

CHAPTER 4

The 1950s, Clark, MO
Starting from the Beginning

So how did a farm boy from central Missouri—the youngest of the raiders, with no combat experience—get selected for one of the most daring raids in military history?

I was born in a two-bedroom house on a small 72-acre farm in central Missouri in 1950. We were six miles from Clark, six from Renick, and six from Higbee. Our mail came through Clark, I went to school at Renick, and our phone came through Higbee. Clark happens to be the birthplace of the famous World War II General Omar Bradley. Our house had been built in 1870. We didn't have indoor plumbing until 1962, when I was twelve.

As far as I'm concerned, there is no greater life than living in the country. Farm life provides the opportunity to learn a lot about life and yourself. You learn to rely on your family and neighbors. We were a typical small—farm family. Eighty acres is not a big farm, and Dad worked at a factory that made small appliances, driving the family car to the big city of Moberly (population 13,000) each day to make ends meet. I remember, Dad was paid in silver dollars by the appliance factory so they could determine where the money was being spent in town. One Saturday morning when I was about thirteen, I counted the silver dollars; he made $90 for a week's work—not much for a family with three boys, but we never missed a meal.

Farm life teaches you to be self-sufficient. We raised cattle, chickens, hogs, and a few horses. We always had a big garden and Mom canned most of our vegetables. Every year, we raised 150 chickens that we butchered at the end of summer, as well as one hog and one steer for pork and beef. We always had plenty to eat. We were not rich, but we always had everything we needed. Growing up, I knew not to ask for things that my family could not afford. Mom and Dad always provided the necessities for us boys. We weren't the only ones—most of our neighbors were just like us. Farm life is not easy, but you learn to work hard at an early age. Of our 72 acres, only about 50 were tillable. Dad rented another 200 acres.

I have many fond memories of living on the farm. When you live on a farm there is always something to keep you busy: fixing fences, overhauling tractors, cutting wood for winter or hauling hay. Everyone has a job and you learn to work as a family. My older brothers Doug and Darrell did the heavy work until I was old enough to help. I have always enjoyed being outside and we didn't have a TV until I was seven, so we had to entertain ourselves.

One of my boyhood friends was Mike Ridgeway. He lived down the road about a quarter of a mile. I remember us being about seven or eight, fishing in one of his dad's farm ponds that was built by the Works Progress Administration. We hunted with BB guns and our dogs until we were nine—then we hunted with .22 rifles. People would drop off dogs they didn't want any more on the 1500-acre wildlife refuge across the road from our dads' farms. Mike and I would find them in the woods and bring them home and keep them as pets. At one point, we had about twelve dogs between us. Our parents were pretty good about letting us keep them. A big treat for us was to ride our bikes to Rucker, about three or four miles from our house, when Mom and Dad would let us. At Rucker, there was a small, one-room country store. My treat was an ice cream soda (15 cents) and a Butterfinger candy bar (25 cents.)

Dad was a hardworking man, but he also enjoyed having fun. When he returned from the war in 1946, he worked as a coal miner alongside his dad in Rock Springs, Wyoming. After he was injured in a mine cave-in, he decided he was not interested in a miner's career and moved back to Missouri, where he had been raised. In 1947, he purchased the 72 acres I came to know as our farm. He attended classes on agriculture at the technical college under the GI Bill.

Since the farm came with two large chicken houses, he naturally went into raising chickens—until an outbreak of Coccidiosis killed off several hundred of them. A later attempt at raising turkeys also proved unproductive. When the Midwest suffered a multiyear drought in the early fifties, he was forced to sell off half his small herd of cattle. At this point, Dad had to supplement his farm income by driving a school bus for the local school in Renick. He later took a job in Moberly at the small appliance manufacturer where he worked for over 15 years while continuing to farm. The state built a prison near Moberly and, in 1967, he went to work as a guard until he retired.

I was nine when Mom went to work for State Farm Insurance at their regional office in Columbia about 40 minutes away. I stayed home by myself. (In today's world Mom and Dad might be arrested for child neglect, letting me stay home at such a young age!) When I turned fifteen, I spent most of my summers working for a neighbor who farmed about 500 acres. My brothers had worked for him until they graduated and then I took their place.

My buddy Charley Cottingham had a Cushman Scooter and we would ride it on the dirt roads. I believe the top speed was only 50. At that ripe age of fifteen, I succeeded in talking my dad into letting me buy a motorcycle. I sold one of my horses, and the motorcycle was mine! I bought a Honda 50 and we had a blast riding those country roads.

I started school at Renick and graduated from Renick High School, as did my brothers. Renick was not a big school; I had 19 in my graduating class. We only had about 130 from 1st grade through 12th. You knew everyone, and you even knew the names of their dogs. I was elected Class President from my freshmen year through my senior year. (I believe no one else wanted the position.) The only sport we had was basketball and, at five-foot-six, I never expected the NBA to offer me a contract.

After graduating from high school, I moved to Columbia to work the summer for my uncle Rodney, who had owned a tree service since 1950. Uncle Rodney had a contract with the phone company to clear the right-of-way for phone lines along the Missouri River. That was a bitch of a job. Poison oak had grown up the poles and along the phone lines. That summer the whole crew had poison oak down our arms, around our waists, and on our chests.

In the fall of 1968, I moved to Louisville, KY to attend a trade school for electronics. I had a job working construction in the mornings and went to school in the afternoon. I did this until January of 1969 when I ran out of money. At that point, I moved back home and went to work for AB Chance making electrical equipment like fiberglass booms and fiberglass buckets in nearby Centralia.

It was the end of February 1969 when a couple of my high school buddies and I were riding around the big town of Moberly and decided to stop in at the draft board and see where we were on the draft list. We had all been in technical school and, back then, when you lost your draft deferment from college, it seemed like you jumped up on the draft list. The lady at the draft board told me that it would probably be April before I would be drafted. I asked her when the next group was scheduled to go, and she told us it would be March. I asked her to add me to the list. So that was it—I had just volunteered for the US Army.

When I got home that day, I told Mom and Dad I had volunteered. I remember Mom crying, sitting in the kitchen. Dad was not really happy about it, but I knew he understood. I had a couple of weeks before I had to leave. My church, First Christian Church of Clark, gave me a going away party and Mom had a big family dinner where I was able to say goodbye to my aunts, uncles and cousins, all of whom lived within about 30 miles of our home.

On March 17th, 1969, the day to report to the Moberly draft office, Mom got me up early and fixed Dad and me a big breakfast before she went to work. There in the kitchen, Mom gave me a big hug and we kissed. She told me she loved me. She told me to be safe. That was a tough day for Mom. As she walked out of the kitchen door to go to work, I could see she was crying.

Dad had taken the morning off to drive me to Moberly so I could catch the Missouri Transit bus to Kansas City for my physical and my swearing in. It was a bright sunny morning, driving to Moberly. Dad and I had a nice talk about what to expect at Army Basic Training. He advised me to take it all with a grain of salt. Dad had served in the Pacific Theater during World War II and had seen his share of combat in the Philippines.

Standing at the bus stop, we hugged and he gave me some more good advice: "Keep your nose clean, your head down, and don't volunteer for anything." Dad wiped back his tears as he walked back to his car.

I was getting on the bus to Kansas City and who do you think was driving the bus? None other than Ralph Chilton. Ralph had been my bus driver from the first day I started school to my last day as a senior. I thought it was very fitting that he drove me to the Army induction station in Kansas City. I never thought about how he must have felt until we said our goodbyes and I noticed that he had tears in his eyes. Then it hit me: Ralph had seen me grow up and now he was dropping me off for the last time.

I never saw him again. Due to health reasons he moved to Arizona while I was in the Army.

I spent the night in a Kansas City hotel along with about 100 other draftees. The hotel was the Hotel Phillips, which had once been the tallest building in Kansas City. It was Art Deco with a sculpture of the Goddess of Dawn in the lobby. I am not sure how it got started, but what began as a little fun that night ended up getting a few us in trouble. As cars passed below us, we would lean out the fourth-floor windows and try to hit the cars with balls of wet toilet paper. As the night progressed, we pushed our luck. We used the rooms' small trash cans to pour water out the windows for the same challenge. A police car passed under us and it must have looked like Niagara Falls. That's when the fun ended—for a little while anyway. We all thought, *What they are going to do? —Draft us and send our butts to Vietnam?*

The next day, March 18th, at the Kansas City Recruit Depot, I learned what "hurry up and wait" is all about. We had our physical and it was exactly what you've heard: strip to your underwear, turn your head, and cough. Afterward, all those who had passed their physical were assembled in a big room and sworn into the Army.

CHAPTER 5

March 1969, Fort Leonard Wood, MO
The Army

AFTER BEING SWORN IN, we stayed the night in that same hotel. The next morning, they woke us at zero-dark-thirty and we loaded another bus that took us to what would be my new home for the next sixteen weeks. It was about 5:30am when we arrived at Fort Leonard Wood. I knew they were expecting us, but I did not know they would have such a warm welcoming committee. That committee consisted of four big burly Drill Sergeants. Our bus stopped, the door opened, and they jumped on our bus and began yelling for us to get our butts off it. Needless to say, they were not in the public relations business! The induction process began. We were told to empty our pockets. I had a small pocketknife about two inches long that I had not removed before I left home. The way they started yelling, you would have thought I had been caught with a twelve-inch Jim Bowie skinning knife. I was immediately surrounded by two of those big burley Drill Sergeants who told me to drop and start doing push-ups as they continued yelling at me. They asked me if I was going to kill them with this big hunting knife. I thought, *What the hell are they talking about? —It's just a small pocketknife!?!* (This was my first taste of Army pressure, working toward its long-term goal of preparing you for combat.)

By now, it was about 6am as we stood in line to get our new wardrobe. We were issued our new nice green uniforms and all the good stuff that comes with it: underwear, socks, boots and blankets. Our new friends, the Drill Sergeants, marched us—or at least we called it marching—over to get our first Army haircut. It took about one minute, but it was free, and you know what they say: you get what you pay for.

My first assignment was to Company D, 5th Battalion, 2nd Brigade. I had only been in the Army a few days when our company was brought into one of our training buildings. There was this big, bad-looking Rambo guy who was looking for volunteers for the Green Berets. I didn't know a lot about the Green Berets, but I did know they were one of the most elite fighting units in the Army. This guy looked as though he could kick any ten of us at once. I thought if I am going to war, I wanted to go with the best, so I raised my hand when he asked if anyone wanted to volunteer for the Green Berets, Special Forces. I knew this would cost me another year of service, but I figured another year is a worthy price to pay to be among the Army's best. I guess I was a poor listener when it came to my dad's advice about volunteering.

On March 21st, 1969, I raised my hand a second time and took another oath to support this great country and the Constitution. I went from a "US number" to an "RA number." US numbers indicates that you were drafted, and an RA number identifies you as Regular Army or as many others would say, Regular Asshole.

This is a good time to reveal my politics and my opinion concerning what this country needs. As I look over my career, I can say unequivocally that the best thing was my decision to join the

Army. I believe the problem with our politicians today is that very few of them have had to lay their lives on the line for this country and don't have a clue what Duty and Honor mean to soldiers. There is no camaraderie like that of the military. Anyone who has ever served will tell you that your experiences in the military will help you in life.

The next few weeks were interesting and, I can even say, fun. I decided that if I was going to be a Special Forces solider, I better get used to the even higher level of harassment yet to come. Like everyone else who had the good fortune of experiencing military training, I quickly learned that this harassment part of the training sucks. I had a bad habit of smiling. Now, this doesn't sound bad until you realize that the DIs' (Drill Instructors) job is to break you to make you. My smiling gave them a good reason to drop me for push-ups. They told me many, many times they were going to wipe that smile off my face. If you see my graduation platoon picture, you will notice I was still smiling. I must admit that they did a pretty good job trying.

My favorite DI was Sergeant Dunham. He was a Vietnam veteran and former Airborne. I once forgot his name, and did I pay for that: I did push-ups repeating his name every rep until he got tired of listening. He told me I would never forget his name and—you know what? –it worked. When he found out that Dwight Palmer (a smart ass 17-year-old) and I were headed to Airborne training, life got a little more difficult. Every time Palmer screwed up, I would receive his punishment along with him. So, every now and then, I in turn would screw up so that he could suffer with me.

I remember when we were doing pugil training, Dwight and I got our butts kicked but good. In pugil training, the platoon makes a big circle and the DI calls two trainees' names. The two students immediately enter the circle to do battle until he calls two more

names. You are only in the circle for a couple of minutes, but it is
like boxing; three minutes of getting the crap knocked out of you
seems like an hour. You have your pugil stick and a cheap, half-
ass helmet. The objective is to beat your opponent to the ground.
Sergeant Dunham called my name and that of one of the biggest
guys. After he kicked my butt, he would call for Dwight and another big guy. After you have been in the circle three or four times,
your arms feel like rubber and your head feels like it's been used
as a soccer ball. The big guys that we were fighting started feeling sorry for us, but Sergeant Dunham told them not to show any
mercy or he would come in the circle and they would have to fight
him. It was part of the training. I guess it's like they say: "What
doesn't kill you makes you stronger." Sergeant Dunham made sure
we were in good shape when we graduated from Basic.

One night, my squad and Sergeant Dunham were cleaning our
weapons. I made the mistake of calling my weapon a gun. Well
there is a saying in the Army: "This is my weapon, this is my
gun; One is for shooting, one is for fun." As soon as I said "gun,"
I knew. I didn't even look up; I just started doing push-ups. My
squad was counting them off. When I hit rep one hundred, I did a
one arm push-up on my right hand and the hundred first one arm
on my left hand. I was in excellent shape.

When I took our PT (Physical Training) test at the end of
Basic Training, I scored a perfect 500 on the test. The last event
of the test was a mile run. My Company Commander was Captain
Kenneth Mostella. He was about six-foot-two and in really good
physical shape. He was an Infantry officer and a Vietnam veteran.
If it were not for him, I may have not scored a perfect 500. He
knew I was close to a perfect 500 going into the mile run so for the
last lap he ran along side of me, pushing me to run faster. Thanks
to him, I made it with seconds to spare. This is what the Army is

about—soldiers helping soldiers. As it turned out I was one of only six in my Battalion who scored a perfect 500 on the PT test.

Of course, there are some aspects of training you *really* don't like. For me, it was the tear gas building at Fort Leonard Wood. While the DI was giving us instructions on how to wear our gas masks and cover up with our ponchos, Dwight Palmer and I were at the back of the class joking around and being stupid. Drill Sergeant Dunhum appeared out of nowhere and volunteered Palmer and me to be the first in the chamber. When the DIs opened the door, you could not see across the room, the gas was so thick. Our instructions were to remove your mask, state your name, rank and serial number, put your mask back on, clear it, and then leave the building. I think I got part of my name out before I felt like I was being choked. We came out of that building with snot running out our noses and eyes burning like fire hardly able to catch a breath. This made a lifetime impression on me.

Another thing I really disliked in Basic Training was police call. Police call is when the platoon forms a line, standing an arm's length apart, and you start picking up anything that is not attached to the ground. I believe the term the DIs used was, "Assholes and elbows! Now pick it up!" This meant cigarette butts. Now, I didn't smoke, but I still had to pick up those damn cigarette butts. My dad told me before I left that Basic would consist of a lot of things that didn't make sense, but not to take it too seriously. What I was going to experience was for my own good. The DIs' job was to make men out of us boys and they did a good job.

I still have memories of KP. Reporting to the mess hall at 4:30am was a bitch. I tried to get the job of Pots and Pans Man or DRO (dining room orderly.) DRO was the cushy job of filling salt and pepper shakers and sweeping the floor. Pots and Pans Man was a dirty job, but as soon as you had washed all the pans, you could leave, so you were usually the first one to go back to the barracks and grab some sleep. Basic Training was an education for this farm boy. I was introduced to people from New York, California, and most states in between. Graduation day arrived and, boy, were we ready for this day to come. Having scored a perfect 500 on my PT test, I graduated from Basic Training as a PFC, Private 1st Class, in May 1969.

CHAPTER 6

In the Back of my Mind:
My Dad in World War II

LET ME PAUSE TO tell you about my father's service in the Army. World War II was when he served. He never talked about the war until one Saturday in July 1997 after he had his stroke and was recovering in the University of Missouri Hospital. My middle brother, Darrell, lived near Columbia, so he and Mom visited Dad through the week. On the weekends I would drive from Kansas City to stay with him.

On that Saturday, for some reason, Dad and I started talking about what he did in the Army from Basic Training until he was released from active duty. Dad spent 36 months in the South Pacific. We talked about what it was like to get shot at and how it felt to shoot another person. Dad was a very laid-back person. It was hard to image him shooting someone. We compared the food the army fed us and the types of weapons we had. We both carried a Colt 45. Our long rifles were very different. We talked about fear while in combat.

He talked about missing his family. He had a son waiting for him and a wife that loved him. My oldest brother, Doug, was born while Dad was at war. Doug was three when Dad first saw him. That was the way it was during that war. You didn't do a tour of just a year. You stayed until the war was over.

Now I know that my dad was awarded the Bronze Star, but I never heard the story of how he earned it. I think I never will. On February 5th, 1998, the saddest day of my life, my parents were both killed in a house fire. Mom and Dad were happily married for 58 years. They lived a good life and enjoyed each other's love to the end.

With their death went all those memories I now wish I could draw upon. And beyond that, all his military records were lost in the fire.

When I later was researching his military time, I contacted the National Personnel Records Center in Saint Louis. I was crushed to find out that, in 1973, the Records Center had a huge fire that destroyed approximately 16–18 million official military personnel files documenting the service history of military personnel discharged from 1912 to 1964.

So I treasure the memory of that conversation about his military service that Dad and I had that Saturday in 1997.

CHAPTER 7

Back in the Summer of '69

AFTER GRADUATING FROM BASIC Training in May 1969, I was sent to my Military Occupation School. My MOS was 12B (Combat Engineer) and this training was at—you guessed it—Fort Leonard Wood. I will admit that Advanced Individual Training (AIT) was much easier compared to Basic. Knowing I was headed to Airborne training after AIT, I kept myself in shape by running and doing push-ups.

After graduating from AIT, I experienced my very first airplane ride. It took me from Fort Leonard Wood to Fort Benning, Georgia. I will never forget it. It was American Airlines and we had the three prettiest stewardesses. This was in the days when the airline stewardesses were young ladies in their tight skirts and cute hats. Being in Basic and AIT for the past sixteen weeks, there weren't a lot of women around to admire. You can't image how a plane full of starved GIs tried to impress our good-looking young airline stewardesses.

FORT BENNING, GEORGIA

Jump school was much as I expected: a lot of running and push-ups when you screwed up and morning inspections. I went through jump school in August.

Allow me to inform you that August at Fort Benning, Georgia, can be rather warm. It was about the second week of jump school and we were having our morning inspection. Due to the heat, we could remove our fatigue shirts and train in our Army t-shirts. It just so happens that the t-shirt the Army provides has a low front, exposing a good part of your chest. This hot morning, the Sergeant doing the inspection walked up to me and asked me why I had not shaved. I replied, "I did shave, Sergeant." Now I had always had a pretty hairy chest. The sergeant reached out and grabbed a hand full of my chest hair and jerked it out by the roots. He pushed it in my face and said, "You forgot to shave this part." If you've never had the hair on your chest pulled out by its roots, let me give you an idea what it feels like: IT HURTS LIKE HELL! But I didn't say a word. He moved to the next solider. However, the next morning, I shaved most of my chest so not one hair was visible. That same Sergeant walked up to me during inspection, looked at my chest, looked at me, smiled and moved on to the next solider. I might add, I kept my chest shaved the rest of my jump school training.

I had the good fortune of going through jump school with some Navy SEALs from Team 2 (if I recall correctly.) When they learned that I was headed for Special Forces training, they decided they would adopt me into their ranks. The water troughs we had were about a foot deep and about 18 inches wide. The SEALs stopped up one of the troughs and filled it with water. Then about six of them grabbed me and dunked me under water until I thought I was going to drown. From then on, they deemed me an honorary SEAL! I guess you might say I had my first taste of water--boarding.

They were actually a great bunch of guys. One day as we were headed back to the barracks after a day of training, one of the SEALs was made to run around the platoon while we did the Airborne shuffle (marching/jogging along to the call of a jody something like, "Two old ladies lyin' in a bed! One rolled over to the other and said, 'I want to be an Airborne Ranger.'") Well the SEALs have a very high degree of esprit de corps. If one of them was dropped for push-ups, they all did push-ups. So, if one SEAL had to run around our platoon, they all would. Think about that: the SEALs were running circles around us as we soldiers did the Airborne shuffle! Now to say this pissed off the Cadre is an understatement. The next thing I knew, we were running what felt like a sprint as the SEALS still ran around the platoon. By the time we made it back to the barracks, we were all exhausted. The Cadre then had the SEALs doing push-ups for the next ten or fifteen minutes. I developed a real appreciation for the level of camaraderie the SEALs have.

After weeks of training and thousands of push-ups, the day had finally come; I was about to make my first jump from a C-141 Starlifter. The cadre asked if anyone wanted to volunteer to stand in the door. I was getting good at volunteering (Forgive me, Dad!), so I stepped forward to stand in the door. Looking out across the DZ (drop zone) surprisingly gave me a chance to let the butterflies calm down in my stomach. Heights did not bother me. While working for my uncle trimming trees, I'd gotten use to swinging from a rope 100 feet in the air. However, there is a big difference between an oak tree and 1500 feet at a speed of 150 knots.

The C-141 was a newer aircraft for jumping. When the door opened, there was a wind deflector that extended about eighteen inches out into the wind stream the entire height of the door. This was to reduce the wind blast as you jumped out, they said. Since this was my first jump, I couldn't tell if it helped or not. The name of the DZ at Fort Benning is Fryar Field. [Some 43 years later, Dan Turner (my Son Tay Raid partner) and I would be at this same field the night my daughter made her first night jump for Airborne training.]

As I looked down at the DZ it reminded me of a big plowed field back in Missouri. It was surrounded by trees on three sides. The parked Army deuce-and-a-half trucks that were there to take us back to the barracks looked like toy trucks from my view. Here I am—in a perfectly good airplane the second time I had ever flown, and I can't even stick around for the landing. I was rehearsing in my mind what I'd been taught the last few weeks. Jump out, keep your feet together, tuck your head, count to four, look up, check that your parachute is open and not twisted, steer your parachute to not land in the trees. The green light came on and I was ready to jump, but the jumpmaster told me to stand by. You see, the Air Force controlled when to turn on the green light, but the jumpmaster controlled when you jumped. I later learned that jumping when the green light comes on could leave you hanging in the trees. My eyes were focused on the DZ when I felt a rap on my helmet. This was the jumpmaster letting me know it was my big moment. In that instant, I forgot everything I was taught. The noise inside the plane is so loud you have to shout to the person next to you. I jumped as far out of the plane as I could and the wind blast hit me with a shock.

The next thing I heard was dead silence. I looked up and saw the most beautiful sight: the inside of my chute. As I drifted to earth on my first jump, my thought was, *This was GREAT!* I looked around and saw others floating in the air. I could hear guys yelling at one another. I spotted the DZ. Soon it was time to see if I could make a perfect PLF (Parachute Landing Fall.) I looked down. The ground was getting closer. I thought back to what I had learned. Put my feet together, eyes on the horizon, get ready to land, "Boom!" My feet hit the ground, my body twisted to my left and I executed an excellent PLF. I jumped up and took off my chute and stuffed it in my kit bag. This was the first of many more jumps to come.

Not every jump I made was this pleasant. I remember one jump when the wind was roaring across the DZ. I hit the ground and was dragged about thirty feet before I could get up and collapse my chute.

To graduate from jump school, I only had to make four more jumps. Happily, I completed those jumps with no injuries.

CHAPTER 8

September 1969
Special Forces Training

"One hundred men we'll test today,
but only three win the Green Beret."

THESE LYRICS TO "THE Ballad of the Green Beret" by Barry Sadler are a very good summary of Special Forces.

One certain night in September 1969, 74 top-notch soldiers—out of hundreds screened—jumped into the DZ at Camp Mackall near Ft Bragg with all our equipment and one change of fatigues. That's all we would have for the next few weeks. We were about four miles from what would become our base camp. It was about 10pm and the welcome committee was ready for us. Now you could tell these guys really looked forward to our arrival. The cadre quickly assembled us and started marching us to camp on this dirt road with our rucksacks and our weapons.

We had been marching about five minutes when the cadre yelled out "Double Time!" We took off and, for the next several minutes, we double-timed down the road. Now, when you have a 40- or 50-pound rucksack on your back and you're carrying your weapon, it sure makes double-timing difficult. The next command they gave us was "Double Time, Halt!" "Face the outside of the road!" "Drop and start pushing Fort Bragg away from your body and don't let your weapon touch the ground!"

The next couple hours consisted of marching, double time, push-ups, marching, double time and push-ups. I and one other student were able to keep up with the lead cadre all the way to our camp. I remember getting there exhausted, and the cadre asked us if we were tired. We looked at each other knowing it was probably a trick question and said, "No." His response was "Good! Then drop and start doing push-ups until I get tired." This was the first time in my military life that I could not muster the strength to do any more push-ups. Thank God that the other troops soon joined us.

They harassed us for a few more hours and finally let us go to sleep around 4am. We were *so* ready for sack time.

The next sound I heard was "Rise and shine ladies!" It was 6am. The two hours of sleep did help, but another six would have been appreciated.

This first day of fun started with us running the Special Forces obstacle course. I had run obstacle courses in Basic and AIT, but this course was one heck of a lot harder. It took me over thirty minutes to complete the course. Little did we know that this would be a regular event for us. Every time a dignitary visited, we had to run the obstacle course to show how it was a part of our training.

By the end of the first day, several students dropped out. Just from the DZ to the camp the first night we lost ten or fifteen. Students drop out for a variety of reasons, some due to injuries; others decide that Special Forces wasn't for them, and some just couldn't make it. This part of Special Forces training is designed to test the students' physical and mental endurance.

It was during the map course that my quest to become a Green Beret almost came to an end. My four squad mates and I had gotten lost. In class and in the field, we had been taught advanced techniques in patrolling, setting up ambushes, and land navigation using a map and compass. For over six hours we had hiked through the swamps of Camp Mackall taking turns carrying a .30 caliber machine gun. As the sun set and dark took over, we couldn't see much more than five to ten feet in front of us. At each leg, our task was to locate a specific marker and then shoot an azimuth to the next marker. In the end it was determined that one of the markers had been removed. We were given another map course and we passed.

Image 3: M1919 Browning .30 caliber

Training was very difficult, but there were some fun times. You were given different duties, ranging from "burning the crap" (which is the formal Army terminology for "cooking/KP duty"), to leadership positions such as Company Commander. I had the opportunity to do both. The advantage of burning crap was you didn't have to do morning PT.

I have always tried to add humor to anything I do. One early morning the company was in formation waiting for the cadre to join us. On that day, I was the student Company Commander. While we were waiting, I shouted out a command that, "Anyone that can't tap dance must be a sissy!" Well, the entire company started tap dancing in place. All of a sudden, they all stopped. I had my back to the cadre building and it was at that time that I realized I was the only one still tap dancing. I stopped and slowly turned around, and there stood the cadre. They did have a sense of humor and got a chuckle out of it, but they told me to drop and start doing push-ups.

LIFE LESSON 1: Add Humor. It really helps when things are getting tough. Sometimes it's not easy to find it within you, but even the POWs somehow found a way to pass some slivers of humor through the cracks in the prison walls. The soul needs it. Make sure you contribute some for the benefit of the people around you.

While at Camp Mackall, we lived in squad tents. One night, my squad was eating some good old C-ration cookies and Kool-Aid before we turned in for some sleep. I was lying on my back in my fart bag and was about to fall asleep, when I felt little teeth bite down on my lip. I flipped a rodent off me and yelled, "RAT!!" The critter went airborne, landed on the cot across from me, and was gone in a flash. We decided that the rat was trying to eat the cookie crumbs and sugar off my lips. The next morning, I told the cadre what had happened. They ordered me to go to sick call and get checked out. The medic told me I was lucky the rat didn't break the skin, so I didn't have to get rabies shots. That was the last time we had cookies before going to bed.

We finally made it through to that long-awaited November day. We were trucked back to Fort Bragg for the ceremony in which would don our Green Berets. You would always know when a newly completed class had arrived back in the barracks. The smell of forty to fifty guys that had not showered for the past eight weeks penetrated the halls. The only bath we took was a dip in the river with your dirty fatigues on. After a dip in the river you put on your other set of dirty fatigues that were at least dry.

As I placed that Green Beret on my head at the graduation ceremony, I was one of only 43 who had lasted through the eight weeks of absolute hell.

From this, I was sent to my Special Forces MOS. In Special Forces there were five MOS options: weapons, engineer, communications, intel, and medical.

Humor is crucial for morale—I say this again because I have personally benefited from it so greatly. In January 1970, while in training for my communications MOS, the entire company was required to present for morning formation. This is the time the Company Sergeant Major disseminates information to the troops. A certain morning, the Sergeant Major announced that someone had turned in a beret they had found and he wanted to know if anyone had lost theirs.

From the back of the formation, one of the trainees hollered out, "What color is it?" The whole company busted out with laughter—except the Sergeant Major. His response was, "Who said that?" The laughter stopped; no one said a word. The next command we heard from the Sergeant Major was, "Drop to the Leaning Rest." The Leaning Rest is the pushup position. After holding that position for about five minutes, the guilty trainee stepped forward and we were all allowed to stand back up. The Sergeant Major did have a sense of humor and let him off with guard duty for the weekend.

After I completed Special Forces MOS training in March 1970, we were all then assigned to a Group. At this time 5th Group was responsible for Vietnam and as warriors, everyone wanted to be assigned to 5th Group including myself. However, there were two Groups at Fort Bragg: 6th Group and 7th Group. I was assigned to 7th Group. Like any good soldier, you do as you are told and make the best of it. I was proud to be a Green Beret.

That summer brought me to Nantahala National Forest, from which I was picked to be a part of Bull Simons' mysterious mission. So, on September 2nd, 1970, as a member of the "Advance Party" we loaded those C-123s, southbound.

When we landed, we were at a remote airstrip in the sands of western Florida, on a secure military operating area many miles away from any civilians. It was referred to only as "Auxiliary Field #3," and we were not allowed to leave the base without permission, which we found would be rarely granted. None of us knew it at the time, but these remote Florida sands had a history of being used for top-secret missions.

CHAPTER 9

History Repeats: The Parallels Between the Doolittle Raid and the Son Tay Raid
World War II

IT WAS 28 YEARS earlier when 80 brave men did their training at Auxiliary Field #1 just down the road from Auxiliary Field #3 where we trained. This group was known as the Doolittle Raiders led by LtCol Jimmy Doolittle. For several weeks in early 1942, these B-25 Mitchell bomber crews trained takeoffs from a simulated Navy aircraft carrier deck, low-altitude bombing and over-water navigation.

These men had made the selfless choice to go on a mission that would likely require many of them to lay down their lives for their country. They knew there was no hope of landing their aircraft in friendly territory. It was on April 18th, 1942, only four months after the surprise attack on Pearl Harbor, that that they launched their sixteen B-25s from the aircraft carrier USS Hornet in the western Pacific Ocean. Their mission was to bomb military targets in Tokyo.

...*but*, just like for the Son Tay Raid, there was a MUCH HIGHER purpose for the mission.

The President knew that the bombs would not cripple any significant percentage of Tokyo's war machine. The President and the commanders had talked through the reality that America would lose the aircraft and possibly some of the Raiders. Then (just as would happen on the Son Tay Raid), ON THE LAST DAY prior to launch, new information (detection by Japanese fishing boats) indicating a lower probability of achieving some of their goals would force the American leaders to make a command decision based upon their highest priority. Even with a lowered likelihood of tactical benefit, the commanders authorized the launch because they knew that the Raid would SEND THE INTENDED MESSAGE TO THE ENEMY AND BOOST THE MORALE OF AMERICANS.

After hitting their targets, all the aircraft involved in the bombing were lost and 11 crewmen were either killed or captured—with three of the captured men executed by the Japanese Army in China. One of the B-25s landed in the Soviet Union at Vladivostok, where it was confiscated and its crew interned for more than a year.

So, in retrospect, was it a success or a failure?

Answer: Like the Son Tay Raid, it was a *success*. The morale of Americans soared at a time when it was *desperately* needed. The Doolittle Raid SUCCEEDED IN SENDING THE MESSAGE.

OUR ARRIVAL AT EGLIN

There were 25 Green Berets in the Advance Party aboard our C-123 from Pope AFB, NC, to Eglin AFB. We landed at around 6am on Wednesday September 2nd, 1970. It was typical Florida weather, hot and humid.

Now, I had never been on an Air Force base. I thought all military mess halls were the same. Let me tell you—I was wrong! This Air Force mess hall was more like a restaurant! I remember at breakfast the cook asked me how I wanted my eggs. I thought, *You must be trying to pull a joke on me.* In the Army, eggs were either cold & scrambled or warm & scrambled. I told him I'd like them over easy. He asked how many and I told him two would do it. I thought to myself, *I'm gonna like this.* They had several different fountain drinks and when they told me I could have seconds, I was hooked.

They bused us to "Auxiliary Field #3" (today it is named Duke Field.) The other Ft Bragg Green Berets would be arriving in another week or so. One of our first tasks was to secure the Tactical Operations Center building, which was only about 200 yards from the runway. The OSI (Office of Special Investigations) guys swept the building for bugs and did their security checks. We placed three rolls of concertina wire around the building, creating only one entrance. We installed a field phone at the entrance for communications to the staff inside. From Thursday September 3rd on, this building was guarded 24x7.

Six of us were given that round-the-clock task of guarding the building. While on shift, we would rotate a guard every two hours: you'd pull guard duty for two hours, then you'd be free to do other things for the 10 hours before your next shift. If I wasn't on guard duty, I was training or sleeping. It was hard work keeping up with training events and the PT events *and* guard duty.

This TOC building that we guarded was where a lot of the Top Secret planning for the raid was accomplished. I never entered it, but inside this building there would be a lot of brass spending the next few months planning the mission.

Our orders were that no one was allowed to enter the building without us verifying their identification and their authorization. Our job was to confirm that they were who they said they were. No matter who they were or how many times they had been in the building, we had to check their ID every time they entered. After confirming their identity, we would call into the building on the field phone and verify whether they were authorized to enter the building at this time. Someone from inside would come out and escort them from our gate into the building.

Now, the Bull wasn't the only legendary officer attached to the Son Tay Raid. Captain Dick Meadows would lead Blueboy Assault Group, which would land directly inside the POW camp walls. Enlisted in 1946, a paratrooper in the Korean War, in the early 1960s, Meadows served a stint with British Special Air Service. In Vietnam, Meadows captured video footage proving North Vietnam Army was infiltrating South Vietnam and impressed General Westmoreland so much that, in 1967, he received a battlefield commission directly to Captain. He was the commanding officer of Ranger School when Bull Simons recruited him for the Son Tay Raid.

Lieutenant Colonel Bud Sydnor was selected by Bull Simons to serve as the Ground Forces Commander (whereas Bull Simons' role would be the on-scene eyes and ears of the Joint Contingency Task Group, in constant contact with General Manor.) LtCol Sydnor had the reputation of a gentleman and a consummate professional.

One day, Brigadier General Blackburn from the Pentagon, Brigadier General Manor (Commander of USAF Special Operations Forces), Bull Simons, and Captain Dick Meadows (both Simons and Meadows have statues at the Army's Special Forces Museum today—see images at the end of Appendix 4) showed up as a group and requested access to the Operations Center. I checked their IDs and called in for someone to come out and escort them in. LtCol Sydnor comes out to the gate. Can you image how I felt? Here I am a 20-year-old buck sergeant standing in the midst of some of the most notable Special Operations Forces officers ever. I remember they treated me as one of them, making small talk with me. After a while, LtCol Sydnor took them inside. This is one of the great things about Special Forces. The officers and enlisted men treat each other with respect. I believe this is because you have to depend on one another when you operate in small teams like Special Forces.

Image 4: BGen Donald D Blackburn created the concept
of the mission to rescue the POWs at Son Tay.

It wasn't until after the mission that I understood what an important job guarding access to the Tactical Operations Center was. Had the information in that building been revealed, it would have jeopardized the lives of the men and the mission. Bull Simons mentioned in his speech on the night of the raid how crucial operational security had been.

LIFE LESSON 2: Your Life is Significant, so be Excellent in Everything you Do. No matter how insignificant you think your job is, it could turn out to be a life-changing position. One of the reasons Capt Dan selected me to be paired with him was that, during all the time I spent pulling guard duty and training, I never complained, but always did what was asked of me. I credit my dad for instilling this attitude in my brothers and me. He always told us, "If you're going to do anything, do your best."

As a member of the Advance Party, another of our tasks was to build this large Mockup of buildings, using target canvas as the walls with doors and with cut-outs for windows. We began constructing it on Thursday Sept 10th and it took us several days to complete. We didn't know why we were having to build it. It wasn't until we did our first walk-through during our initial training that I realized how it would be used. Even then, we had no idea that it was a dimensionally perfect replica of all the buildings and walls of the POW camp in Son Tay, North Vietnam.

We built it on what is known as Range C-2, formerly a strafing range used by the Air Force.

Image 5: This photo shows both Aux Field #3 (on the left) and the range where the Mockup was built (on the right.)

Image 6: We built the Mockup with the type of cloth that the Air Force used for building strafing targets. Recall that the interviewers asked me if I could weld. In the photo you can see how we put chains on some "walls" to practice freeing people using cutting torches. Major Tom Macomber is standing on the north side of the "Quiz Room." You can see the northwest guard tower behind him.

Image 7: The Mockup. In the top photo ,the nearest
"building" likely represents the northwest tower.

Image 8: Shown at the Mockup are Master Sgt Joe
Lupyak (Redwine), Sgt 1st Class Donald Wingrove
(Blueboy), Major Thomas Macomber (Security at
Aux Field #3), 1st Lt James Paine (*Peach 3*.)

Kemmer   Lawhon

Image 9: Shown at the Mockup are Master Sgt
Thomas Kemmer (Blueboy), and Sgt 1st Class
David Lawhon (Greenleaf.) The white tires were the
markers of the landing zones for the helicopters.

In addition to the "buildings" that we constructed, there was earthmoving equipment that completed a "road by the Son Tay compound and a canal/river" on Thursday Sept 10th. By Tuesday Sept 15th, we constructed "Helio Landing Sites #1 and #2" with white tires dug into the ground to mark the landing sites. (The TOC log records these details.)

HISTORICAL NOTE FOR SON TAY RAID RESEARCHERS:

Multiple books and historians perpetuate an inaccurate story that we took the Mockup down every day. The concern was that the Soviet reconnaissance satellites that pass over Eglin each day might be able to determine what we were planning. I can clear up that misconception—we never took it down. It is true that we were concerned, but those concerns were satisfied by a simple experiment. An Air Force reconnaissance aircraft took some high-resolution photos for us while the Mockup was installed. Those photos proved that the Mockup could not be seen clearly enough by even the best high-resolution imagery.

I can tell you—as someone who constructed it and who used it for months—from the time that we arrived September 2nd through at least November 16th (the end of our time at Aux Field #3), we did not take down the Mockup. (Also see Sgt Robert Hobdy's and Sgt Pat St.Clair's explanations of this in Appendix 4.)

Image 10: This photo was taken by a USAF reconnaissance jet to help in the determination that we would *not* need to take down the Mockup. The photo was taken from an aircraft northwest of C-2 looking to the southeast.

IF YOU ARE PARTICULARLY INTERESTED IN MILITARY HISTORY...

Let me offer you an option at this point. Since I am telling you my story, I have not shared much of the behind-the-scenes information of the big picture, the overall plan. This overall plan was known only to the President, the Secretary of Defense, the Joint Chiefs of

Staff, the four leaders of our Special Forces contingent, and a small group of Air Force planners. If you are the type of technical person who really wants to know those details ahead of time, feel free to look in Appendix 1: A "30,000 ft View" of the Mission.

CHAPTER 10

September 1970
The First Month of Training

ON WEDNESDAY SEPTEMBER 9ᵀᴴ, about a week after we arrived as the Advance Party, the other 78 (or so) Green Berets arrived and we started our training (the log recorded for Thursday Sept 10th states, "Day 01 of training.") The first 30 days of training were intense. Each day started with PT, followed by running the Meadows Mile. Dick Meadows loved to run and he led many of our runs. Now I like to run, but not like Captain Meadows. If you were not in shape, you soon would be. I think this was one of the reasons I was selected as one of the raiders.

I was, by no means, the biggest man. In fact, I was second shortest. The shortest raider was also the oldest NCO: Master Sergeant Galen "Pappy" Kittleson. Pappy was no stranger to combat. Pappy and I had several things in common. We were both short and stocky built. We'd both grown up on a farm in the Midwest. In World War II, Pappy was the youngest man in the raid on the Cabanatuan POW camp in the Philippines. I was the youngest man on this raid, 25 years junior to Pappy.

[John Gargus' book *The Son Tay Raid: American POWs in Vietnam Were Not Forgotten*, on page 24, explains a little about me being the youngest raider.]

Pappy was a quiet man, but he always knew what he was doing. He made history on the Son Tay Raid as the only American soldier to be on four POW raids. Pappy was well respected by everyone.

[On a side note, Pappy visited my family after he retired. In his hometown of Toeterville, Iowa, he started a group called the Alamo Scouts. It was for kids that were considering the military or kids who could just use some direction in their lives. Pappy suggested to my daughter that she should come to his summer camp to see if she would like the military. Sadly, Pappy died a couple of months before Hana was able to attend his training camp. I attended Pappy's funeral and it was amazing how many men from Pappy's Alamo Scout group attended to show their love and respect for him. There were doctors, military men, an FBI agent, and many friends and family. Pappy had left an impact on a lot of people. Ross Perot paid for his headstone listing many of his accomplishments. At Pappy's funeral, someone asked me if I was Pappy's son—I was truly honored to receive that compliment! Pappy was a true American hero!]

Being in good physical shape is important to any solider who is going into combat. One of the raiders, Sgt 1st Class Jake Jakovenko, went beyond the rest of us. I believe there was a good reason why Jake was selected to carry an M-60 machine gun, our heaviest gun. Jake was what you would think of when you picture a Special Forces soldier. He was over 6 foot, with a big barrel chest and shoulders about two axe handles across with a waist of maybe 30 inches.

After our morning PT and the two- or three-mile run, while the rest of us where resting up from the PT, Jake would add more as his own personal workout. We would watch Jake place his feet on the second or third step and knock out fifty or one hundred push-ups, depending on how he felt. To say Jake was in good shape would be an understatement.

Our training began with us walking through our positions over and over again in daylight. During the first month, there were several changes to how we performed our mission. Each person had specific tasks to perform. Not only did we have to know our own role, but we had to know the role of the man to our left and right and where they would be when the firing started. Capt Dan and I were a two-man team. As the RTO for Redwine Security Group my job was (as Capt Dan put it): "I want you an arm's length from me or *I will be the one* who'll shoot you!" And if you knew Capt Dan, he would have, so you can bet I stayed damn close to him. The primary job of our two-man team was to make our way to the Communications Building as fast as we could to neutralize the people inside before they could radio for reinforcements. We had two buildings to clear (Buildings 11 and 12 on the diagram in Chapter 16) before we could get to the Communications Building (7A on the diagram.)

The technique we used for clearing a building was different from what our troops use today. As a two-man team, we would first toss a concussion grenade into the building. Why use a concussion grenade and not a frag grenade? The answer is very simple. The buildings we were clearing of bad guys were not made of concrete, but of a thin material that a piece of frag would fly through. Capt Dan would stand to one side of the doorway and I would position myself to the other side across from him. When the concussion grenade exploded it would generally blow the door open or in some cases completely off.

As soon as the grenade exploded, Capt Dan would dive to the floor at the threshold firing into the room from top left to bottom right. At the same time, I would step over him firing top right to bottom left. By this we created an X covering all the space in the room. Capt Dan would remain on the floor, and I would back out and shine my flashlight into the room so Capt Dan could confirm that we had neutralized everyone.

I would then put in a new clip, depending on if I'd fired any tracer rounds. Capt Dan taught me that, in combat, you don't have time to count how many bullets you fired. The technique is to first load five tracer rounds and then finish filling the magazine. When you're in a firefight and you see the tracers smoking out the end of your barrel you know you need to change magazines. See any tracers: change out your clip.

LIFE LESSON 3: In your Work, always be Training and Improving. During the first month of our training, there were several changes made to how we approached our positions. I learned a very important lesson: Invest the time in training—it pays off. Just like a football team trains for the big game, we were training for our big game. The major difference: our lives depended on how well we performed. Training sometimes gets boring, but when the bullets start flying in both directions, you're sure glad that you know what is expected of you and your team members.

As one of the six guys assigned to guard the Tactical Operations Center, I started to see that I might miss out on some key training. If I wanted to have a chance of getting selected for one of the Assault Force teams, I had to train when I was not pulling guard duty. Security was so tight that we didn't know who we would be rescuing or in what part of the world the mission would take place. There was a lot of speculation that it might be an attempt to free prisoners in Cuba based on the three-hour flying time of the mission.

I had been training and pulling guard duty for about a month when I got my chance to speak up. I was checking Colonel Bull Simons for access to the TOC building. While we were waiting for an escort to take the Bull in, he asked how things were going for me. I knew that he was only going to pick some of us for the actual mission, so I said, "Sir, I didn't volunteer to come here and pull guard duty. If I wanted to pull guard duty, I could have stayed at Fort Bragg." Now the Bull always had a two-inch cigar that he chewed on. He looked me right in the eyes and said, "Young man, hang in there. Things are going to change pretty soon." After he went into the building, I thought to myself, *What in the hell did I just do? First I chewed out two Sergeant Majors back at Ft Bragg, trying to get on this mission. Now I just told a Colonel—and not just any Colonel, but Bull Simons—that I was tired of pulling guard duty. I just bitched to the Bull about pulling guard duty!?* I thought, *Well I'll probably end up pulling guard duty the rest of my time in the Army.*

However, what he said was true. Within the next week, things did change.

The first cut was made on Friday September 18th. They selected 51 men, and an additional 10 men were identified as backup that could be used in any of the different elements. I was selected to be a part of the Redwine Security Group. I would be the RTO for Captain Dan Turner. No more guard duty for me! The three Groups were each placed in their own areas in the barracks building to help build the team concept.

LIFE LESSON 4: Have Patience and Aggressiveness and Contentment. Guarding the TOC, we were not allowed to know the "Why." As I saw my opportunity slipping away, I was aggressive, hungry to be in the middle of the action. That's OK—it's not a fault to be aggressive. It's a virtue—if you can choose in your heart and in your mind to be at peace and to be thankful, trusting God with the outcome.

In our training at Ft Bragg we used blanks, but for our training here at Aux Field #3, we used live ammunition. I remember one day we were throwing frag grenades and one of the guys got hit with some shrapnel. It was only a minor cut, but it drove the point home that we needed to stay sharp. By the end of the first month, we had practiced until every person knew not only his own position, but also the job of every person around him and Alternate Plans.

Then we started practicing at night.

CHAPTER 11

October 1970
The Second Month of Training

On Tuesday October 6th, we flew a "Full Profile," including a three-hour flight, launching at 8pm, flying around Lower Alabama, air refueling, followed by a full ground assault on the Mockup. Then we exfiltrated with a flight back to Aux Field #3 where we did a mission debriefing at 8am.

Image 11: Nighttime training at the Mockup.

When we first started training using the helicopters, the plan called for Capt Dan to be the first man off and for me to be the second. Now, I had watched enough war movies to know that the first men off any vehicle get killed. For a couple of weeks, we trained this way. I thought, *Oh shit, we aren't even going to make it off the chopper.* I can now admit that every time I stepped off the chopper, the thought went through my mind of getting zapped before my foot even hit the ground.

Then after a few rehearsals, the plan changed to where Capt Dan and I were the <u>last</u> two off the chopper. All of the sudden, I thought, *Damn, now that I'm the last guy off, the bad guys will get their sights locked on. I will get nailed for <u>sure</u>!* Eventually I had to admit that, if the good Lord wants me, He doesn't care if I am the first, last or in the middle. My Maker is going to bring me home when it's my time.

LIFE LESSON 5: Be Prepared for Death. Don't worry about it. You can't completely control it. Make sure that the day you meet your Maker is not the first time you've been introduced. If you are prepared at all times, you're free to live life fearless.

WHY DAN SELECTED ME

It wasn't until I began to write this book that I asked Dan Turner why he selected me to be his right-hand man. The following is his response: "During training, I had noticed you and your gung-ho attitude. You responded positively to any and all tasking, didn't give any bull shit excuses and got things done without a lot of supervision. You were in great physical shape if I needed you to carry my butt out. Plus, there was that intangible thing, the stuff that you can't really define. When I looked in your eyes, I knew I

wanted you as my RTO. There was just something about the way
you carried yourself that told me you were way beyond the experience level of an average 20-year-old. The only approval I needed
was LtCol Bud Sydnor and he approved without any questions."

I owe Dan a lot. He took a kid, still wet behind the ears with no
combat experience, and turned me into a soldier. He told me, "You
stay an arm's length from me and cover my butt." I felt very safe
with him at my side. I trusted him to do the same for me. I know
there were times when he probably thought, *Is this damn kid going to perform when needed?* Well I had the opportunity to prove
myself a couple of times and I am glad to say we both made it back
safe.

> [Dan has passed away now. He and his family be-
> came a part of our family. We stayed in close contact.
> When my daughter graduated from jump school, Dan
> was there with me to see her fifth jump at 1:30am at
> the Fryar Field Drop Zone. Hana didn't know Dan
> and I were going to be at the DZ that night. She was
> on the last stick to jump. Dan took a great picture of
> her as she hiked to the trucks with all her gear. (See
> Hana's picture in Chapter 21.)]

In October, we were each given a "Singlepoint" sight to mount
on our weapons. This technology had never before been used in
the military. It provided a red dot on your target during the day
and a green dot at night. It requires no electricity. Instead, its optics
collect the ambient light (even at night), creating a single colored
dot. You cannot see through the tube. Looking through the tube,
you would only see the colored dot (when aligned correctly) on a

black background. When you used the Singlepoint, you kept both eyes open and your mind would superimpose the dot on the target.

Image 12: Most of the Son Tay Raiders carried the CAR-15, shown here with the 30-round magazine, which were rare in the DOD inventory. Although 30-round magazines are now common, they were new technology in 1970. The "first generation" of 30-round magazines, called constant curve magazines, had feeding problems. The magazines we used were "second generation" and had to be specifically ordered for the mission from Colt Arms Company (because these magazines were not available through normal supply channels). We even had to fabricate our own pouches (from Claymore mine bags) to carry these magazines because they were so new to the Army. The 30-round magazines reduced the number of times I would need to reload in a firefight. Some of the Son Tay Raiders used electrical tape to secure their slings, reinforce the mount on their Singlepoint sight, and to keep dirt out of the muzzles of their rifles. This Son Tay CAR-15 replica was constructed by Eric Fordon of Enhanced Tactical Arms. It was researched by Dr. Earl Burress, Jr., Owen Lincoln, and Augee Kim. The photography by Colin Blount.

SINGLE POINT

Single POINT
DO NOT SIGHT — JUST POINT

The Singlepoint sight can be mounted on any standard rifle using conventional mounts with split 1-inch rings.

PHOTOS COURTESY OF GUNS & AMMO MAGAZINE

The Singlepoint mounted on Armalite's AR-18.

DISTRIBUTED BY: **ArmaLite, Inc.**
118 East 16th Street, Costa Mesa, Calif. (714) 548-7701
WASHINGTON OFFICE: Suite 404, 1700 K Street, N.W., Washington, D.C. (202) 296-3565

Image 13: ArmaLite's Singlepoint sight (red/green dot optics—
red during the day and green at night.) Note the date.

BK Moore

Image 14: Master Sgt Billy K. Moore has an ArmaLite
Singlepoint sight. Notice some used amber/
red goggles and others used clear goggles.

FRIDAY NIGHT FIGHTS

Friday night was our time off. After the first month, almost all our training was at night and, because of the urgency, we trained on Saturdays and even some Sundays. One day in early October, the training schedule posted on the bulletin board at the entrance to the barracks read, "Friday Night Fights."

Most of the fights were guys just popping off steam from the week of training. Like any military base, our small compound had a bar where we gathered to have drinks and blow off steam. At the bar, there was a jukebox but every once in a while, they would bring in a band. They did that for us about four times, as I recall. Sometimes, some young ladies would show up. Looking back, many of us now believe that the ladies who showed up were DOD employees there to see if we would divulge any information about what we were doing. I guess they thought that we single young bucks, after drinking a few beers, might have loose lips. Well we might have been young and filled with alcohol, but we kept our mouths shut.

I do remember a few good fights. One late Friday night, Sergeant Bass got into a fight and it moved outside the bar. Sergeant Bass was one big boy (about 6'3" and 250 lbs) and the last guy I would want to fight. There, outside the bar, he had a knife in one hand just daring anyone to take it away from him. Well it wasn't long until a couple of young Air Force Security Police showed up in their little blue jeep. Now, the two of them couldn't have weighed more than 130 lbs each. Their job was to disarm Sergeant Bass and take him to the Air Force brig. We thought, *This should be fun to watch*, and it was. After about fifteen minutes of the fly boys trying to talk Sergeant Bass into dropping his knife, one of our NCOs suggested the best approach would be for them to get back in their jeep and let us take care of our own. It was pretty easy to see that these two cowboys were not going to take Sergeant Bass anywhere. After the Air Force Police left, Sergeant Bass was talked in to putting away his knife by one of our NCOs. We all went back in the bar and had a few more drinks.

One night when the band was playing, someone tossed a smoke grenade on the dance floor. The band stopped playing and ran out as if there were a fire. Sgt Arlin Olson and I sat and watched the grenade burn. It only took a few minutes for the whole dance floor and the bandstand to be full of smoke. I am not sure who tossed the grenade, but it did burn a hole in the dance floor. It didn't stop anyone from drinking and after the smoke cleared the band came back in and played some more. The next morning LtCol Sydnor gave us all a good ass-chewing, but no one ever knew who threw the smoke bomb.

There was one other interesting incident that sticks in my mind. Our barracks were two-stories, the World War II style, with one big open bay for all of us. I was on the first floor and our beds were lined up on each side of the room. It was about 1:30am when I was awakened by crashing noises just four bunks down from mine. It was three NCOs wrestling a Master Sergeant to the floor in our barracks. Apparently, the Master Sgt, after quite a few drinks, had a disagreement with Bull Simons at the bar concerning how the teams should perform their mission and was frustrated that the troops were being kept in the dark. The discussion got heated and the NCO came back to his barracks to get his weapon to persuade the good Colonel to use his ideas. The guys in the barracks held the NCO until he eventually cooled down.

The next morning, the Bull and the NCO were on the PT field. The Bull had the NCO's heals locked at attention while he chewed his butt up one side and down the other. The Bull convinced him that he should not disagree with him again—at least not with a threat of bodily harm. The Bull did not let this effect his relationship with the NCO or anyone else. The Bull always said he didn't want a bunch of Boy Scouts. We always looked forward to Friday Night Fights!

The following entry was made in the official TOC Record of Events. I believe this was that very discussion with that very Master Sergeant!

27 Oct 70 (Tuesday)

1715:   COL Simons discussed grievances with operational personnel and discussed progress.

Image 14A: This entry is on page 12 of the "Record of Events (Log), U.S. Army Element, JCTG (JCS)," the book kept at the Tactical Operations Center building

SUNDAYS

Sundays were days that we had to ourselves for sleeping in or playing basketball or just hanging out. Due to our security situation we could not go anywhere. There were a couple of weekend days that we were loaded into deuce-and-a-halfs with the back covered and taken to a deserted beach where we could swim, barbeque, and drink beer. It was a good break from being stuck at Aux Field #3.

I remember I would get up, go over to the bar jukebox and play "Sunday Morning Coming Down" by Johnny Cash. It was a meaningful song to listen to on Sunday. Under normal circumstances, Sunday was when I would call my folks. During this whole time, we were not allowed to communicate with anyone. Before leaving Fort Bragg, I had called them and explained to them I was going on a training mission and would call them when I returned, but that I did not know when that might be. I figured my dad would understand that I was doing something more than training, but he never let on. [In fact, it wasn't until the day at the University Hospital when we finally talked about our military experiences. That's when he told me that he suspected I was doing something dangerous, but he didn't dare say a word to Mom.]

BARBARA

I am not sure, but it was rumored that our phone calls were monitored and our mail read. It didn't bother me. I only called my folks on Sundays and I didn't get any mail. (I did borrow Sgt Tyrone Adderly's mail. His lovely wife Gloria would send him scented letters and I would stick them under my pillow so I could smell them when I slept. He was always good about letting me borrow them.)

> [Note: Two months later in December, Tyrone ends up in the East Room of the White House being awarded a medal by the President of the United States! See a photo of the televised event in Adderly's contribution in Appendix 4.]

There was one occasion when, after a day of training, we landed back at Aux Field #3 and there were some Air Force guys taking pictures as we exited the chopper. We were walking toward our barracks when two black sedans pulled up, and four guys dressed in civilian clothes jumped out of the sedans and took the camera away from the Air Force guys, pulled the film out, and then handed back the camera. We had not seen these four civilian clothes guys, but they apparently were always there like sentinels, looking out for us. We thought it was cool that they had our backs.

Security was tight. We were kept in the dark.

Then, on Monday October 19th, we were introduced to Barbara. She was a sight to behold! Everyone had been wanting to lay eyes on her. She was the talk of the week. She was housed in a separate building away from us and each of us was required to study her so that we had a mental image of every inch of her. Barbara was a model. And someday, Barbara would be famous.

When I was with her, I used a prism to study her so that, when the time was right and I exited the chopper, I would be oriented to everything around me. It was time well spent. You see Barbara was a precise scale replica of a military compound (the Son Tay POW camp), created from CIA photographs taken from Buffalo Hunter drones and SR-71 manned reconnaissance aircraft. It was codenamed "Barbara" after Barbara L. Strosnider, a secretary from the United States Air Force Directorate of Plans, at the Pentagon where the model was created.

The CIA had done an excellent job of detailing the terrain and buildings at the camp. One item that really fascinated me was the bicycle that was parked in front of the Communications Building that Capt Dan and I had to neutralize as quickly as we could before enemy reinforcements could be alerted. On the night of the raid, as we approached the actual building—sure as heck—the bicycle was there!

The intel we had was amazing and the intel community deserves praise. Sadly, there are too many armchair quarterbacks who have a political agenda when they criticize the intel.

[You can see a full color "pin up" of Barbara in Sgt Ken Ruud's contribution at the end of Appendix 4.]

E & E EXERCISE

On Wednesday October 21st, we did another Full Profile—this time with our ArmaLite sights which placed the green dot on your target—launching at 10pm. Observing were BGen Blackburn (who created the concept of the raid at the Pentagon) and BGen Manor (the raid's Mission Commander; USAF Commander of Special Operations Forces.) By 1am the mission was complete.

At the end of this run, we began a Field Training Exercise of E&E (Escape and Evasion, in case we were trapped behind enemy lines) beginning at 9am that morning, October 22nd.

During one of our training exercises, we had the opportunity to use a jungle penetrator for rescue. Here's how it works. The chopper will hover over you at 100 to 150 feet. A hoist extends out from the right-side doorway. The PJ (AF pararescueman) in the chopper will lower the penetrator to the ground (it's sleek and can't get caught in the jungle branches.) You let the penetrator hit the ground before you touch it. The aircraft and the jungle penetrator builds up a huge static charge, so it will shock the crap out of you if you don't let it ground out first. As soon as it hits the ground, you stand it up and fold out one of the three seats.

If there are two of you being extracted, you grab each other's web gear and hold on until you are hauled inside the chopper. Now, what normally happens is, the chopper hovers stationary until you're securely inside the chopper. It so happened that Sgt Arlin Olson and I were kind of the team's jokers, so I believe they saw this as the opportunity to have a little fun with us. They flew us around like this for about ten minutes before they started pulling us in. That was a fun ride.

On another day, our assault groups were divided into 4- or 5-man teams. We were taken into the woods on the Eglin ranges with C-rations and were told to rendezvous at a certain lake in a couple of days. We all met at the lake and someone had the idea of catching some fish to eat. Now, when a bunch of Green Berets go fishing, they usually catch their limit. The trick is the bait you use…and we just happened to have a few concussion grenades. We tossed a couple of them into the lake, and the fish just floated to the surface. Now all we needed was for someone to swim out and collect our dinner. So, Staff Sergeant Larry "Tiny" Young and I blew up an air mattress, stripped off, and swam out to do the job.

While we were collecting the fish, the local Game Warden pulled up in his jeep on the lake dam. He got out of his vehicle and walked around so he could see what we were doing. Now, this guy was about as wide as he was tall. When he saw what we were doing he yelled at us to stop. We had all these fish… and we were pretty hungry... All of the sudden, there was a rapid Ack!Ack!Ack! right over our heads in the general direction of the Game Warden. One of our guys on the shore had picked up his M-16, placed it on "Rock & Roll" and fired about fifteen rounds over our heads into the water. It scared the hell out of Tiny and me, but not as much as it did the Game Warden. I have never seen a fat man move so damn fast. He jumped back in his jeep and took off! We all had a good laugh…and fish for dinner.

We ran another Full Profile launching at 10pm on Friday November 6th. All went very well on that run.

CHAPTER 12

Monday November 16th, 1970
Pack your Bags and Pray

WE WERE TOLD TO pack our gear—that we were leaving Eglin AFB for our new undisclosed location the next day.

We didn't have a chaplain in our group, but we did have Master Sgt Galen "Pappy" Kittleson. Pappy announced that he would be holding a prayer service in the barracks. Pappy was respected by all the raiders and officers from the Bull down the chain of command.

In World War II, Pappy had been an Alamo Scout (precursor to the Green Berets), just like Bull Simons. They both were on the raid that freed 500 POWs (survivors of the Bataan Death March) from the Cabanatuan POW camp in the Philippines. There's a 2005 major motion picture about it called *The Great Raid*. Pappy was pretty famous in the Army, particularly in Special Forces.

When I walked into the barracks where Pappy was holding the prayer service, it really struck me, how many of these seasoned soldiers were there to pray on their knees to our Father in heaven. I can tell you there were no atheists in our group.

The next morning, Tuesday November 17th, they loaded us up in covered deuce-and-a-halfs and drove us to a larger landing field, the main airfield of Eglin AFB. We unloaded inside a large hangar. Inside that hangar was a C-141 Starlifter, which we boarded. I remember, the seats were like those on civilian planes, except they faced the back of the plane. We still didn't have a clue as to where we were headed. We all joined in singing the John Denver chorus, "I'm leavin' on a jet plane. Don't know when I'll be back again." In this case, it was so true.

It was a long flight. We landed in California to refuel but had to stay on the plane.

The next place we landed was Alaska. We were allowed to unload while they refueled our plane. A few of us went outside for few minutes, but it was so damn cold and we were not really dressed for winter weather. We had just come from 75-degree temperatures wearing our jungle fatigues. Our uniforms were sterile—there was no military rank or anything that identified us as US Army soldiers. We didn't wear our Green Berets—only our regular Army head gear.

On these flights, we had a serious craps game going on. I believe it was Sgt 1st Class Leroy Carlson who converted a cardboard box into a craps table. Talk about a floating craps game!

Our next landing was Japan, but we had to stay on the plane.

The next stop would be our new home for the next few days. It was a long flight and we didn't get much sleep, but at last we touched down at our final destination.

CHAPTER 13

Wednesday November 18ᵗʰ, 1970
The CIA Compound in an
Undisclosed Country

IT WAS NOVEMBER 18ᵀᴴ at about 3am, when we stepped off the C-141 directly into a large hangar. They loaded us into what I thought were bread trucks. The air in this dark land had a sweet tropical smell, warm and humid. The old warriors thought we were in Southeast Asia but were not certain. We never knew it until many years later, but this was the CIA Compound at Takhli Royal Thai Air Force Base.

When our trucks arrived at some barracks, most of us went straight to bed. Our trip had taken 28 hours.

I woke up around mid-morning and went outside to see what our new home looked like. My first thought was that we were in a prison. There was a 10- to 12-foot fence around the compound with razor barbs on the top. I didn't know which country we were in, but the scenery was beautiful. There were lush green mountains that surrounded us and the air was filled with the smell of flowers.

It didn't take long to find the chow hall. I had a good breakfast with a couple of other raiders. There was a bar with some pool tables and one big snooker table.

[I had not played snooker since leaving Missouri. There was a pool hall near our farm in the small town of Clark where the farmers played when it rained and was too wet to do their work in the fields.]

I shot a couple of games of snooker and eight ball. I sat around and listened to some of the seasoned warriors guessing the country. I knew one thing for sure: we weren't in Kansas anymore, Toto. We were told to relax and get some rest. There wasn't much to do for the next couple of days, but we all knew that we were getting closer to what we had been training to do for the past three months. I was thinking about my family and friends back home. I thought about Mom and Dad, where they would be right now. We were all excited about what our mission might be. For the past three months we had rehearsed, rehearsed, and rehearsed, and we were ready to go do our job.

CHAPTER 14

Friday November 20th, 1970
The Day of the Launch

WE WERE AWAKENED AT 6am, had breakfast, and went about our morning as normal. We were told to be at the mess hall at 11am, a little earlier than normal lunch. During lunch, we were told to go to our barracks immediately after we finish eating and get some sleep. To ensure we got sleep, LtCol Joe Cataldo, our doctor who would be going on the mission and into the compound with us, required every one of us to take a sleeping pill as we exited the mess hall. As we walked toward the barracks, the old timers explained that they had never had to do that before. It was pretty clear that this would be the night.

I spent the rest of the afternoon walking around the compound and talking with other raiders about what they thought was going on. The time passed very slowly that afternoon.

By 5pm, everyone was awakened from our bunks and told to get to the mess hall for dinner then meet in the Theater at 1800 hrs.

By about 1730, we started filling the Theater. You could tell everyone was getting pumped for what we were about to learn.

Everyone was talking and making guesses. By this time, we all knew we are going on some kind of rescue mission. We just didn't know the when, the where, and the who.

At 1800, the Bull and LtCol Sydnor walked on the stage. The room got dead silent when the Bull began to talk. Bull was a man of few words. The briefing Theater was a short walk from our barracks. Inside, it had rows of simple wood seating like 2x10 boards on short metal poles—no seatbacks. It would seat around 100. There was an elevated stage with a screen. We had watched a movie there just a couple of days prior.

BULL TELLS US OUR MISSION
Bull reveals a large map (it was the area around Hanoi) and says,

"We are going to rescue 70 American Prisoners of War, maybe more, from a camp called Son Tay. The target is 23 miles west of Hanoi.

This is something our American Prisoners of War have a right to expect from their fellow soldiers. We are all part of the same military family. We want these men to know that they are not abandoned by their military family. No man should feel that way. That's why we are going in there after them.

*You are to let nothing, **nothing** interfere with the operation. Our mission is to rescue prisoners, not to take prisoners.*

If there's been a leak, we'll know it by the time the second or third chopper sets down. If we're walking into a trap, if it turns out that they know we're coming, don't even dream about walking out of North Vietnam—unless you've got wings on your feet. We'll be 100 miles from Laos. It's the wrong part of the world for a retrograde maneuver. If it happens, I want to keep this force together. We'll back up to the Song Con River if we have to and, by God, they're welcome to come across that damned open ground. We'll make them pay for every foot across that sonofabitch."

For about four seconds, you could have heard a pin drop. Then, like a cannon shot, everyone bursts out, shouting, whooping & hollering, slapping each other on the back, raring like broncos, yelling "Let's go get 'em!"

Bull tries to bring us back to earth by explaining, in no uncertain terms, that he estimates each man has a 50/50 chance of returning alive from this mission. He states that this is *strictly* a volunteer mission. If any man has a reason that he should not go on this mission, he should decide now. (Not a single man backed out.)

The whole meeting, including LtCol Sydnor's portion, lasted no longer than 10 minutes.

[Looking back on this today, it is impressive to know the dedication these men had to fellow warriors. It is just as impressive to know that young people in today's military have that same commitment.]

Image 15: Bull Simons

At 2100, the bread trucks took us to a hangar that we used as our staging area. We checked our weapons. I carried a Colt M1911, a .45 caliber pistol. My machine gun was a CAR-15 with eight 20-round magazines and five 30-round magazines. I used the tips I'd learned from Capt Dan on how I should load my magazines:

first load five tracer rounds and then finish filling the magazine. The last thing you want to do is charge into a building with less than five rounds in your magazine. The seasoned warrior was looking after my butt.

I strapped on two frag grenades and ten concussion grenades. Capt Dan told me if we ended up needing to use the frags, well, we were probably in some deep shit. So I hoped I did not have to use them. We used the concussion grenades in clearing the buildings. My next task was to check the batteries on both my radios. I checked my handset and my headset on my PRC-25. That's the way we were to communicate with LtCol Sydnor's ground command team. The headset allowed me to listen to the radio traffic and still fire my weapon and toss grenades.

Each raider carried a survival radio, a PRC-90. When you turn these radios on, they send out a warble tone that allows a SAR (search and rescue) team to pull you out of a hot situation (although the chances of being rescued that deep in enemy territory were slim to none.) Among the 56 raiders we had 92 radios.

RAIDERS EQUIPMENT LIST

The following is the equipment the raiders had. You might say we could host our own war with plenty of fire power.

	Inventory	Ammunition
2	M-16 Rifles	1,200 rounds
48	CAR-15 Rifles	18,437 rounds
51	Colt 45 Pistols	1,162 rounds
4	M-79 Grenade Launchers	219 rounds
4	M-60 Machine Guns	4,300 rounds
2	12 Gauge Shotguns	100 rounds
15	Claymore Mines	
4	Demo Charges	
213	Hand Grenades, including Frag and Concussion	
12	Wire Cutters	
2	Chain Saws	
17	Machetes	
11	Bolt Cutters	
1	Heavy Duty Bolt Cutter	
2	Cutting Torches	
5	Crowbars	
34	Miner's Lamps	

I also checked my flashlight, my goggles and my Blood Chit. Having never been in combat, I wasn't really sure what this Blood Chit was used for. Capt Dan told me, "Let's hope you won't need it." Blood Chits date back to WW I. Mine was a bright yellow silk with the American flag on one side and the following words in several different languages on the other side:

I am a citizen of the United States of America. I do not speak your language. Misfortune forces me to seek your assistance in obtaining food, shelter, and protection. Please take me to someone who will provide for my safety and see that I am returned to my people. My government will reward you.

After we had checked out our equipment, we then checked our buddy's gear. Since I was the kid of the group, many of the seasoned warriors came up to Capt Dan and me. They told Capt Dan, "Bring the kid back in one piece." They all told me, "Don't hesitate," and to watch Capt Dan's back. I can tell you the morale was very high. For the past few months all we had done was train, train, and train. We were all ready to go bring home our American POWs. It was our Super Bowl...with a life-or-death outcome.

We loaded onto the C-130 that then took us to Udorn Royal Thai Air Force Base, where our helicopters were prepped and ready, awaiting us.

CHAPTER 15

2317 hrs, Friday November 20ᵗʰ, 1970
The Helicopter Flight from Udorn
RTAFB to Son Tay

WHEN OUR C-130 LANDED at Udorn at 2300, we were immediately ushered to our respective HH-53 choppers. The engines were running, but eerily, all the aircraft lights were off. The code name and call sign for Redwine's bird was *Apple 2*. I moved to the front of the bird for the three-hour flight. I could smell the jet fuel as the rotors were spun up. I took my radio off and leaned back against my troop seat along the side of the chopper.

At 2317, with all the Green Berets aboard, *Apple 2* lifted off, forming up with the other five helicopters and *Lime 1* and *Lime 2*, the 4-engine C-130 Hercules tankers that would take us to the border of North Vietnam. During our training, we had only made the full three-hour-long flight twice (a "Full Profile"). The idea, I think, was to keep us from trying to figure out where we might be going. What I remember about that night was how hot it was and that the sky was very clear.

On that long chopper flight from Udorn to Son Tay, I spent a lot of time in prayer. You can learn a little bit about yourself, seeing what your mind latches onto when you know that in a few hours you might be meeting your Maker. God has been an important part of my life as long as I can remember. My mother's side of the family attended church pretty regularly, compared to my dad's side. The Bucklers like to drink, dance, and party. Not to say they didn't believe in God—they just liked to celebrate a little more. After the death of my Grandpa (Mom's dad), we stopped attending Grandpa's church in Cairo, Missouri, about 20 miles from our farm. We started going to church in nearby Clark.

My Sunday School teacher was Emma Ridgeway. She was not only my teacher but our neighbor. The only grandparent I remember was my mom's dad. My other grandparents passed away before I was born. To me, Emma was as close as a grandma. Emma taught our Sunday School from my freshmen year through my senior year.

I was sixteen when I accepted Christ as my savior. I have always known He was with me.

After about an hour of flying, most of the guys were lying back against the sides of the chopper. Some guys had their eyes closed, either praying or sleeping. I thought to myself, "These men are true warriors." Many of the raiders were married; some had kids my age or older. There was not a lot of small talk. I figured each man was thinking of his family. Each one knew the risk he was taking. We were no different than other warriors before us. Our military is filled with men and women who are willing to risk their lives to protect this great country. I sat back and had a nice talk with the Big Man upstairs. I asked Him to protect us tonight.

This was the longest three hours I had ever experienced. I thought about Mom and Dad and how they would feel if I didn't make it back. I wondered what they would think when they read the letter I had written to them before I left. I thought about what Dad told me when I left for the Army: "Don't volunteer for anything." So what did I do? I volunteered for Airborne, then for Special Forces, and now for this raid.

I thought Mom and Dad would be heading to the Moose Lodge this weekend for a Saturday night outing. Mom and Dad loved to dance and they went dancing just about every Saturday night since I could remember. I was about seven or eight when I learned to dance at the Moose Lodge.

I thought about Doug, my oldest brother, who served in Navy submarines for nine years. After repeated tours of spending several months undersea, he decided to change careers and went to work in the computer industry.

I will never forget how upset my brother Darrell's wife was when he received his draft notice. I imagine she felt like so many other wives did when that letter came for the person they love. Darrell took his physical but, due to a back problem, he didn't pass. One winter, Darrell and I were playing ice hockey with some of my Grandpa's golf clubs. We used a corncob for a puck. I accidently racked Darrell on the chin with my club. He turned and cracked me upside the head right above my eye, and blood flowed down the side of my face. He immediately packed snow on my cut and told me not to tell Mom and Dad. I still have the scar today.

I thought about how my brothers and I fought and the crazy things we had done on the farm.

I thought about the times I hunted squirrels with Dad. I thought back to the first squirrel I killed. I had shot him about nine times, and when Dad and I were skinning it he said, "We might get lead poison when we eat this one."

Mike Ridgeway, one of my best friends back home was getting married tonight. I thought how far Clark, Missouri, is from where

I was tonight. I thought, *Well if I do make it out of this, I will never forget his wedding anniversary date.* It's funny what goes through your mind.

I thought about my buddy Charlie Cottingham and the fun we had as kids. I thought about the first job we had working for his dad cutting corn out of beans with a corn knife. Back before they had the chemicals that are used today, some farmers would pay us kids to cut the corn that came up 'volunteer' out of the beans. Our corn knife looked like a big old machete and we'd walk the bean rows, getting the corn. We were about 10 years old and made two bucks a day, a free lunch and a cold bottle of Double Cola.

There's Johnny Adams and me, riding my old Honda 50 on the dirt roads around Clark.

I thought back on the times Mike and I spent riding our horses in the woods around our farms.

I guess I was trying to take my mind off the mission, because I couldn't stop mentally rehearsing my duties for the mission over and over and over. I got up to stretch my legs and look out the window. I could see the other choppers in the moonlight. It was like we were doing just another rehearsal, so prepared we were. But this was the live run. We were actually going in. I sat back down, said another prayer for us, and waited for us to arrive at Son Tay, North Vietnam.

CHAPTER 16

0219 hrs, Saturday
November 21st, 1970
Alternate Plan Green

THE 170 REHEARSALS WERE about to payoff. We had prepared in case one of the choppers had mechanical problems or was
taken out of service by a SAM (Surface-to-Air Missile.) Alternate
Plan Green was for a scenario where Greenleaf Support Group
(which included Colonel Simons) was out of service. Alternate
Plan Blue was called if Blueboy Assault Group was out of service.
As you can guess, there was also an Alternate Plan Red, in case we
didn't make it. The planners had decided that if we lost one chopper the mission would continue, but if we lost two choppers, we
would abort the mission.

The plan was for *Cherry 1* (the MC-130 that took over the formation at the North Vietnam border and led all the helicopters
from there into Son Tay) to fly over the camp and drop flares to
illuminate the entire compound. The Mk 24 Magnesium Flare has
a parachute and descends very slowly and provides two million
candlepower for three minutes.

As the choppers landed, they would kick up dirt, sand, and debris. For this, we wore ski goggles similar to some used in World War II. The lenses were amber/red or clear. The amber/red was preferred by some guys because it helped to preserve their night vision, given all the explosion flashes, flares, and lights.

Son Tay, on the outskirts of Hanoi, was one of the most highly defended areas in the world. Near Son Tay was a SAM site and eight AAA (anti-aircraft artillery) sites.

When *Cherry 1*, with its *very* precise navigation electronics, left the formation just prior to arrival at Son Tay to climb and deploy the flares, the chopper formation drifted due to winds. At the moment when the helicopter formation was to break up (about a quarter mile from the landing) and each helicopter was to go to its own landing spot, they were actually closer to a different set of buildings that coincidentally looked _very_ similar to the Son Tay POW camp. The set of buildings was a military facility used for training and was referred to in our training briefings as "the Secondary School." In briefings, all had recognized the potential for mistaking it for the Son Tay POW camp. The other helicopters recognized it as such, but—in the chaos of no-lights, no-radio, nighttime battle with explosion flashes and flares—the helicopter farthest to the right (*Apple 1*) didn't catch that fact. *Apple 1* could not see the other helicopters change course at the last moment. While the other helicopters corrected back toward the Son Tay POW camp in a sharp 90-degree left turn, *Apple 1*, carrying the 22 men of Greenleaf Group which included Colonel Bull Simons, landed at the Secondary School!

Landing at the Secondary School may have been extremely lucky for the other raiders. The Greenleaf team didn't know they had landed at the wrong compound. As they exited *Apple 1*, they responded with the same intensity as if they were landing at the

Son Tay POW camp. It is thought that the soldiers at the Secondary School were training North Vietnamese Army officers. But as the firefight unfolded, it became clear to the Greenleaf Group that these soldiers there were not Vietnamese. We now believe that they were Chinese or Russian, based on their physical size. With these men located so nearby (only 400 yards south of the actual Son Tay POW camp), it is likely they would have rushed as reinforcements within minutes to fight the Americans at the POW camp. As it was, Greenleaf had already poked the bear, so the only thing for them to do was to eliminate as many of the enemy as possible. It is estimated that Greenleaf Group neutralized at least 40 and possibly more than 100 North Vietnamese or Chinese or Russians at the Secondary School. One thing is for sure: Greenleaf put a damper on any plans they had for their graduation ceremony.

All told, Greenleaf Group spent only eight minutes (from 0220 to 0228) on the ground at the Secondary School, as *Apple 1* quickly recognized its mistake and transported them to the correct LZ, only a one-minute flight away.

This is why (as you read at the opening of this book) we had to implement Alternate Plan Green. **Now, we pick up the story…**

CHAPTER 17

0220 hrs, Saturday
November 21st, 1970
Insertion: Landing at the
Son Tay POW Camp

(To the reader: The first page of this section will be
familiar, as will the photo. But it's worth refreshing
the timeline now, with a few extra details.)

WHEN WE WERE JUST about to land, I heard the chatter in my
headset. The voice of Sgt 1st Class Howell came through. He was
the RTO for LtCol Sydnor, the ground force commander for the
raid: "Alternate Plan GREEN." "I repeat: Alternate Plan GREEN.
Do you copy?"

This was only the first of the bad news I would hear tonight.

I responded, "SAY AGAIN?"

Sgt 1st Class Howell: "Alternate Plan GREEN. Alternate Plan
GREEN. Over."

I said back into my hand mic, "Roger. Alternate Plan Green.
Over."

I thought to myself, *Holy crap. This can't be real.* I turned to Capt Dan and told him we were going to Alternate Plan Green. Capt Dan gave me that, "Oh Shit" look and calmly told me to pass the announcement on to the others in Redwine.

Alternate Plan Green meant one thing to all of us on the Redwine chopper: We knew we had 22 fewer men. There would be a lot less fire power as we hit the ground. Whether Greenleaf Group had mechanical problems or had been shot down, we knew the mission, including the Alternate Plans. With or without the 22 men of Greenleaf Group, we were going to execute the mission and would now have to perform their role as well as ours.

LIFE LESSON 6: Don't be "Indispensable." Always be training a backup person for your job and always be learning to be a backup for your teammates. This applies to any job in life. The graveyards are full of "indispensable men."

Image 16: The minigun.

At that moment, the minigun in the door to our right fired off a few hundred rounds. For those of you not familiar with a minigun, it's a gun that fires 4,000 rounds of 5.62mm ammo per minute. It has an electrically driven, rotary breech to feed the ammo belt at lightning speed. Now my heart was already pounding but the sound of that minigun firing two feet from me really took me to a new level.

I adjust my headset and the "Prick-25" (PRC-25 FM Radio) on my back, I feel for my ammo pouches, I check for my frags and my concussion grenades, I place my finger on the Safety to make sure that I have my Safety OFF and that my CAR-15 is set to AUTO. I make sure I have the 30-round magazine well seated and I chamber a round. In training, I've done this hundreds of times, but this is "it." My first time in combat, this is no game. I'm not scared as much as I am excited. This is the moment I have trained for, the reason I joined the Green Berets. I can't let Capt Dan down or the other Raiders.

As the RTO for the Redwine Security Group, my job is to stay close to Capt Dan. He is the commander of Redwine and I am expected to protect his backside.

The tail gate is lowered; the chopper is feathering to the ground. We are about to touch down on the enemy's homeland and there is no rescuing us if there has been a security breech. I feel the chopper settle as it has done so many times in training. Redwine Group is unloading exactly as we have practiced over 170 times. The major difference is that, this time, the bullets are flying in BOTH directions.

It is amazing how fast you can exit a chopper.

Capt Dan and I start off the tail of the chopper, the last two men off. I am literally one step to his right side as we run. Our boots have just started splashing the rice paddies when a North Vietnamese Army soldier fires at us from the very building we were to clear first (7B in the diagram below). A couple of bullets zip by us.

A natural reaction: I place the green dot from my ArmaLite Singlepoint Sight on the guard's chest and fire three rounds—he immediately falls to the ground. In that instant, what the seasoned warriors taught me really paid off: Don't hesitate. I imagine most warriors, in your first time 'down range,' wonder in the back of your mind how will you respond in the moment. Would I freeze when faced with the decision to kill or be killed? I had only just stepped onto the enemy's ground and I had my first kill. There'd be more to come as we cleared the buildings. It's true you don't forget your first kill.

[In his book *The Son Tay Raid: American POWs in Vietnam Were Not Forgotten*, John Gargus states on page 207 that he believes that this was likely the first of the many kills—all crucial to the success of the mission—in the Son Tay POW camp compound.]

Capt Dan thanks me as we charge toward our first building.

I am following Capt Dan with bullets blazing and men moving to their positions. Alternate Plan Green is proceeding. We hear our chopper *Apple 2* loudly lift off the rice paddies to wait about a mile away until they are called back to take us home with the POWs we came to free. In the back of our minds: *If these birds get battle damage, it will be a long walk back to friendly lines.*

No time to think about that. We move forward to clear our designated buildings. Nearest to us is Master Sgt Joe Lupyak and his Redwine Element 2 (which includes him, SFC Tyrone Adderly and SFC Billy Martin.) Each of us knew this was going to be much more difficult than it was during training. These are buildings that Greenleaf Group would have neutralized according to the original plan and they were to have 14 of their men on this task. Under Alternate Plan Green, five on our team are now going to have to do it. They also had more fire power: Sgt 1st Class Jake Jakovenko was carrying an M-60 bipod machine gun which we don't have on our team.

What we *did* still have was the element of surprise. Bull Simons told us if there was a security leak, we would know it by the time the second chopper landed. We turned out to be that second chopper and we are operating like a well-oiled machine.

Capt Dan is directing our Redwine Group, comprised of four Elements, and is making sure we are getting our job done. As a virgin to combat and as Capt Dan's RTO, I stay close to him. You have to respect and trust the men with whom you go to battle.

This is where the months of training pay off. We know what we have to do next. Alternate Plan Green means that the bridge to the north of the POW camp will remain open to enemy reinforcements crossing it, since we simply don't have enough Raiders to send someone to blow it. Over the radios, LtCol Sydnor directs our A-1 Skyraider pilots to light it up with Rockeye missiles. If anyone tries to cross it, the A-1s will open up with 20 mm cannon (which they can do with intimidating accuracy.) These fly boys are cocky, but they're damn good at their job.

> [One day while in training, we asked them to bring in rounds as close as they could so we could see how good they were. They brought rounds in within 30 to 40 feet of us. Scared the crap out of me. I was sure glad they were on our side.]

What amazes me is that, in all this chaos, only one of us Green Berets gets wounded. That is Sgt 1st Class Joe Murray. Joe is a member of Master Sgt Herman Spencer's team (Redwine Element 1, which also includes SFC Noe Quezeda, SFC Jerry Hill and SSG Tiny Young) whose job is to secure the area south of south wall. That's the wall closest to where the helicopters dropped us off and later will pick us up. MSgt Spencer is carrying a 40 lb block of C-4 explosives slung over his shoulder. It is to be used to blow the bridge. It turned out to be a good shield for him. As we landed and spilled out of our helicopter, Spencer and Murray immediately rushed toward their objective, the guard shack (Building 8D in the diagram below) by the south wall. Spencer took a couple of rounds from a guard with an AK-47 in the block of C-4 he was carrying. Joe Murray would not be that lucky.

When Spencer was dealing with that guard, that delayed Spencer such that Joe arrives at the guard shack alone. The building needs to be cleared immediately, before the enemy troops inside can all emerge. So, Joe decides to use a frag grenade instead of a concussion grenade. As he is about to toss it in the window, he feels his leg push forward with a burning sensation. Joe tosses the frag grenade in, neutralizing the guard shack. He then turns to eliminate the threat. Spencer, now arriving, fires his machine gun first and eliminates three guards. [Joe was the only Army Raider to receive a Purple Heart.]

For Capt Dan and me, the objective is to get to the Communications Building (7A in the diagram) as fast as possible to prevent them from calling for reinforcements. It's a good fifty meters ahead of us and it's an open area with no cover. We have two buildings to clear before we clear the Communications Building. We were told that we would not take any North Vietnamese Army prisoners and to neutralize everyone. We will be coming back through this same area and the Bull doesn't want anyone preventing us from getting back on the choppers. To do this, we have to ensure that there is no one alive to ambush us on our way back.

Capt Dan and I are getting closer to the Communications Building. We can see the Main Guard House is on fire and people are running away from us. Clearing the Main Guard House was the job of another Redwine element and they apparently are succeeding. We still have two more buildings to clear. The first one (Building 11), is empty. The second one (Building 12), has a few North Vietnamese Army soldiers.

I toss a concussion grenade into the room, and as soon as it explodes, Capt Dan drops to the floor and I stand in the door straddling him. We create a crossing fire with me firing fully automatic from right to left and he from left to right. He yells, "Clear!" and I back out and shine my flashlight so he can confirm we've neutralized everyone. Because there are a number of them, we do a closer check that all are neutralized.

In the clearing of buildings at Son Tay, Capt Dan and I are the only two-man team. Depending on how close you are to the grenade when it explodes it can bust your ear drums and pretty well mess you up. In Building 12, as I'm confirming everyone is dead—it's a grim task (whatever you are thinking right now, it's far more grim than that)—a guard raises his weapon behind me. Capt Dan neutralizes him. There is no doubt: With that decisive action, Capt Dan saved my life.

Approaching 0228, LtCol Sydnor receives notification that Greenleaf Group is *not* out of commission. We can hear *Apple 1* landing and are told to hold fast until the Greenleaf elements get to their original planned positions. With 22 men of Greenleaf team, including Bull Simons, we are back on track. Within one minute, Greenleaf has secured the Guard Quarters (7B) per the plan and takes over their roles that the Redwine team members have been handling for them.

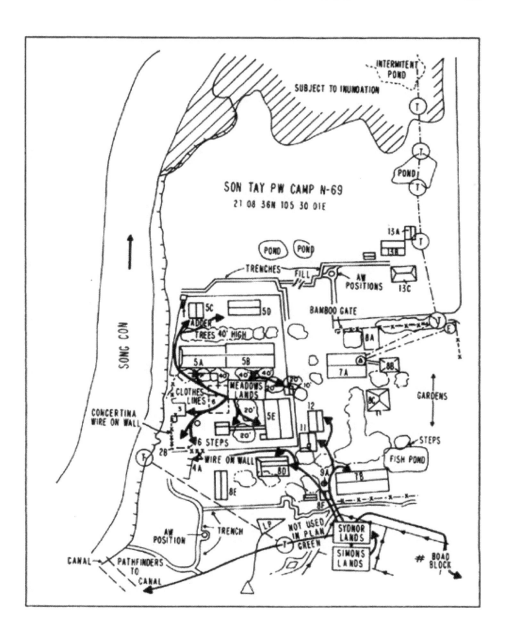

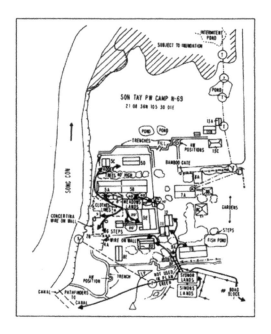

Actual Movements of the Green Berets as recorded in a JCS report.

Blueboy Assault Group (Capt Meadows)

Redwine Command/Security Group (LtColSydnor)

Greenleaf Support Group (Col Simons)

The nighttime guard force was estimated to be one guard per watchtower and a minimum of two guards in the compound with relief personnel in 5E.

The outside force could number up to two platoons, located primarily in
* The Guard Quarters (7B),
* Kitchen (11) and Guard Mess (12),
* Communications Building (7A),

Automatic weapons positions at
* South Wall
* East Wall
* North Wall

Image 17: Image from the DoD/JCS After Action Report. Expanded on the prior page.

At 0229, we had just reached the Communications Building when I heard on my headset, "Negative items." I told Capt Dan. He asked me, "Are you sure?!"

"Items" was the code word for POWs.

It didn't make any sense.

The next radio call I heard was at 0230: "Begin extraction to choppers." We entered the Communications Building without tossing a grenade. It was empty.

At this time, we started our move back to the LZ for extraction. We still moved with the assumption that there could be more enemy soldiers lying in the bushes.

While the helicopters were en route returning to extract us, one of Redwine's roles was to clear the planned LZ by cutting down certain light poles. That task revealed one frustrating surprise. We had brought a chainsaw to cut down certain wooden telephone poles, but Sgt 1st Class Charles Masten and Sgt 1st Class Ronnie Strahan were to blow up a tall, concrete light pole.

The moment that Masten and Strahan had finished placing the four one-pound packets of C-4 explosive, were ready to blow, and were confirming that they should activate the fuse, Apple 1 was arriving (this was happening at 0228)! They waited until Apple 1 had landed, offloaded Greenleaf, and departed. Ensured of safety, they detonated the C-4.

As the pole rose into the air in a huge flash of light, Masten and Strahan could see that this was NOT a light pole—it had four large high-tension power lines! Dancing sparks were everywhere as the four huge power lines hit the rice paddies—the very rice paddies in which our soldiers and POWs would be marshalling to load the returning choppers!

Were we going to have to find a new location for the LZ? Masten, Strahan, and Capt Jim McClam, as MACO (Marshalling

Area Control Officer) immediately set about ensuring they understood the location of all the lines and whether they were hot. After
assessing the situation and ensuring there were no other potential
hazards, they began placing the "beanbag lights" in an area suit-
ably distant from the power lines.

LIFE LESSON 7: Don't be a Complainer. The world is moving on and needs people to solve problems. Evaluate your situation, make a decision, and execute any new plan without complaining and feeling sorry for yourself.

As everyone returned to the LZ waiting for the helicopters, we had
a few minutes to gather people and equipment to load on *Apple 1*
and *Apple 2.*

    We had several items that you don't normally take into battle.
For instance, Staff Sgt Tiny Young carried a backpack of oxyacet-
ylene torch tanks for cutting through steel doors and chains. The
Navy uses these aboard ships and we'd borrowed some of these
for the mission. They were very effective. The issue was, nobody
wanted to be too close to Tiny in case a bullet hit one of his tanks.
We brought compound bolt cutters. We all would much rather use
those, if we could, than be near Tiny!

    The wall around the camp was estimated to be 10 to 12 feet
high and made of red brick. The plan called for us to blow a hole in
the wall near the southwest corner of the camp to bring the POWs
out to the choppers. We had several strands of "det cord" (detonat-
ing cord) about 12 feet long. They braded them together and then

secured them to the wall. What do you think was used? Yes, you guessed it: duct tape! They had tested other options but the det cord with duct tape worked best and was easy to carry.

There were two other areas where we used explosives:

1. The HH-3 helicopter *Banana* that brought the Blueboy Assault Group was intentionally "crash landed" inside the compound courtyard per the plan. That HH-3 needed to be demolished to deny the enemy anything useful. That's why we had MSgt Spencer's 40 pounds of C-4 with a 10-minute fuse timed to detonate long after we all lifted off North Vietnamese soil on *Apple 1* and *Apple 2*.

2. There was also a bridge that was north of the camp that needed to be blown up early in the raid by the Greenleaf team to cutoff an access route for enemy reinforcements.

CHAPTER 18

0237 hrs, Saturday
November 21ˢᵗ, 1970
Extraction: Bright lights over Hanoi

"No POWs" WAS NOT something that we had spent time thinking about. I could hear chatter on my headset. I heard the RTO for Bull say that Bull was coming into the compound. Bull had to verify it with his own eyes that there were no POWs.

At 0237, *Apple 1* landed facing east toward Hanoi and loaded Redwine Group and Blueboy Group (their helicopter had been the HH-3 *Banana*, whose mission was to crash land inside the walls of the camp, with Blueboy storming out in all directions.) Capt Dan and I were the last ones to board. The two of us sat at the tail of the chopper, loading door fully down and open, with a minigun mounted right between us manned by an Air Force PJ (pararescue/ gunner.)

At 0240, we lifted off and turned west. Looking out the open tail, we had a front row seat with a bird's eye view of Hanoi. I will never forget that view. I couldn't believe how big Hanoi was and how close we were to it. It was like looking at any major city in America. We were only about twenty miles from the capital of North Vietnam. I compare it to the view when I flew into Washington DC while stationed at Fort Belvoir. For the past thirty minutes, we had owned a piece of the enemy's capitol city. Never before had the North Vietnamese Army been violated like this. That's when it really hit me what we had just done.

As we were rising only a minute or two after liftoff, suddenly our chopper took a hard dive to the left. What looked like a telephone pole with a bright red fireball shot by us. I yelled over to Capt Dan, "WHAT THE HELL WAS THAT!?!" Before he could answer, the gunner standing between us yelled that it was a SAM. Now, I was scared while on the ground, but now I was *really* scared. On the ground, I have a fighting chance. But being in a chopper at 600 ft, you feel like a sitting duck. Thank God for some of the best pilots we could have had. These guys knew how to handle it. We soon were out from the threat, into the dark jungle mountains, and headed for Udorn.

During the next three hours on the flight back to base, I had plenty of time to replay what we had done that night. Like the rest of the Raiders, I was very disappointed that we came home with no POWs. I kept thinking, *What went wrong? Why? When had the POWs been moved?* That flight returning to Udorn seemed a lot longer than the flight to Son Tay. We had been so extremely pumped up about our mission. To find no POWs was the last thing that would ever have crossed our minds. Beyond the two wounds received (USAF Tech Sgt Leroy Wright's ankle was broken during *Banana's* crash landing, and Sgt 1st Class Joe Murray), America's only casualty that night was our morale.

Arriving at Udorn, there in the pre-dawn dark, we sat on the flight line for a while. I don't remember much about that time at Udorn before heading back to the States. I do not believe we did any kind of debrief there. I think each of us had to write a description of our actions on the ground. Capt Jim McClam explained years later that he was on the After-Action Team and that he read every individual After-Action Report for Greenleaf and Redwine Groups. Capt Dick Meadows did the same for the Blueboy Group. We all were required to sign a letter re-emphasizing the secrecy.

A LONG FLIGHT HOME TO FORT BRAGG

To say we were disappointed would be an understatement. Some of us talked about how maybe we should have gone on into Hanoi— we were thinking crazy thoughts like that. That's how confident we were.

We got some rest at Udorn for a couple of hours. We flew a C-130 from Udorn to Takhli, where we were briefed again in the auditorium on what to say, and more importantly, what *not* to talk about. We packed our duffle bags, secured our equipment, and had a few hours to relax. The C-141 that we boarded was one that had been prepped for Medevac, ready to bring the POWs home. Now its mission was to bring us to Eglin.

All the After-Action Reports were finalized at Aux Field #3 where we spent two days before heading home to North Carolina on C-123s.

CHAPTER 19

Monday November 23rd, 1970
Returning

IN CONTRAST, LANDING AT Pope AFB, NC, a couple of days later was a very happy time. It was happy for the Raiders and for all the people awaiting us: family, friends, and the Army support personnel there to process us back into our normal world at Fort Bragg.

In fact, for me personally, that is the most memorable moment. It was not the training or the day of the launch or the landing at Son Tay. For me, it was the landing at Pope AFB. I will never forget what I witnessed that day. I was a single guy, so a couple of my buddies came to pick me up. But, standing there on the flight line, when I looked around at the men unloading from the airplane and I saw their wives and children running out to meet them, it really hit me. The Bull had warned us that we had a 50/50 chance of not coming home—a 50/50 chance of this moment never happening. If there had been a security breach, it was unlikely that we could have been rescued. These warriors had laid their lives on the line to rescue fellow warriors.

Image 18: The Raiders arrive at Pope AFB, NC, Monday
November 23rd, 1970, two days after the Raid.

Image 19: The Raiders arrive at Pope AFB, NC, Monday
November 23rd, 1970, two days after the Raid.

Image 20: The Raiders arrive at Pope AFB, NC,
Monday November 23rd, 1970, two days after the Raid.
Master Sgt Joe Lupyak (Redwine) with his family.

Image 21: The Raiders arrive at Pope AFB, NC,
November 23rd, 1970, two days after the Raid. Staff Sgt
Lawrence "Tiny" Young (Redwine) and his family.

Image 22: The Raiders arrive at Pope AFB, NC,
November 23rd, 1970, two days after the Raid.

THE WHITE HOUSE CELEBRATION CEREMONY

Four days after the Raid, on Wednesday November 25th, 1970, President Nixon honored the Son Tay Raid by having the following representatives in a televised ceremony in the White House's East Room (see the photo in Adderly's Memorable Moment in Appendix 4):

USAF Brigadier General Leroy Manor
Army Colonel Bull Simons
Army Sergeant 1st Class Tyrone Adderly (the representative of all us Green Berets)
USAF Technical Sergeant Leroy Wright (the representative of the aircrews)

FORT BRAGG, DECEMBER 9, 1970

I remember being told to report to the parade field in my dress greens for an awards ceremony. It was a nice, sunny, cool day when Secretary of Defense Melvin Laird personally presented the medals to the members of the Son Tay Raid. There I stood, spit-shined jump boots, jump wings, expert rifle badge, and the 7th Special Forces Group ribbon.

BGen Henry Emerson, the commander of Special Forces at Fort Bragg, thanked the Raiders for their courage and dedication. We had reflected well on the Green Berets. Here is a list of those Green Berets awarded the Silver Star:

CAPT Thomas W. Jaeger, CAPT James W. McClam, CAPT Dan H. McKinney, CAPT Eric J. Nelson, CAPT Glenn R. Rouse, CAPT Daniel D. Turner, CAPT Udo H. Walther, 1LT George W. Petrie, Jr., MSG Galen C. Kittleson, MSG Joseph W. Lupyak,

MSG Billy K. Moore, MSG Herman Spencer, SFC Donald D. Blackard, SFC Earl Bleacher, Jr., SFC Leroy N. Carlson, SFC Anthony Dodge, SFC Freddie D. Doss, SFC Jerry W. Hill, SFC Marion S. Howell, SFC John Jakovenko, SFC Jack G. Joplin, SFC Daniel Jurich, SFC David A. Lawhon, Jr., SFC Gregory T. McGuire, SFC Billy R. Martin, SFC Charles A. Masten, SFC Donald R. Wingrove, SFC Joseph M. Murray, SFC Noe Quezada, SFC Lorenzo O. Robbins, SFC Ronnie Strahan, SFC Salvador M. Suarez, SFC Donald E. Taapken, SFC William L. Tapley, SFC Richard W. Valentine, SSG Charles G. Erickson, SSG Kenneth E. McMullin, SSG Walter L. Miller, SSG Robert F. Nelson, SSG David Nickerson, SSG Paul F. Poole, SSG John E. Rodriquez, SSG Lawrence Young, SGT Terry L. Buckler, SGT Gary D. Keel, SGT Keith R. Medenski, SGT Franklin D. Roe, SGT Patrick St.Clair, and SGT Marshal A. Thomas.

The following are comments Secretary Laird spoke to all the airmen and soldiers. In the audience were the leadership of Fort Bragg, family members, and the press.

"We are here to honor brave and dedicated men. We confer on them today awards that express their country's gratitude and admiration. The mission for which these men volunteered called for undaunted courage and deep compassion. They were asked to go deep into enemy territory to search for—and if possible, to rescue—their comrades in arms who are prisoners of war. They performed their mission flawlessly. From the outset, the President, the nation's top military leadership, and I gave total and unqualified support to this mission. I knew—as these men did—how grave were the risks they willingly undertook. I knew—as these men did—that there was a chance of disappointment—and even of failure.

"But the reasonable chance to return to freedom Americans held captive made this mission well worth the risk. If a similar chance to save Americans were to arise tomorrow, I would act just as I did in approving and supporting the effort at Son Tay."

Fort Bragg, North Carolina

Parade and presentation of decorations by the Secretary of Defense Melvin R .Laird.

Image 23: Secretary of Defense Melvin Laird honors
the Raiders at Ft Bragg, December 9th, 1970.

Image 24: Secretary of Defense Melvin Laird honors
the Raiders at Ft Bragg, December 9th, 1970.

Image 25: The bulletin for the ceremony in which
Secretary of Defense Melvin Laird honors the
Raiders at Ft Bragg, December 9th, 1970.

SEQUENCE OF EVENTS

1015-1145   Honor/Award Ceremony   - Main Post Parade
                                          Field

1200-1230   Reception and Luncheon - Fort Bragg
                                         Officers Open Mess

1430-1510   Observe Airborne Operation - Sicily Drop
                                             Zone

Image 26: The bulletin for the ceremony in which
Secretary of Defense Melvin Laird honors the
Raiders at Ft Bragg, December 9th, 1970.

The following individuals are to be awarded the
Distinguished Service Cross:

Lieutenant Colonel Elliott P. Sydnor
Captain Richard J. Meadows
Master Sergeant Thomas J. Kemmer
Staff Sergeant Thomas E. Powell

The following individuals are to be awarded the
Air Force Cross:

Lieutenant Colonel John V. Allison
Lieutenant Colonel Warner A. Britton
Major Frederic M. Donohue
Major Herbert D. Kalen

The following individuals are to be awarded the
Silver Star:

Lieutenant Colonel Joseph P. Cataldo
Captain Thomas W. Jaegar
Captain James W. McClam
Captain Eric J. Nelson
Captain Dan H. McKinney
Captain Glenn R. Rouse
Captain Daniel Turner
Captain Udo H. Walther
First Lieutenant George W. Petrie, Jr.
Master Sergeant Galen C. Kittleson
Master Sergeant Joseph W. Lupyak
Master Sergeant Billy K. Moore
Master Sergeant Herman Spencer
Sergeant First Class Donald D. Blackard
Sergeant First Class Earl Bleacher, Jr.
Sergeant First Class Leroy N. Carlson
Sergeant First Class Anthony Dodge
Sergeant First Class Freddie D. Doss
Sergeant First Class Jerry W. Hill
Sergeant First Class Marion S. Howell
Sergeant First Class Donald E. Taapken

Image 27: The bulletin for the ceremony in which
Secretary of Defense Melvin Laird honors the
Raiders at Ft Bragg, December 9th, 1970.

Sergeant First Class John Jakovenko
Sergeant First Class Jack G. Joplin
Sergeant First Class Daniel Jurich
Sergeant First Class David A. Lawhon, Jr.
Sergeant First Class Billy R. Martin
Sergeant First Class Charles Masten
Sergeant First Class Gregory T. McGuire
Sergeant First Class Joseph M. Murray
Sergeant First Class Noe Quezada
Sergeant First Class Lorenzo Robbins
Sergeant First Class Ronnie Strahan
Sergeant First Class Salvador M. Suarez
Sergeant First Class William L. Tapley
Sergeant First Class Richard W. Valentine
Sergeant First Class Donald R. Wingrove
Staff Sergeant Charles G. Erickson
Staff Sergeant Walter L. Miller
Staff Sergeant Kenneth E. McMullin
Staff Sergeant Robert F. Nelson
Staff Sergeant David Nickerson
Staff Sergeant Paul F. Poole
Staff Sergeant John E. Rodriquez
Staff Sergeant Lawrence Young
Sergeant Terry T. Buckler
Sergeant Gary D. Keel
Sergeant Keith R. Medenski
Sergeant Franklin D. Roe
Sergeant Patrick St. Clair
Sergeant Marshal A. Thomas

The following individuals of the United States Air
Force are to be awarded the Silver Star:

Lieutenant Colonel Albert P. Blosch
Lieutenant Colonel Royal A. Brown Jr.
Lieutenant Colonel Herbert R. Zehnder

Image 28: The bulletin for the ceremony in which
Secretary of Defense Melvin Laird honors the
Raiders at Ft Bragg, December 9th, 1970.

Major Eustace M. Bunn
Major Irl L. Franklin
Major John Gargus
Major James R. Gochnauer
Major Alfred C. Montrem
Major Kenneth D. Murphy
Major Harry L. Pannill
Major Edwin J. Rhein
Major Richard S. Skeels
Major John C. Squires
Captain John M. Connaughton
Captain David M. Kender
Captain Norman C. Mazurek
Captain Thomas L. Stiles
Captain William D. Stripling
Captain Thomas R. Waldron
Master Sergeant Harold W. Harvey
Master Sergeant David V. McLeod, Jr.
Master Sergeant Maurice F. Tasker
Technical Sergeant Dallas R. Criner
Technical Sergeant Billy J. Elliston
Technical Sergeant William E. Lester
Technical Sergeant Charlie J. Montgomery, Jr.
Technical Sergeant Paul W. Stierwalt
Technical Sergeant Jimmie O. Riggs
Technical Sergeant Lawrence Wellington
Staff Sergeant Daniel E. Galde
Staff Sergeant Melvin B. D. Gibson
Staff Sergeant Aron P. Hodges
Staff Sergeant Donald LaBarre
Staff Sergeant James J. Rogers
Staff Sergeant Angus W. Sowell III

The following individuals are to be awarded the
Distinguished Flying Cross:

First Lieutenant George W. Williams
Chief Warrant Officer Ronald J. Exley
Chief Warrant Officer Jackie H. Keele
Chief Warrant Officer John J. Ward

Image 29: The bulletin for the ceremony in which
Secretary of Defense Melvin Laird honors the
Raiders at Ft Bragg, December 9th, 1970.

Even though the following people were not in attendance at the Ft Bragg ceremony, I want to point out their role in the Raid. There are so many people who deserve honor that we cannot possibly list them all--we ask your forgiveness. For a most authoritative listing, we highly recommend John Gargus' book *The Son Tay Raid: American POWs Were Not Forgotten*. The following are people that are not heralded elsewhere in this book, (though some of their direct peer colleagues are) and they well deserve a mention:

McComb, Randy S., SSgt (Apple 2 crew)
Fisk, Wayne L., SSgt (Apple 4 crew)
McGeorge, William M., Capt (Apple 5 crew)
Eldridge, John J., SSgt (Apple 5 crew)
Waresh, John C., Major (Peach 1 crew)
Senko, Robert M., Capt (Peach 2 crew)
Paine, James C., 1Lt (Peach 3 crew)
Skelton, Robert H., Capt (Peach 4 crew)
Sutton, William R., Capt (Peach 5 crew)
Boots, Larry C., Spec 6 (crew of alternate Banana, a UH-1H)
Wood, Allan H., Spec 4 (crew of alternate Banana, a UH-1H)
Kornitzer, William J, Major (Lime 1 crew)
Frank, Richard E., Capt (Lime 1 crew)
Felmley, Jerry T., Major (Lime 1 crew)
McNeff, Charles P., Capt (Lime 1 crew)
Bomans, Johnie, MSgt (Lime 1 crew)
Keel, Holley V., MSgt (Lime 1 crew)
Swinson, Aaron, SSgt (Lime 1 crew)
Waters, Samuel L., Sgt (Lime 1 crew)

DINNER AT THE O'CLUB

A couple of days later, all the Raiders were invited to the Fort Bragg Officers' Club for a formal dinner. For me, the low-ranking E-5 NCO, this was going to be quite a treat and I thought I should invite a date. A little before I'd left for Eglin, I had broken up with the young lady I had been dating. Her father was a full bird Colonel in the 18th Airborne. Her father and I got along great. He was a mustang (he entered the Army as an enlisted man and then become an officer.) Her mother, however, was not impressed with her daughter dating an NCO.

It just so happened that Sgt Blackard of the Redwine Group had a daughter that he suggested I might want to take to the Officers' Club for that dinner. It didn't take much arm twisting for me to say yes to taking her. She was a very nice, very pretty lady. The guest speaker at the dinner was the four-star General William Westmoreland. With this kind of brass as the guest speaker, every officer on Fort Bragg wanted to be there. The Club that evening was packed. The Raiders were the special guests and we were seated at our own special tables. For a country boy from Missouri this was a pretty fancy shindig.

I went to the PX (the Post Exchange) to purchase the proper medals for my dress greens. The guy behind the counter was a little reluctant to sell them to me. I was looking over the different medals that I was going to buy. I pointed to the Combat Infantryman Badge, the Vietnam Campaign ribbon, and the Silver Star. He looked at me and said, "Are you sure you don't want to get the Medal of Honor while you are buying these?" That's when I told him that I was one of the Son Tay Raiders. I am not sure he believed me, but he did sell me the medals.

Like many dinner speakers, after a few minutes the speech gets boring and this was the case with General Westmoreland. Now, most people will sit and listen as the speaker rambles on…and then there are people like Master Sgt Herman Spencer. MSgt Spencer, after patiently listening to the General for 20 or 30 minutes, decided he had heard all he needed to hear. MSgt Spencer stood up and took his wife's hand and proceeded to walk out, saying he had heard enough. General Westmorland stops talking and watches, along with every other eye in the room, as MSgt Spencer walked out. I can tell you that this was very typical of Spencer. He was not political. He was a warrior. When the bullets start to fly, he is the guy you want on your team. The Raiders all knew Spencer…and probably wanted to do the same.

CHAPTER 20

December 1970
Veterans, you have a mission:
Listen to Veterans

THEY GAVE EACH OF us 30 days of leave (uncharged against our balance), so I went home for the whole month of December. Back home in Missouri, we talked a little about the mission, but not much. It's funny how some people don't understand the significance of a combat raid. I wasn't going to try to impress it upon them. Most of my friends had not gone into the military, so I didn't have any significant conversations with them about the Raid. Some had gotten married and were busy with their own lives. My dad was a good listener for me. He expressed his pride. And after a few beers at the Eastside Tavern in Moberly, he even told some of his friends what I had done.

But to tell you the truth, after about four or five days, I was ready to head back to Fort Bragg and my Army buddies.

LIFE LESSON 8: Veterans, we all have a Mission: Listen to your fellow Veterans. My hope is that the contributions you read in Appendix 4 help to achieve this. It's important for the veteran, but it's also important for the listener. It's important for America. Good stories and bad, they need to be told. Please take my request to heart and talk with a veteran.

LIFE GOES ON

The next week, I was back at D Company, 7th Special Forces Group at Fort Bragg.

During one of the morning formations I was ordered to report to a MSgt Kraemer at the Matta Mile course at 1300 hrs and be ready to do some running. The Matta Mile was a three-mile course in the North Carolina sand. When I arrived, there were seven others who also were ordered to attend the meeting. At this meeting I was introduced to the sport of orienteering. MSgt Kraemer explained that it was a timed terrain course that tests a person's skill using a topographical map and compass to navigate from point to point in unfamiliar terrain.

This was my first orienteering course of many to come. Among the eight of us that ran the course, I had the second-best time. It was like most other Army positions; I was now an official member of the Special Forces orienteering team.

For the next year, our team represented the Green Berets in several races. I loved it. MSgt Kraemer was our team Daddy and he could run all day. We had our own tack building and training schedule. Every morning started with a nine-mile run on the sandy hills of the Matta Mile. Then every afternoon we ran a three- to five-mile orienteering course.

By December of 1971, our team had represented Special Forces in several orienteering meets. This is how I fared:

I finished 15th in the US Military Championship (all branches.)

I finished 7th in the US Championship (civilian and military with teams from Sweden, Norway, Canada, Czechoslovakia, and others.)

I finished 45th in the Canadian Championship (open to all countries and to both civilian and military.)

The irony: During Special Forces School, I (along with three other students on my team) was almost booted out of the school because we failed the field map course! This would have denied me the chance to become a Green Beret. In the end, it was determined that someone had removed a crucial sign on the course that directed our team to the next waypoint.

CHAPTER 21

January 1972
Separating from the Army

WHEN I HEARD IN December 1971 that the Army was offering early-outs, that really appealed to me. I felt ready to do my own thing and not be told what to do all the time. I took advantage of the opportunity, separating January 5th, 1972.

I started Junior College on January 7th back home.

After completing all my required Junior College classes, I transferred to Columbia College. In December of 1974, I graduated and started the search for a job.

Jobs were hard to find in 1974, but I had a connection. I had attended a reunion of the Son Tay Raiders and POWs in San Francisco in 1973. It was sponsored by Ross Perot. At the reunion, Mr Perot had stated that if he could ever help any of us, we should contact him. I decided to take Mr Perot up on his word. I wrote a letter to Mr Perot and within a week I had an interview in Dallas with Mr Perot's people. A week after that, I had a job offer to work for EDS (Perot's Electronic Data Systems) at a facility in Camp Hill, Pennsylvania.

That is where I met Al Sock, who also worked for EDS. After a few months, Al and I were asked to move to EDS' San Francisco facility. We had become roommates in Pennsylvania and we ended up being roommates in San Francisco too. In 1976, I made a job move that brought me to Kansas City, MO, where I worked in sales for the next four years selling computer furniture.

In 1980, Mr Greg Kallos made me a job offer. Mr Kallos is the best boss I ever had. I worked for Mr Kallos for five years until he sold his company.

In 1989 I took a big leap of faith and started my own business. I had a great silent partner, Mr John Hose, for the first few years and then I bought John out. 31 years later, the doors are still open! We've been blessed with great employees and great customers.

MY MARSHA

I was 34 when I met the love of my life. I had dated several good women in my single years, but never married. I had decided that I was just going to be a single man. In September of 1984, I was a board member of the Kansas City Data Processing Management Association. We had concluded our monthly meeting and we went out to the Long Branch Saloon. It was a Wednesday night and the place was packed. Two of our party had to leave, which opened up a couple of seats.

Well, these two hot ladies, Marsha and Mary were walking through, looking for a place to sit. So being the gentlemen we were, we offered to share our table. They had been to a movie and had stopped in (to meet guys, I am sure.) We did our best to entertain them. They were trying to guess my profession and they both decided I was a truck driver. For the night, I let them think that I was a truck driver. To this day I still sign all birthday, Easter and Valentine cards, "Your Truck Driver." After a few drinks and some good laughs, Marsha had to powder her nose. Now, I am not a stalker, but I had to release a little pressure too, so I escorted her to the little girls' room. I waited outside the ladies' room to escort her back to our table. I also thought this would be a good time to ask her for her phone number. She was a little reluctant, but I am a good beggar.

Marsha and Mary worked together at a local hospital. I sent flowers to both of them the following day. Marsha was divorced and had a good looking five-year-old son, Aaron. We had our first date in September and in March we vacationed in Hawaii.

For that vacation, we stayed with a woman who was an old Kansas City friend of mine who had moved to Hawaii. This friend's nickname was "Mad Dog." --And she fit the name.

We were going to make it a scuba diving trip. I had taken my open water certification dive in Hawaii several years before. Marsha decided that if she was going to Hawaii, she should take her classes in Kansas City and then take her open water test in Hawaii. After she passed her open water test, we went to Hanauma Bay, which is a great place to dive or snorkel.

Now, I had decided to surprise Marsha and ask her to marry me while we were in Hawaii. I talked with Mad Dog about it and told her I was going to ask her on our first dive. Mad Dog, who was a dental hygienist, gave me a great idea. She gave me a piece of red dental floss that I tied to the engagement ring. I placed the ring in a 35 mm film canister and stuffed it in my wetsuit.

We swam out to a place called Witches Brew and dropped down to the bottom at about 30 feet. As we began our descent, I pulled the ring out of the film canister and used the dental floss to dangle the ring in front of Marsha. Technically, she never said the word "Yes," but she did place the ring on her finger! (You know, everything looks three times bigger underwater.) By the time we swam back to the beach, several people had heard that we'd gotten engaged on our dive.

I knew, the first time I met her in that bar in Kansas City, that I would marry this lady. She had a quick smile, was a lot of fun (and had a nice butt.) The following October, we married in my hometown of Clark, Missouri. The lady that taught our Youth for Christ became an ordained minister, so we asked her to marry us. She was so nervous—this was her first wedding to officiate. We had a church full and it was a really fun wedding and reception. My Best Man Dennis Canote and Lanny Barton and I were celebrating pretty good that night. My parents were loyal members of the Moberly Moose Lodge and after the reception we were to meet there at the Moose. In my celebrations with my buddies, we showed up at the Moose—but I had left my new bride at the hotel where the reception was held. Needless to say, I'm still paying for that mistake after 30 plus years of marriage. (I had also failed to reserve a room for the night! Thankfully, my friend Terry Asbury gave me his room. I was new at this husband job and would do better in the future.)

After the wedding, we returned to our new home in Holt, a little town about forty miles northeast of Kansas City. The city girl got a taste of life in the country.

We had a few acres. A neighbor kid, Clay Othic, hunted and trapped on our land. That same kid grew up to be an NCO in the Rangers. He ends up in the battle of "Black Hawk Down" in the heart of Mogadishu, Somalia. He was wounded in the battle. He later joined Delta Force and ran several missions in Afghanistan. What are the odds of two people a generation apart, warriors in battles like ours, living only six hundred meters apart?

MY SON AARON

Today, my son Aaron is grown, with a family of his own. I can't express the pride I have for Aaron and his wife Gayle and my first granddaughter Annika. Aaron and Gayle met while attending college at Northwest Missouri State University. After graduation, Aaron took a job in parks & recreation in Tampa, Florida. Aaron and Gayle have been gypsies moving to different parts of the country. From Tampa they moved back to Greenwood Missouri where he worked for North Kansas City's department of recreation. West Palm Beach Florida was their next move, as he worked in their department of recreation. Their next move was to Burleson Texas working in their parks & recreation department. After that, they moved to Forney Texas where he worked for the City of Rockwall in their parks & recreation department. His next move brought them back to Missouri where he was (you guessed it) Director of Parks & Recreation for the City of Maryville.

The call to return to Texas could not be shook. With wife and child, they moved to Cleburne Texas where he is now the Director of Parks & Recreation and loves his job. Gayle works for the Texas Home School Association and Annika is being homeschooled. Aaron and Gayle are great examples of how taking a chance on a new job and new city can help you on your road to success. Aaron was never afraid to take an educated risk to better his family's future. Today, I believe they have made Texas their home.

MY DAUGHTER HANA

Hana is our daughter. Marsha homeschooled Hana from third grade through senior year. For all you fathers reading this, I can tell you that one of the most difficult experiences you will have is giving your daughter's hand in marriage. The love a papa has for his only daughter is hard to describe. Giving Hana away at her wedding in December 2012 was the hardest thing I ever did, even though I knew that they loved each other and that Nick would do whatever he could do to make her happy.

Hana has always been what I call "the quiet leader." I coached her in soccer and volleyball and watched her lead by example. I was not surprised when she became the first female battalion commander in the long history of the University of Central Missouri ROTC program.

2nd Lt Hana Buckler was married December 18, 2012 to 2nd Lieutenant Nick Modrell. Nick was completing Infantry training at Fort Benning and Hana was finishing Chemical training at Fort Leonard Wood. They both graduated in February and were stationed at Fort Bragg.

But when Hana was deployed to Afghanistan—Oh Man! Having been in heated situations, I knew what could happen. I prayed for her—and for all our troops—everyday, as I do today. I was afraid for her, but I was so very proud of her too.

In March 2013, Hana was deployed to Afghanistan with the 4th Brigade of the 82nd Airborne. She was stationed at Forward Operating Base Pasab just outside the city of Kandahar in the Zhari District, which at the time had the second highest casualties.

Hana was the brigade Chemical Officer and Force Protection Officer. Her primary responsibility was maintaining the surveillance assets throughout their area of operation to ensure the safety of our soldiers. Hana told me about being deployed: "Other than missing my husband and family, what I missed most about America was using a normal toilet and taking long showers and real American food." The first thing she ate when she returned home was steak and mashed potatoes. She had the opportunity to make several friends from all walks of life. One friend got baptized there in an old storage container that they used as the baptismal. She said, "NCOs were truly the backbone of the unit and made my deployment and my whole military career. It would have been much different without the support and mentorship of some really great NCOs."

Image 30: Hana upon completion of her night jump at Fort Benning GA. Capt Dan Turner and I observed. This photo was taken at about 2:30am by Dan Turner.

The one major enhancement the military has today is the ability to communicate. We were able to use Skype, text, and Facebook, unless there was a blackout. There are both good things and bad about being able to see her smiling face: you also see her expression on the bad days. As her Papa, I wanted to tell her everything was going to be okay. But being half a world away, I could not protect her. That, I trusted, was in God's hands. I knew there were a lot of people praying for her and the other troops.

God answered our prayers. She returned to Ft Bragg just as she'd left, except a lot wiser. Not long after she returned, Nick, who is in Civil Affairs, was deployed to Afghanistan.

Nick left active duty as a 1st Lieutenant; Hana left as a Captain.

At the time of the writing of this book, Hana is a deputy sheriff in Johnson County KS. She has worked in the jail and on patrol, and is currently in the training department. She was also one of the squad leaders in the 2020 riots in Kansas City. Nick is currently a fireman in Overland Park KS. They have my second granddaughter, Toni Lynn, and she is just like her mother. I have been blessed!

CHAPTER 22

Today
Honor in this current generation

THERE IS A VERSE in the Bible that says, "Greater love has no man than this, that a man lay down his life for his friends" (John 15:13). The men on the Raid had that kind of love. It was my honor to serve with them. They didn't do it for money or for medals or for fame.

LIFE LESSON 9: Sacrificial Living. That scene as we arrived at Pope AFB back in November 1970 really made an impression on me: It's not only the soldiers but also their wives who are heroes. These families are the type of people our world needs—people who know this life is not just about their convenience. I am thankful for what these families (and also those of first responders in civilian life) do for our country and for freedom around the world.

Consider this: My father never told me what military action prompted our country to bestow upon him the Bronze Star. To this day, I have found no one that can tell me the story. And, I never really made the time to discuss with my father the military action that resulted in my Silver Star. I'm not saying anyone has to tell people about it. I'm not saying it is right or wrong to keep it inside. People have to decide that for themselves.

But the reason I'm writing this book is to show clear proof that Americans serve in our military because of Honor, because they love their country, because they love God, and (in the case of the Son Tay Raid) because our POWs deserved to know that they were not forgotten. As a nation, we are profoundly blessed to have men and women of that same caliber today—and I know this very personally—preserving American values of Freedom in the younger generations. They are among us, serving in our military forces. And when we call upon them, they are the noble Americans…who will go.

APPENDIX 1

A "30,000 ft View" of the Mission

THE RAID ON THE POW camp near Son Tay, North Vietnam, was to be conducted in the dark of night, achieving maximum surprise and shock with a singular focus upon ensuring the guards would not have time to execute the POWs. A quarter moon with clear skies is what the planners felt would be perfect for covert ingress, with just enough visibility to maintain the aircraft formation and to refuel the helicopters.

The choppers were to fly in the draft of an HC-130P tanker (call sign *Lime 1*) to the border of North Vietnam. Then the choppers would shift over to draft behind an MC-130 Special Operations mother ship (call sign *Cherry 1*) that would lead us to Son Tay and drop flares to light up the POW camp at "H-Hour"—the moment of surprise. *Cherry 1* would then turn south to drop a "Firefight Simulator" a half mile from the POW camp as a decoy to draw local forces away from the POW camp. Beginning right from engine startup and taxi, there would be no radio communication between any of the choppers or C-130s; there would be no lights on the aircraft. We would be flying just above the jungle and below the enemy's radar, "terrain masking" along the hills and valleys.

Just a few minutes before H-Hour, there was to be a huge diversionary bombing operation conducted by the Navy in Hai Phong on the east side of Hanoi. The Navy aircraft would be dropping merely incendiary devices, but it was fully effective to draw the majority of defensive focus away from the west from which we would be sneaking in the back door. This diversion would be handled by the aircraft carriers USS Oriskany, USS Ranger, and USS Hancock. All military branches combined, there were over 130 aircraft used in the raid. This was the largest air assault in the Vietnam War.

There would need to be F-4s over Son Tay flying "MiGCAP" (Combat Air Patrol), protecting the helicopters and C-130s from enemy fighters (MiGs). There would need to be F-105 Wild Weasels protecting all aircraft from SAMs. There would need to be Airborne Command and Control Aircraft like EC-121Ts to coordinate everyone once past H-Hour and provide real-time communication and intel to ground commanders, including BGen Manor back at Monkey Mountain at Da Nang AB.

The Assault Force would consist of one HH-3 "Jolly Green Giant" (call sign *Banana*) and five HH-53 "Super Jolly Green Giants" (call signs *Apple 1 – Apple 5*). The plan required three guard towers to be obliterated quickly and for the Green Berets to immediately get to the cells to ensure the POWs would not be shot by guards. To accomplish this, *Banana* would "crash land" right into the courtyard _inside_ the POW camp and the Blueboy Assault Group would storm out with guns blazing immediately and precisely on their rehearsed targets.

Apple 1 would carry Greenleaf Support Group, which included Colonel Bull Simons. *Apple 2* would carry Redwine Security

Group. Both *Apple 1* and *Apple 2* would land just outside the south wall of the POW camp and take out the exterior buildings. *Apple 3* was to be the gunship that would fly 25 feet above the POW camp precisely at H-Hour and come to a near-hover and obliterate the two tallest guard towers (on the northwest and southwest corners). Then *Apple 3* would move outside the south wall to fire upon the guard barracks. *Apple 4* and *Apple 5* were spares, ensuring there would be more than enough room if there were more POWs than estimated.

For all this, we would also need A-1E Skyraiders (call sign *Peach 1 – Peach 5*) attacking the known military facilities within a mile of the POW camp. This would support the elements of Green Berets who had the mission of securing the roads to ensure no North Vietnamese reinforcements could arrive.

Blueboy Assault Group's priority was to gain control of the POWs as quickly as possible. They had to eliminate the guards and search all the cells for POWs. Captain Meadows was to announce on a bull horn, "We're Americans! Keep your head down! We're Americans! This is a rescue! We're here to get you out! Keep your head down! Get on the floor! We'll be in your cells in a minute!"

Once they had control of the POWs, they would take them through a hole in the compound's west wall blown by Master Sgt Billy K. Moore of Blueboy.

The planners estimated that enemy reinforcements would be overwhelming within thirty minutes. Greenleaf Group had the Bull, who would have two RTOs with him at all times. Greenleaf's mission included blowing up the bridge over the Song Con River. This bridge was to the north of the POW camp and it needed to be blown to deny the camp any reinforcements. Intel estimated that there were about 12,000 North Vietnamese military members within just a few miles of Son Tay. Greenleaf would also secure buildings north and east of the road and meet up with a Blueboy element at the camp's main entrance gate on the east. In addition, they were to clear the main guard barracks.

Redwine Security Group had LtCol Sydnor and his two RTOs. They were to establish a command post just outside the south wall. Capt Dan Turner's elements in Redwine were to secure the building outside the south wall and to secure the south wall's doorway. We would secure the irrigation pump house and the area north of it. Redwine would also cut down the light poles to make a better, wider LZ for the choppers' return. We'd also disable the Communications Building. Doctor LtCol Joseph Cataldo was with Redwine. He would quickly check the POWs' health to determine their condition and needs at the LZ before they were put on helicopters.

In summary, this mission was unprecedented in military history. Army, Air Force, Navy and Marine Corps resources would have to be in concert during the hours leading up to and during the Raid—not just executing their portion of a plan, but in constant encrypted communication, nimble enough to adjust in real-time. The only military structure organized with that that kind of authority and resources was at the very top of the pyramid—the Joint Chiefs of Staff. It took another 17 years (and setbacks in Desert One and Grenada) for a consensus to develop regarding the creation of a command able to execute such missions: US Special Operations Command. USSOCOM was established April 16th, 1987 and is proving itself with a series of successes which include the raid on the Osama Bin Laden compound.

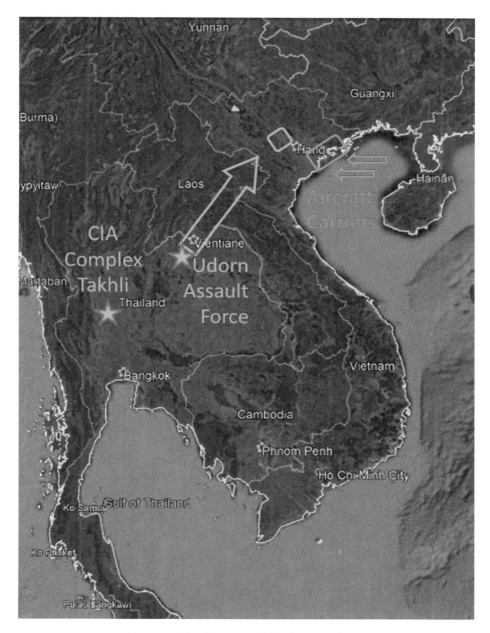

Image 31: Geographical overview.

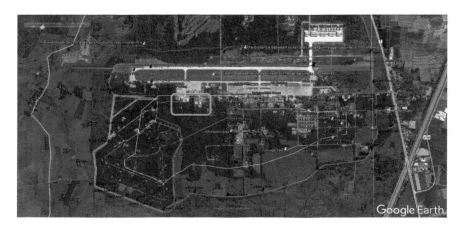

Image 32: Takhli Royal Thai Air Force Base. The
green circle indicates the CIA Compound with the
Raiders' barracks and the Theater where Bull Simons
gave his speech at 6pm, November 20th, 1970.

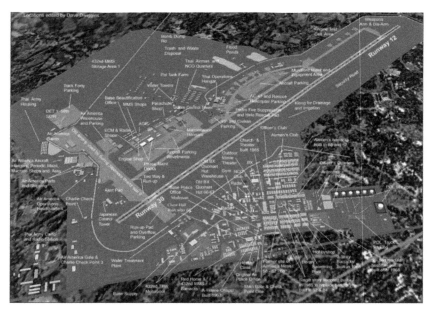

Image 33: Udorn Royal Thai Air Force Base, where the
helicopters and *Lime* HC-130Ps were pre-flighted and waiting
for the Raiders for the launch at 10pm, November 20th, 1970.

In his textbook *Spec Ops,* Admiral McRaven analyzes eight classic special operations to teach today's special operators.

Six missions are from WWII:
- the German commando raid on the Belgian fort Eben Emael (1940)
- the Italian torpedo attack on the Alexandria harbor (1941)
- the British commando raid on Nazaire, France (1942)
- the German glider rescue of Benito Mussolini (1943)
- the British midget-submarine attack on the Tirpitz (1943)
- the rescue at the Cabanatuan POW camp, the Philippines (1945)

Two missions are post-WWII:
- the raid on the Son Tay POW camp, North Vietnam (1970)
- the Israeli rescue of skyjacked hostages in Entebbe, Uganda (1976)

Adm McRaven, who commanded a US Navy SEAL team, uses these examples to teach six essential principles:

Simplicity, Security, Repetition, Surprise, Speed and Purpose.

Image 34: To show how the Son Tay Raid is taught to Army, Navy, Air Force, and Marine special operations forces, see here the listing of the eight missions studied in this textbook. This is a summary of the Table of Contents of the textbook written by former commander of USSOCOM, Admiral William McRaven, *SPEC OPS Case Studies in Special Operations Warfare: Theory and Practice.*

APPENDIX 2

Success or Failure: A challenge to historians to refuse to use the word "failure" in analyses of the Son Tay Raid

IF YOU TALK WITH the Raiders, they will tell you how disappointed we were when we returned to Udorn with no POWs. One thing we did know: If the POWs had been at Son Tay that November night, we would have brought them all home. For many years, many of us felt as if we had let the POWs down.

Then, when the POWs were finally returned in 1973, the truth was revealed. America found out that the Son Tay Raid caused the North Vietnam government to end the use of outlying POW camps. They saw how committed America was to bringing their POWs home. The outlying camps would be vulnerable. Within three days after the Son Tay Raid, all the POWs were consolidated into two POW camps: the camps known by the POWs as the famous Hanoi Hilton and The Plantation, both right in the center of Hanoi.

President Nixon summed up the purpose of the Son Tay Raid: "What these men have done is a message, a message to the prisoners of war still in North Vietnam, to their wives and their loved ones, some of whom are here, that the prisoners of war have not been forgotten and that we will continue to do everything we can at the diplomatic table and in other ways to attempt to bring them back home." (ref: www.nixonfoundation.org)

President Nixon, the Secretary of Defense, and the Chairman of the JCS, Admiral Moorer, made the decision with full knowledge that the North Vietnamese government was regularly moving the POWs around. The National Command Authority authorized the mission because it was not solely about getting the POWs (only about 15% of the POWs in North Vietnam would have been rescued)—it was primarily about sending a message to ALL THE OTHER POWS who would not be rescued in this mission. THE RAID WAS A SUCCESS.

The North Vietnamese government was shaken. The POWs were now put in large cells together, 40 to 50 POWs to a cell. Solitary confinement had been the norm to this point. Now, years of solitary confinement, communicating only with the Tap Code, had come to an end. This resulted in a huge improvement in the POWs' morale!

They could communicate face to face. The POWs were able to take care of the wounds and sicknesses of other POWs. They immediately organized themselves into what they named "the 4th Allied POW Wing." Together, they chose the motto "Return with Honor." They held makeshift church services. To pass the time and keep their minds sharp, they held college level courses including French, Spanish, even calculus, choosing the most knowledgeable POWs to teach as they could.

USAF Captain Lee Ellis, a POW for five years, said it this way:

"**The night of Nov 20/21 at Camp Faith, we POWs were awakened in the middle of night, hearing explosions, aircraft, SAMs launching, and several minutes of chaos.** We could not have guessed that our old camp at Son Tay just a few miles up the road was entertaining guests—uninvited guests for sure. **The next morning, we saw fear in the eyes of our guards and turnkeys and within forty-eight hours, we were loaded up and moved back to Hanoi. For the first time ever, we were in large groups.** We had 335 POWs in seven large open area cells in one compound. Quickly we established communications and named this part of the Hanoi Hilton—Camp Unity. It was a compound that had formerly been occupied by Vietnamese prisoners. **Our leaders formed the 4th Allied POW Wing and morale shot up as life completely changed.** In my cell of 53 guys—most of whom had been at Son Tay—we used our varied talents to organize classes using the best qualified as teachers. We studied subjects like French, Spanish, German, Engineering, and even studied differential calculus using pieces of broken brick tiles as chalk to work problems on the concrete slab floor. Suddenly, life had changed as **we set goals and went to work.**

Though we were not rescued by the raid **in many ways our sanity and teamwork were saved by that event. We will always be indebted to the Raiders for what they did for us.**"

USAF Major Jon Reynolds (later a Brigadier General), a POW for seven years explains in his forward to Bill Guenon's book *Secret and Dangerous,* that within four days after the Raid, all the POWs were joined together in Hanoi: "Men who had been in solitary confinement for over four years found themselves with roommates for the first time. Morale soared. The Vietnamese were visibly shaken." The Son Tay Raid was "the best thing that ever happened to us. God Bless the Raiders."

The Commander of US Special Operations Command (USSOCOM), US Navy Admiral William McRaven, in his textbook *Spec Ops: Case Studies in Special Operations Warfare: Theory and Practice* states, "The raid on Son Tay is the best modern-day example of a successful special operation and should be textbook material for future missions."

US Navy Commander Jeremiah Denton (later an Admiral and then a US Senator), a POW for seven years, said, "The Son Tay Raid was the greatest thing that happened in Vietnam."

(*The Raid*, Ben Schemmer, pg 287)

President Nixon's letter to Secretary of Defense Mel Laird, the day before the launch.

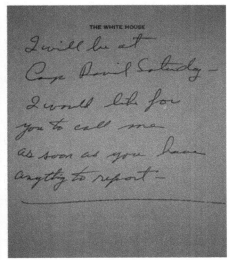

Image 35: From Bill Guenon's book *Secret and Dangerous*, pages 100 – 102. "Mel, as I told [Chairman of the Joint Chiefs of Staff Admiral Thomas] Moorer after our meeting yesterday, regardless of results the men on this project have my complete backing and there will be no second guessing if the plan fails. It is worth the risk and the planning is superb. I will be at Camp David Saturday. I would like for you to call me as soon as you have anything to report." As he promised in this memo, President Nixon honored the men and the success of the mission publicly, with no second guessing. He gave the green light for the mission, knowing that it was worth the risk that no POWs would be rescued, because the highest priority was to send a clear message that AMERICA WILL COME FOR ITS OWN.

Image 36: Thankful for the success of the mission. Three days after the Son Tay Raid, President Nixon stood publicly to honor the Raid in a televised ceremony in the White House. (l-r) LtGen John Vogt (JCS Staff Director), CJCS Admiral Thomas Moorer, Colonel Bull Simons, BGen Leroy Manor, President Nixon, Secretary of Defense Melvin Laird, and National Security Advisor Henry Kissinger. The handwritten note: "To my friend Leroy Manor with best wishes and congratulations for a job well done. Mel Laird"

America thanks the Son Tay Raiders

US House of Representatives,	"House Resolution 1282,"	Dec 7th,1970
US Senate	"Senate Resolution 486,"	Dec 19th, 1970

Whereas *increasing numbers of American military personnel remain in captivity in North Vietnam in circumstances which violate the Geneva Convention of 1949 on Prisoners of War and offend standards of human decency, some having so remained for as long as six years ; and*

Whereas *the government of North Vietnam and the National Liberation Front have refused...*
to identify the prisoners they hold,
to allow impartial inspection of camps,
to permit free exchange of mail between prisoners and their families,
and to release seriously sick and injured prisoners, as required by the Geneva Convention, despite repeated entreaties from world leaders: now therefore be it

Resolved, *that the official command, officers, and men involved in the military expedition of November 21, 1970, seeking release from captivity of United States prisoners of war believed to be held by the enemy near Hanoi, North Vietnam, be commended for the courage they displayed in this hazardous and humanitarian undertaking which has lifted the hopes and spirits of our brave men imprisoned and fighting, as well as Americans everywhere.*

Image 37: These excerpts are key portions of the Resolutions passed by the US House of Representatives and the US Senate in December 1970, honoring the success of the mission in lifting "the hopes and spirits of our brave men imprisoned and fighting, as well as Americans everywhere."

APPENDIX 3

Reunions

MANY HAVE COMPARED THE Son Tay Raiders with the Doolittle Raiders. We both trained at Eglin AFB at secret Auxiliary Fields only a few miles apart. The men on both raids were all volunteers for an undisclosed mission. Both raids sent a message to our enemies that the United States will do whatever it takes. The reunions of the Son Tay Raiders have a feel similar to the reunions of the Doolittle Raiders.

In 1973, Ross Perot hosted a reunion of the POWs and the Son Tay Raiders. The location for the first reunion was San Francisco. Mr. Perot paid for all the transportation cost, as well as rooms at the Fairmount Hotel for all the POWs, Raiders, and their wives. There was a ticker tape parade in the streets of San Francisco. People lined the streets showing their appreciation for the POWs and Son Tay Raiders. There was a banquet dinner that included guests such as Red Skelton, Clint Eastwood, John Wayne, Ernest Borgnine and the Andrews Sisters.

We have had several reunions since Mr. Perot's. The 44-year reunion was held in Kansas City, Missouri, and its success was due in part to the support of officers and NCOs at Fort Leavenworth and the Kansas Speedway and NASCAR. Pat Warren, President of the Kansas Speedway, and NASCAR hosted the POWs and the Son Tay Raiders and their wives. We were introduced to the NASCAR fans at the Kansas Speedway and on national TV. This year 2020, we are celebrating the 50th anniversary of the Son Tay Raid. The POWs, the support personnel, and the aircrews are all like family for us.

"Bull" Simons on a street parade.   *POWs with their wives and families in the parade*

Navy and Air Force POWs enjoy a cable car ride

Image 38: The first reunion. Held in San Francisco, it was organized by and paid for by Ross Perot.

Image 39: The first reunion. Held in San Francisco,
it was organized by and paid for by Ross Perot.
(l-r) Leroy Carlson (Blueboy), Terry Buckler (Redwine), Chuck
Erickson (Greenleaf), Tyrone Adderly (Redwine). Behind
Adderly is his wife Gloria, whose scented letters were so
appreciated. Photo provided to the author by Ross Perot's staff.

Image 40: The first reunion. Held in San Francisco,
it was organized by and paid for by Ross Perot.

APPENDIX 4

Memorable Moments told by the Men who were There

[AUTHOR'S NOTE: I want to thank everyone that contributed their memorable moments and their comments about the Raid. The Raid was a success. Like the Doolittle Raid, it sent the message to our enemies that America will come for you. The POWs got the message as their lives improved and their morale soared. It succeeded because everyone involved made sure the Raiders had everything they needed.]

THE FOLLOWING STORIES WERE provided by the Green Berets, Air Force and Navy aircrew and support personnel and, most importantly, POWs who were at Son Tay, Camp Faith, the Hanoi Hilton and the other camps. I hope you enjoy reading these words from the men themselves.

This photo was likely
taken here.

Image 41: Blueboy Assault Group members at
Aux Field #3 around Oct 20th, 1970.

Image 42: Blueboy Assault Group at Aux
Field #3 around Oct 20th, 1970.
1. Bruce Hughes 2. Anthony Dodge
3. George Petrie 4. William Tapley 5. Billy Moore
6. Lorenzo Robbins 7. Tom Jaeger
8. Pat St.Clair 9. Tom Kemmer
10. Don Wingrove 11. Pappy Kittleson
12. Dick Meadows 13. Kenny McMullin

Blueboys in HH-3 Banana

Image 43: This photo was taken during training at
Eglin. The green and white checkered box contains a
"Firefight Simulator," a decoy of fireworks to confuse the
enemy. The welding tanks are for the cutting torches.

Image 44: Capt Dick Meadows, Commander of Blueboy
Assault Group. Note the amber/red goggles, the ArmaLite
Singlepoint sight, and bullhorn. When Blueboy landed inside
the courtyard, Capt Meadows used the bullhorn to make sure
the POWs would quickly understand what's happening.

SGT PAT ST.CLAIR, BLUEBOY

As a member of the Blueboy Assault Group, I was in *Banana*, the HH-3. The flight in was almost surreal. We were flying a few feet off the wing of one of the C-130s and when I would look out the window, it seemed as if we were one-and-the-same aircraft. Brilliant flying by both aircrews. Since this was my cherry blast into combat, my pucker factor was a little tight. Going in, it was my job to lie on the port side of the ramp and fire my carbine on full auto at the northwest guard tower. On our first approach, we buzzed the wrong compound (the Secondary School). Our pilots corrected immediately and we came in on the actual POW camp. We hit so hard I saw sparks and was flung out of the aircraft. Robbie (Sgt 1st Class Lorenzo Robbins) immediately pointed me in the right direction and we assaulted the northeast tower. Those first few seconds were chaotic with the guards running around everywhere. They were immediately eliminated.

Early on, the lack of American voices coming from the buildings was troubling. After searching our assigned areas, the realization that we hit a dry hole was sinking in. After a complete search of the compound with no POWs found, we exited through a hole in the compound's west wall blown by Master Sgt Billy K. Moore. We rallied at the LZ and loaded on *Apple 1* for the flight out.

The flight egressing was exhilarating in its own right. I had no idea those big HH-53s could do the maneuvers they performed while dodging the SAMs.

Afterwards we were quite somber. The realization of rescuing no POWs left us with the feeling that we had let them down.

Three years later, in San Francisco, the POWs assured us that, in truth, it was a great success.

I may now know the root cause of Tech Sgt Leroy Wright's injury during the crash landing of *Banana*. I did not see it happen, but I may have inadvertently contributed to it. Here's what has been written about it. In Benjamin Schemmer's book *The Raid*: "The impact was so hard that a fire extinguisher tore loose from the bracket and hit Kalen's flight engineer, Technical Sergeant Leroy Wright, with such force that it broke his ankle." And in John Gargus' book *The Son Tay Raid*: "Air Force TSgt. Leroy M. Wright, *Banana*'s flight engineer, was the only man who suffered a significant injury which he completely ignored during the excitement of the moment. One fire extinguisher tore loose from the wall of the helicopter and smashed his ankle. He paid little attention to his pain until after he departed in *Apple 1* for the return trip." I was unaware of his injury until I read about it in Schemmer's book in 1980.

Fast forward to three years ago. Fellow raider, Jim McClam, and I visited Dan McKinney, my team leader on the raid, out in Montana during the last week of his life. We spent days reminiscing about our times together in the Army and he recalled to my memory an incident that happened just before the raid. He was tasked to add another fire extinguisher to our aircraft. He chose me to assist him. The mounting bracket had four screw holes and we were not allowed to drill any holes in the aircraft. We were told there were holes in the bulkheads that would fully accommodate the bracket. We searched high and low and could only find holes that lined up with two—but not all four—of the mounting bracket holes. We mounted the bracket as firmly as we could using only two screws and strapped the extinguisher into it. Dan asked me if I thought it was that extinguisher that injured Leroy. We'll never know, but in all likely hood it was. I regret that I never got to share that with Leroy.

A Historical Note to clear up myths: For a month, I was on the detail that maintained the Mockup. It was not—and I say again—it was NOT taken down and put back up daily. It's like the myth that we had mattresses on the floor of the *Banana* aircraft.

Image 45: In 2003—33 years after the Son Tay Raid— Command Sgt Major Pat St.Clair (second from left) is reunited with *Apple* 1 (tail number 357, now in the National Museum of the Air Force), the very helicopter on which he departed the Son Tay POW Camp. St.Clair is flanked by leaders at Camp Lemonier, Djibouti, in Africa, where his unit was deployed.

CAPT TOM JAEGER, BLUEBOY

Memorable Moment One: I was part of the Blueboy Assault Group, assigned to secure the large building of POW cells on the southeast corner of the camp (Building 5E; the POWs called it "the Cat House"). After we had searched the cells and found no POWs, I notified Capt Dick Meadows. I was told to leave the POW compound and to help prepare for extraction. I was responsible for leading the Blueboy Group to the *Apple 1* HH-53 extraction point and accounting for the number of raiders boarding the aircraft. Because of this role, I was given a headset so I could talk with the *Apple 1* pilot. When we lifted off, I was standing at the rear of *Apple 1* beside the minigun. The tail ramp was open. The crew chief was lying on the floor watching out the tail. Then I see an orange light coming up from the ground getting closer to the aircraft. I did not know what it was. Then I hear the crew chief yell, "SAM! SAM! Get down! SAM!" over my headset.

The pilot immediately commenced evasive maneuvers diving down and to the left attempting to dodge the SAM. Because I was standing, I was immediately thrown to the right and back toward the open ramp. At the last second, I grabbed the webbing on the side of the helicopter just in time to prevent myself from drifting out the ramp to the ground below. At that same instant, I noticed the yellow flash of the SAM as it sailed by the side of *Apple 1* missing us by what seemed like two meters! Thinking of that moment years later, I realized how close we came to crashing to the ground in a ball of fire and remaining in North Vietnam forever. These are the risks.

Memorable Moment Two: As part of the Blueboy team, I was to fire on the south guard tower as the helicopter descended into the POW camp. In preparation for this, at ten minutes prior to landing at Son Tay, I kicked out the right window of *Banana* and took a prone position above the landing gear. What a fantastic feeling! I am lying there at 1,000 feet, feeling the cold night air at 105 mph. We were in the heart of enemy territory 20 miles west of Hanoi, knowing that a SAM could, at any second, blow us out of the sky!

Image 46: An HH-3 displayed with the window removed
over the right landing gear, as was done during the Raid.

A minute later, I noticed a military convoy of 25-35 trucks below us headed east in the direction of the Son Tay POW camp. My
initial thoughts were that our mission may have been compromised
and the North Vietnamese intended to let us land and then destroy
us in place. The *Banana* pilot surely saw the same convoy, was
likely thinking the same thing, but continued toward the target. I
looked ahead and saw the MC-130 *Cherry 1* which was to illuminate the target area with flares.

I then saw that we were approaching a complex of buildings.
As we got closer, I saw a two-story building just below us. The
pilot slowed down as if preparing to land. I thought, "This is not
the POW camp!" In our three months of training, there was no
two-story building in the POW complex. We slowed down to about
three knots at 50 feet. Looking down I saw an old man in the courtyard next to the tall building taking a leak. He looked up at us as if

wondering, "What are they doing?" *Banana* then turned north and picked up speed, heading to the Son Tay POW compound.

After the Raid, I learned that the Greenleaf Group flying in *Apple 1* behind us had landed in that compound next to the tall building. They offloaded, firing at every moving thing in sight. Then they reloaded and headed to the correct site, the Son Tay POW camp.

Memorable Moment Three: When we volunteered for the Son Tay mission, we were only told it was dangerous. We trained hard for three months without being told what the actual mission was. One morning in the second week of training at Aux Field #3 (mid-September), Capt Dick Meadows, my roommate, asked me to assist him and LtCol Sydnor at the Mockup training site. While at the training site I overhead Dick accidentally say "prisoners" three separate times talking with LtCol Sydnor. That afternoon Dick asked me to not mention his "prisoner" slip-up to anyone. I told him I would not. From that morning on, I tried to think about what mission would involve rescuing prisoners. American POWs in North Vietnam obviously came to mind, but I thought it was impossible to put a 56-man raiding force on the ground deep into the heart of North Vietnam and expect that we could get out with the POWs. I thought the more likely mission would be to rescue American POWs thought to be held in caves in the Laotian tri-border area, something my FOB-2 recon team had attempted several times but were shot out each time. I guessed wrong.

It was wonderful news when Colonel Simons finally told us our actual mission. Each of us was ecstatic and never considered opting out of the most worthwhile mission any of us had ever been given. We had all volunteered for a dangerous, undisclosed mission. We had trained hard for three months and flown halfway around the world. We were aware of the risks if the mission was compromised and if things went wrong. Some or all of us might become POWs ourselves. Some might have to evade back to safety—some or most might never make it back to safety.

During the flight from Son Tay back to Thailand, after finding no POWs, I felt the greatest disappointment of my life. It never occurred to me that there might be no POWs in the camp and, as a result, our returning without POWs was heartbreaking. There was no talk on the flight back to Thailand and mostly silence on the 20-hour flight from Thailand back to Eglin. After risking everything we were returning without our POWs.

I assumed that the President and senior military leadership would want to keep secret what we had just attempted. I wondered how each of us could spend the rest of our lives without saying anything about it. I was so relieved and elated that the President decided to proudly make our POW rescue attempt known to the media. I now feel grateful that the POWs were immediately aware of our attempt to free them, that that gave them hope, that they knew they had not been forgotten, and that in future wars our POWs will know that we will never forget them and will make every attempt to return them to safety. It is the least a country can do for its servicemen and it is worth the risks.

Image 47: Blueboy Assault Group exiting *Banana*. The gunship *Apple 3* is exiting after its strafing. *Cherry* 1 has just deployed the flares. Painting: "Surprise at Son Tay" by Ronald Wong.

Image 48: Blueboy Assault Group exiting *Banana*. The helicopter is facing the Cat House. To the left is Beer Hall, Quiz Room, and Opium Den. Painting: "The Raid, Blueboy Element" by Michael Nikiporenko.

This photo was likely taken here.

Image 49: Greenleaf Support Group members
at Aux Field #3 around Oct 20th, 1970.

Image 50: Greenleaf Support Group at Aux
Field #3 around Oct 20th, 1970
1. Richard Valentine 2. Jack Joplin
3. Robert Nelson 4. Marshall Thomas
5. Jimmy Green 6. Jake Jakovenko
7. Walt Miller 8. Keith Medenski
9. Gary Keel 10. John Rodriguez
11. Frank Roe 12. Udo Walther
13. Don Taapken 14. Eric Nelson
15. David Nickerson 16. Leroy Carlson
17. David Lawhon 18. Glenn Rouse
19. Earl Bleacher 20. Sal Suarez
21. Dan Jurich

Image 51: These key leaders were spread among the three Groups. The photo was snapped while in Florida. (l-r) Captain Richard A. "Dick" Meadows, Colonel Arthur D. "Bull" Simons, Lieutenant Colonel Elliott P. "Bud" Sydnor

STAFF SGT TOM POWELL, GREENLEAF

What do you remember most about training?

Rehearse, Rehearse, Rehearse…

We rehearsed our mission over and over again…then we rehearsed the "Alternate Plan Red" in case their aircraft was shot down or for any other reason didn't show…as fate would have it, the force had to put Plan Green into effect due to *Apple 1* (with Greenleaf Group aboard) mistakenly landing at the Secondary School. Once Greenleaf was reinserted to the primary target, then Greenleaf had to conduct a passage-of-lines with Redwine.

What do you remember about the flight to Son Tay that night?
I was thinking, "We will have the POWs home for Christmas… what a Christmas present for their families. I would not miss this flight for the world."

What was the craziest memory you have of our time as a unit?
"Friday Night at the Fights." It gave the boys a chance to let off a little steam. I remember one night when things got a little out of hand and someone called the Air Force Security Police. They showed up in their bus and Sgt Major Minor Pylant met them and said, "Boys you don't want to get involved in this. I will handle it." They made a quick assessment and abruptly left.

What do you want your kids and grandkids to know about the Raid?
He was a soldier who did the right thing.

Why did you volunteer for the Raid?
At the time, I didn't know Colonel Simons personally, but I did know him by reputation. Anything that he was involved in had to be significant for the Army and quite possibility for our nation. To paraphrase Tyrone Adderly, "That knock at the door was an opportunity of a lifetime, and not just someone making a lot of noise."

Is there anything else you want to share?
Every American held in captivity has the right to expect their fellow Americans will come to their aid.

SGT 1ˢᵀ CLASS JAKE JAKOVENKO, GREENLEAF

I always had a problem coping with the fact that we did not bring them home. But then I met those brave POWs and heard what they said: "You may have not gotten us home, but you did made things a lot better for us."

My other most memorable moment was when Colonel Bull Simons told us where we were going and what we were going to do! The standing ovation from the Raiders: "Let's Get Them Home!"

Another was at one of our reunions; I believe it was at Eglin. Leroy and I were talking and a lady came over and stood for a few seconds and said, "So my dad was a POW. I was only eight years old in 1970." Then, with tears in her eyes, she hugged both of us and said, "Thank you." I believe Leroy and I both had tears in our eyes. The POWs will be my heroes forever with humble respect.

SGT 1ˢᵀ CLASS FRANK ROE, GREENLEAF

During our infiltration it seemed to take a long time for our helicopter *Apple 1* to land after we got to the site. Upon landing (at 0220), I squeezed out of the HH-53 but it landed so close to a rice paddy dyke that the tailgate could not be completely lowered. The pilot moved the helicopter forward to allow the tailgate to come down.

I was already out of the helicopter when I noticed that my two target buildings were not where I expected them to be. I moved through the compound as I thought that we may not have landed where we had rehearsed. After getting further into the compound, I encountered some resistance. I moved to the edge of the compound. I could see action (at the actual Son Tay POW camp) approximately 400 yards away. I took a position near the largest building and encountered more resistance. After what seemed like 15 minutes (actually at 0227) we re-boarded the HH-53 and went over to SonTay (lifting off at 0228).

Upon arriving (at 0229), we took up a defensive perimeter as our targets had already been neutralized by Redwine Group. Once we had been notified that there were no POWs in the camp and charges had been set on *Banana* (the HH-3 which had been crash landed intentionally inside the camp), we got the word to re-board our HH-53 *Apple 1*. On the way to re-board, I decided to get rid of the 40 lb bolt cutter I had been carrying during the mission.

Because of the way our perimeter was set up, I was directed to load near the middle of the Greenleaf Group. During the head count, Capt Walther thought that we were one person short. After several recounts, it was determined that all personnel were present. I found out later that they thought I was the one missing (probably because I fell asleep before the head count). During our exfiltration flight, the pilots had to take evasive action because we were targeted by SAMs. It was kind of a rough ride. However, we were able to return to the launch site without further incident.

This photo was likely
taken here.

Image 52: Redwine Security Group members
at Aux Field #3 around Oct 20th, 1970.

Image 53: Redwine Security Group at Aux
Field #3 around Oct 20th, 1970
1. John Lippert
2. Freddie Doss 2a.(behind 2) Ron Strahan
3. Greg McGuire
4. Joe Murray 5. Noe Quezada
6. Tyrone Adderly 7. Terry Buckler
8. Billy Martin 9. Joe Lupyak
10. Dan Turner 11. Don Blackard
12. Herman Spencer 13. Charlie Masten

Grimes and Sydnor at Eglin

Image 54: Major Keith Grimes (chief weather
advisor) and LtCol Bud Sydnor.

SGT TERRY BUCKLER, REDWINE

My most memorable moment has nothing to do with the training,
the flight to Son Tay, or the fire fights on the ground, or dodging
the SAMs during egress. It is this: When we landed at Pope AFB
and the Raiders were exiting from the plane, I paused to watch as
the Raiders were reunited with their families. It hit me like a ton
of bricks: Many of these men were married and many had children
my age or younger. I thought, "My God, these men were willing
to lay their life on the line for the POWs and could leave their
family without a husband and father." I will never forget watching
wives and children running to hug their loved one as they exited
the plane.

SGT 1ST CLASS TYRONE ADDERLY, REDWINE

Memorable Moment 1. After finishing a session of physical training led by Master Sgt Galen "Pappy" Kittleson, I went to pick up
my blouse, which was folded neatly on the ground. Once I had it on,

I felt something crawling on my back. I struck at it and made contact. I immediately felt a pain, similar to an electric shock. Then I felt movement again. My automatic response was to do something, so I repeated the same action that I took the first time—with the same result, only more painful! Now I was scrambling to remove my shirt: I discovered a good size black scorpion!

I told our medic, Sgt 1st Class Jack Joplin, but he didn't have his first aid bag with him. He told me to meet him at the club and he would take care of it, so I did. His prescription: he gave me a shot glass full of whiskey.

2. En route to Son Tay, I had a great view of the refueling of *Apple 2*. I was amazed at such a dangerous maneuver made to look somewhat easy (kind of?) In May 2019, I had the opportunity to meet the pilot Colonel John Pletcher, and we talked about how expertly that was accomplished.

3. I had the privilege to sit next to our ground force commander, LtCol Sydnor en route to the target. When we were over Son Tay, I will never forget, the door gunner and the sound and fury of his minigun, setting the guard tower ablaze and at the same time cutting it in half as it collapsed to the ground.

4. As soon as we hit our target, (The Pump House), Billy Martin and I were ready to move to our next objective when we received a message from our security team leader, Joe Lupyak, that Alternate Plan Green was activated. We began moving with urgency toward the compound with Joe Lupyak leading the way under sporadic small arms fire crackling around us. It appeared to come from the vicinity of the well, inside the compound. As part of Alternate Plan Green, I zig-zagged across the battlefield to link up with Terry Buckler to pick up a bag containing hand grenades in preparation for close quarters combat. I returned to my element as quick as possible.

As we continued moving toward the compound our team came under continuous fire from a building on our right side. I asked Joe to pause for a minute to give me an opportunity to sight my Grenade Launcher (M79). I fired a first round and it was on target, right through the window. It set the whole place ablaze. I fired another, as we were moving with the same result. I will never forget what Joe said, as memory gives way to time. I'm sure that Joe said, "G-D Tyrone you were right on it!"

As we closed in, I linked up with Leroy Carlson of Greenleaf. We came from opposite ends of the compound, and a scary moment happened. We both came into what could have been a blue-on-blue incident, if not for our superb training. We were both in the "high ready position" and ready to fire! In that moment, we were both relieved to recognize it was fellow team member. We took up our security positions in the vicinity of the well until we received the message for extraction.

Image 55: Tyrone Adderly is second from the right.
The White House, November 25th, 1970, four days
after the Raid. With President Nixon are (l-r):
USAF Brigadier General Leroy Manor
USAF Technical Sgt Leroy Wright (the
representative of the aircrews)
Sgt 1st Class Tyrone Adderly (the
representative of all us Green Berets)
Colonel Bull Simons

Image 56: (l-r) USAF Tech Sgt Leroy Wright, President Nixon, Sgt 1st Class Tyrone Adderly, Secretary of Defense Melvin Laird, Chairman of the Joint Chiefs of Staff Thomas Moorer.

SGT 1ˢᵀ CLASS RONNIE STRAHAN, REDWINE

In-bound to Son Tay, there were several sudden turns and yaws. Our group, Redwine in *Apple 2*, peeled off to the left and no more than 30 seconds later, "Alternate Plan Green!" was passed down the line. On landing (at 0220), we hit the ramp to execute our part of the assault. Charlie Masten and I were the pathfinders (to mark the LZ). We had to go with Plan Green. I was carrying about 10 pounds of composition C-4 to blow the power line tower down. Charlie went to the Pumping Station to clear it. I was about to initiate the charge on the power line when an HH-53 (*Apple 1*) carrying Greenleaf came directly overhead and rotated to land (0228). I waited until all Greenleaf had exited, and the helo had departed then gave the "FIRE IN THE HOLE!" shout three times. After the tower was down, I started setting up the recovery LZs.

As I was running to put out the beanbag lights for the recovery, I came upon a guy in a place I had not anticipated. I shouted,

"Coming through!" and Jack Joplin said with a chuckle, "Come on through, Ronnie!"

We had Alternate Plans if any of the groups did not make it to Son Tay, but as I recall there was never a plan for a group to come in after the assault had started. It just takes some adjustment from some good SF troops. I will never forget Jack Joplin with his calm demeanor, on watch with the hearing protectors on his head and almost laughing at me.

I do wish we could have got our guys back. It was a somber ride back to Thailand, and yes, maybe we did some good for the POWs' treatment, but there will always be a sense of failure for not getting some our finest back that night.

SGT 1ST CLASS BILLY MARTIN, REDWINE

I was a machine gunner. The most memorable moment of the Raid for me was when we first landed at Son Tay and we went to Alternate Plan Green. While Tyrone Adderly and I were running in, I stumbled and stuck the barrel of my machine gun in the mud. Adderly grabbed my harness and kept me from falling. Adderly could outrun me but he stayed right by my side. At the same moment, we were taking fire from the barracks. Joe Lupyak was yelling for me to fire with my machine gun. I thought I needed to change the barrel because it might be full of mud. I knew there was no time for that, so I started firing.

Tyrone, Joe and I made it to the berm and started putting down a wall of fire. Just then, Don Blackard's rocket hit the truck coming toward the camp. We continued there until we were called off.

We did not find out that there were no POWs until we got into the chopper.

CAPT JIM MCCLAM, REDWINE

1. I remember waking from a nap aboard our HH-53 while we were flying around Alabama late at night simulating the three-hour trip from Udorn RTAFB Thailand to Son Tay, at the end of which we would be landing and conducting our ground assault on the Mockup. I looked out the right front window where the minigun was and saw a C-130 next to us. I could not believe what I saw. It looked like our HH-53 was between the left wing and the tail of the C-130! I distinctly remember rubbing my eyes in disbelief that we were so close to the C-130. I could almost reach out and touch the C-130. Later, I learned there was another HH-53 in the same position on the right side of the C-130! The Air Force Special Operations pilots were indeed practicing their TIGHT formation flying. This tight formation flying was used on the night of the Raid during our three hour flight from Udorn, Thailand, into North Vietnam as a tactic to reduce the radar signature so our aircraft would present less of a radar pattern to the North Vietnamese should it be detected.

2. As MACO (Marshalling Area Control Officer), I carried a PRC-77 radio and monitored the ground command frequency. During the Raid, I heard Capt Dick Meadows (at 0229) report over the radio, "Negative Items." At that moment, I realized that there was a great deal more small arms firing occurring around the Son Tay compound than I ever heard during our many rehearsals. A terrifying thought entered my mind: "Oh no, this is a trap!" We never rehearsed having no POWs to rescue. The thought passed quickly as LtCol Sydnor had Dick make a second sweep of the compound to ensure there were no POWs. We began our exfiltration.

As MACO, I was also responsible for ensuring no one was left on the ground before the last HH-53 departed. LtCol Sydnor and I were at the tailgate of the last HH-53 (*Apple 2*) and the count of

Raiders was off. I let LtCol Sydnor know that we were short at least two if not three of Raiders. LtCol Sydnor had both HH-53s recount those aboard while he and I surveyed the pickup zone. Using my telescope night vision device, I spotted two or three guys on our right flank but could not determine if they were our guys or bad guys. LtCol Sydnor had me cover him while he checked out the guys. Thank God they were our missing team members and we all got out safely (at 0245).

3. After our return to Eglin AFB, I remained behind with Colonel Simons, LtCol Sydnor, and Capt Dick Meadows to prepare the After Action Report. During this time, we heard a recording made by one of the HH-53 pilots on their command frequency during the raid. The portion of the recording I distinctly remember and will never forget is the minute or so just after the exfiltration from Son Tay, as we were gaining altitude aboard the HH-53. I was looking out the tail of the HH-53 at what appeared to be a flaming telephone pole coming out of the ground and rising into the air. In the moment, I had no clue what I was seeing. The HH-53 immediately took a dive toward the ground and I lost sight of the object rising into the air. The recording we heard at Eglin solved my mystery. As we listened to the recording, there was a shout, "SAM! SAM! Dive right." I realized what I had observed during the exfiltration was the firing of a surface-to-air missile by the North Vietnamese. The realization was startling and, although back safe at Eglin, I was more scared than any time during the actual raid.

SGT ROBERT HOBDY, TRAINING SUPPORT ELEMENT AT EGLIN AFB

I was one of the guys who guarded the elements training and using the Mockup. I was disappointed that I didn't get to be one of the 56. I was chosen to research and train the elements in the use of the radios for the mission. After the Raiders left for the mission, I remained behind in Florida with other members of the support element and trained in the Mockup daily—as if the rest of you guys were still there training. We even did some live fire and air support training with the A-1s. Any satellite viewer would think that all us Green Berets were still in training at Aux Field #3, thus hiding the timing of the mission. The mockup was made of 2x4s and burlap cloth and was NOT taken down each day. I hope this helps clear up the myth that the Mockup was disassembled each day. (I did help tear it down once—at the end when we packed up and left Aux Field #3.)

SGT DAVE ADAMS, TRAINING SUPPORT ELEMENT AT EGLIN AFB

As many of you know, I never left Duke (my fault). But as far as support went and far as training went, I know a little bit. I don't remember who else was supposed to play the part of the POWs, but we were supposed to act scared and not know who they were and yell and act stupid. (That's the easy part for me!) Well needless to say: Guess who the rescuer for me was? Yup, you got it. Jake Jakovenko. So, I'm yelling and screaming and Jake is telling me he is there to help me and to take me home and whatever and I am still acting like an ass (again, easy for me) and refusing and acting afraid. Suddenly, I get the ass end of a CAR-15 coming at my face at about Mach 2. It stops about an inch from my face and Jake says "Look asshole, I am here to help you! Cut that shit out and let's go!!" I remember leaving the Mockup, but I don't remember getting back to the barracks. I know it has been 49+ years since it happened, and my memory is going bad, but I still remember what the butt of that rifle looks like.

Reasons for the Son Tay Raid (continued below)

Camp	Last	First	Camp	Last	First	Camp	Last	First	Camp	Last	First
Plantation	Anderson	John	The Zoo	Bailey	Jim	Fornats,	Badua	Candido	HH Room 1	Bagley	Bob
Plantation	Anton	Francis	The Zoo	Byrne	Ron	var camps	Balagot	Arturo	1	Barrett	Tom
Plantation	Anzadula	Jose	The Zoo	Chauncey	Arv	"	Cayer	Marc	1	Bell	Jim
Plantation	Archer	Bruce	The Zoo	Gideon	Will	"	Diehl	Bernhard	1	Black	Cole
Plantation	Baird	William	The Zoo	Hiteschew	Jim	"	Schwinn	Monika	1	Bolstad	Dick
Plantation	Brande	Harvey	The Zoo	Martin	Ed (SRO)	US Civilians	Adkins	Clodeon	1	Bomar	Jack
Plantation	Budd	Leon	The Zoo	Nasmyth	Spike	var camps	Daves	Gary	1	Burer	Art
Plantation	Burgess	Richard	The Zoo	O'Dell	Don	"	Keesee	Bobby	1	Burns	Don
Plantation	Cius	Frank	The Zoo	Sawhill	Bob	"	Manhard	Phil	1	Burns	Doug
Plantation	Chirichigno	Luis	The Zoo	Smith	Brad	"	Meyer	Lewis	1	Burroughs	Dave
Plantation	Daugherty	Thomas	The Zoo	Estes	Ed	"	Olsen	Robert	1	Carpenter	Al
Plantation	Davis	Thomas	The Zoo	Barnett	Bob	"	Page	Russell	1	Christian	Mike
Plantation	Deering	John	The Zoo	Blevins	John	"	Rushton	Tom	1	Collins	Quincy
Plantation	DiBernardo	Jim	The Zoo	Mehl	Jim	"	Spaulding	Richard	1	Doss	Dale
Plantation	Drabic	Peter	The Zoo	Hyatt	Leo	"	Stark	Larry	1	Duart	Dave
Plantation	Elliott	Art	The Zoo	Profilet	Leo	"	Weaver	Eugene	1	Everson	Dave
Plantation	Ettmueller	Harry	The Zoo	Berg	Kile	"	Willis	Charles	1	Fleenor	Ken
Plantation	Flora	Carroll	The Zoo	Stavast	John	"	Benge	Mike	1	Flescher	Bud
Plantation	Frank	Martin	The Zoo	Vogel	Dick	The Gym	Sirion	Praphan	1	Hall	George
Plantation	Gostas	Ted	The Zoo	Davis	Ed	The Gym	Uom	Chem	1	Hardman	Bill
Plantation	Gouin	Donat	The Zoo	Friese	Larry	"Zero" 0	Bean	Jim	1	Kerr	Mike
Plantation	Guy	Ted	The Zoo	James	Gobel	"Zero" 0	Flynn	John	1	Hickerson	Jim
Plantation	Harker	David	The Zoo	Miller	Edwin	"Zero" 0	Gaddis	Norm	1	Hubbard	Ed
Plantation	Hefel	Daniel	The Zoo	Osborne	Dale	"Zero" 0	Winn	Dave	1	Hutton	Duffy
Plantation	Henry	Nathan	The Zoo	Uyeyama	Terry	"Zero" 0	Nguyen (S	"Max" Dat	1	Kopfman	Ted
Plantation	Helle	Robert	The Zoo	Profilet	Leo	Double 0	Alvarez	Ev	1	Lewis	Earl
Plantation	Horio	Thomas	Zoo or Veg	Mullen	Moon	Double 0	Black	Neil	1	Lilly	Bob
Plantation	Jacquin	Juan	Zoo or Veg	Andrews	Tony	Double 0	Borling	John	1	Makowski	Lou
Plantation	Kerns	Gail	Zoo or Veg	Baldock	Chuck	Double 0	Brazelton	Mike	1	McDaniel	Red
Plantation	Kobashiga	Tom	Zoo or Veg	Biss	Bob	Double 0	Browning	Tom	1	Merritt	Ray
Plantation	Kushner	Floyd	Zoo or Veg	Cherry	Fred	Double 0	Coffee	Jerry	1	Metzger	Bill
Plantation	Lenker	Michael	Zoo or Veg	Clements	Jim	Double 0	Cormier	Art	1	Mullen	Moon
Plantation	Leopold	Steve	Zoo or Veg	Norrington	Giles	Double 0	Carey	Dave	1	Myers	AJ
Plantation	Lewis	Robert	Zoo or Veg	Hughey	Ken	Double 0	Davies	Jack	1	Plumb	Charlie
Plantation	Long	Julius	Zoo or Veg	Pirie	Jim	Double 0	Johnson	Harry	1	Rehmann	Dave
Plantation	Malo	Isaako	Zoo or Veg	Shanahan	Joe	Double 0	Kiern	Pop	1	Rice	Chuck
Plantation	McMillan	Isiah	Zoo or Veg	Sullivan	Dwight	Double 0	Lane	Mike	1	Runyan	Al
Plantation	McMurray	William	Zoo or Veg	Thorsness	Leo	Double 0	McDaniel	Norm	1	Russell	Kay
Plantation	McMurray	Cordine	Zoo or Veg	Abbott	Joe	Double 0	Mecleary	Read	1	Schulz	Paul
Plantation	McPhail	Don	Zoo or Veg	Hoffson	Art	Double 0	Monlux	Harry	1	Shattuck	Lew
Plantation	Mehrer	Gustav	Vegas	Sticher	Walt	Double 0	Ratzlaff	Dick	1	Shuman	Ned
Plantation	Miller	Roger	Vegas	Long	Steve	Double 0	Robinson	Bill	1	Seeber	Bruce
Plantation	Montegue	Paul	Vegas	Bedinger	Jim	Double 0	Sigler	Gary	1	Sima	Tom
Plantation	Newell	Stanley	Vegas	Brace	Ernie	Double 0	Wells	Norm	1	Smith	Dewey
Plantation	Nowicki	James	Vegas	Leonard	Ed	Double 0	Woods	Deane	1	Southwick	Ev
Plantation	O'Connor	Mike	Vegas	Harnavee	Chaicharn	Triple 0	Gartley	Mark	1	Spencer	Larry
Plantation	Parsels	John	Vegas	Lamar	Jim	Triple 0	Brown	Paul	1	Stark	Bill
Plantation	Perricone	Richard	Vegas	Franke	Bill	Triple 0	Ingvalson	Roger	1	Stavast	John
Plantation	Pfister	James	Vegas	Mobley	Joe	Triple 0	Mayhew	Bill	1	Sterling	Tom
Plantation	Purcell	Ben				Triple 0	Miller	Edison	1	Thorsness	Leo
Plantation	Rander	Donald				Triple 0	Schweitze	Bob	1	Tyler	Chuck
Plantation	Ridgeway	Ronald				Triple 0	Wilber	Gene	1	Van Loan	Jack
Plantation	Rose	Joe							1	Vissotzky	Ray
Plantation	Sooter	David							1	Vohden	Ray
Plantation	Sparks	John							1	Waddell	Wayne
Plantation	Tabb	Robert							1	Waltman	Don
Plantation	Thompson	Dennis							1	Young	Jim
Plantation	Thompson	Jim									
Plantation	Tellier	Dennis									
Plantation	Ziegler	Roy "Dick"									
Plantation	Branch	Mike									
Plantation	Chenoweth	Robert									
Plantation	Daley	James									
Plantation	Elbert	Fred									
Plantation	Kavanaugh	Able									
Plantation	Rayford	King									
Plantation	Riate	Alfonso									
Plantation	Young	John									

Image 57: The following is a listing of the US POWs who were in prison on the night of the Raid. The locations, however, reflect those of each POW on November 23rd, 1970, two days after the Raid (notice no POWs remain in Camp Faith on November 23rd as the North Vietnamese Army was in

the process of consolidating all POWs into two camps deep in Hanoi). This list was made possible only by the solemn commitment made by the POWs to memorize the names of all the other POWs. POWs recited these names upon their return in 1973, to ensure an accounting for their brothers, both the surviving and the dead. (Names provided by retired Navy Captain Mike McGrath of the NAM-POWs organization)

Reasons for the Son Tay Raid (continuation)

HH Room 2		HH Room 3		HH Room 4		HH Room 7	
Austin	Bill	Alcorn	Ray	Abbott	Will	Anderson	Gary
Ballard	Ted	Baker	Moe	Abbott	Bob	Brady	Al
Baugh	Bill	Boyd	Chuck	Barbay	Larry	Coker	George
Brodak	John	Brenneman	Dog	Bliss	Ron	Coskey	Ken
Brunhaver	Skip	Bridger	Barry	Boyer	Terry	Craner	Bob
Buchanan	Hubi	Brudno	Al	Berger	Jim	Crayton	Render
Butler	Phil	Brunstrom	Al	Burns	Mike	Crow	Fred
Campbell	Burt	Butler	Bill	Chapman	Harley	Crumpler	Carl
Chambers	Dennis	Carrigan	Larry	Copeland	HC	Daniels	Verlyne
Cordier	Ken	Chesley	Larry	Crecca	Joe	Daughtrey	Norlan
Cronin	Mike	Clark	John	Eastman	Len	Day	Bud
Daigle	Glenn	Clower	Doug	Ellis	Jeff	Denton	Jerry
Davis	Ed	Collins	Tom	Gruters	Guy	Doremus	Rob
Doughty	Dan	Curtis	Tom	Haines	Collie	Dramesi	Jim
Driscoll	Jerry	Donald	Myron	Hall	Tom	Dunn	Howie
Ford	Dave	Dutton	Dick	Hill	Howie	Fellowes	Jack
Gerndt	Jerry	Ellis	Lee	Horinek	Ray	Finlay	Jack
Hall	Keith	Fer	John	Hinckley	Bruce	Franke	Bill
Halyburton	Porter	Fisher	Ken	Jensen	Jay	Fuller	By
Heiliger	Don	Flom	Fred	Kramer	Galand	Gillespie	Chuck
Hess	Jay	Forby	Will	Lebert	Ron	Guarino	Larry
Jones	Bob	Fowler	Hank	Luna	Dave	Gutterson	Laird
Jones	Neal	Frederick	John	Marvel	Jerry	Hughes	Jim
Karl	Paul	Gaither	Ralph	McManus	Kevin	James	Charlie
Knutson	Rod	Galanti	Paul	Means	Bill	Jenkins	Harry
Lasiter	Carl	Glenn	Dan	Mechenbie	Ed	Johnson	Sam
Lengyel	Laurie	Goodermo	Wayne	Milligan	Joe	Kasler	Jim
Lockhart	Hayden	Gray	Dave	North	Ken	Kirk	Tom
Lurie	Al	Greene	Charlie	Parrott	Tom	Lamar	Jim
McCuistion	Mike	Harris	Smitty	Perkins	Glen	Larson	Swede
McGrath	Mike	Hatcher	Dave	Peterson	Doug	Lawrence	Bill
McNish	Tom	Heilig	John	Pitchford	John	Ligon	Vern
McSwain	George	Hivner	Jim	Pollack	Mel	McCain	John
Meyer	Al Benno	Jayroe	Jay	Ringsdorf	Ben	McKnight	George
Morgan	Scotty	Jeffrey	Bob	Rollins	Jack	Moore	Mel
Moore	Denny	Key	Denver	Ruhling	Mark	Mulligan	Jim
Myers	Glen	Madison	Tom	Sandvick	Bob	Pollard	Ben
Naughton	Bob	Mastin	Ron	Shively	Jim	Risner	Robbie
Neuens	Marty	McKamey	JB	Simonet	Ken	Rivers	Wendy
Newcomb	Wally	Moe	Tom	Smith	Wayne	Rutledge	Howie
Nix	Glen	Peel	Bob	Stackhouse	Charlie	Schoeffel	Pete
Norris	Tom	Pyle	Tom	Stafford	Al	Shumaker	Bob
Purcell	Bob	Ray	Jim	Sullivan	Tim	Stockdale	Jim
Purrington	Fred	Reynolds	Jon	Sumpter	Tom	Stockman	Hervey
Pyle	Darrel	Schierman	Wes	Tangeman	Dick	Stratton	Dick
Sehorn	Jim	Seeber	Bruce	Terrell	Dave	Tanner	Nels
Shankel	Bill	Smith	Gene	Tomes	Jack	Webb	Ron
Singleton	Jerry	Stirm	Bob	Torkelson	Loren		
Spoon	Don	Storey	Tom	Waggoner	Bob		
Stier	Ted	Stutz	Leroy	Walker	Cliff		
Talley	Bunny	Swindle	Orson	Wendell	John		
Terry	Ross	Temperly	Russ	Wideman	Bob		
Trautman	Konnie	Thornton	Gary	Woods	Brian		
Venanzi	Jerry	Tschudy	Bill				
Wheat	Dave	Warner	Jim				
Williams	Irv	Writer	Larry				
Wilson	Glenn						
Zuhoski	Charlie						

USAF 1ST LT J.H. "SPIKE" NASMYTH, POW 1966-1973

<<Make sure also to read Spike Nasmyth's book *2,355 Days: A POW Story* >>

You'll never know how much I admire all you guys who were on the Raid mission. I met some of you at a party thrown by Ross Perot in San Francisco many years ago. You're a bunch of studs.

I was in Hanoi six-and-a-half years. I spent time at the Hanoi Hilton, then five years plus at "the Zoo" POW camp, then back to the Hilton. I was at the Zoo the night of the raid, Cell 5 of the cellblock we called The Barn. My cellmates were USAF Major Will Gideon and Navy Lt Commander Ed Martin. A rumble of bombs woke us, then all hell broke loose—Ack Ack (AAA), SAMs, everything they had started going off. Fighter planes roared by.

We started figuring out what we were going to do if it was commandos coming to rescue us. Will the NVA guards try to kill us before the commandos get to us? We figured that if the commandos come, we've got a fifty-fifty chance of making it. We've been here for five years now. The fifty-fifty is better than the 100% chance of being stuck here forever. We might as well be dead forever as be a prisoner forever! The consensus was, "Bring on the commandos! Give us a fifty-fifty shot at making out of here. No one wants a 100% chance of rotting in a communist jail forever."

Then, the noise stops suddenly. We're waiting. It's real late. We don't hear another sound. Nobody comes.

The guards were clearly shaken by what they heard. They were digging holes like mad; it was a real show to watch. At dawn, the NVA are still running around. You've heard of a Chinese fire drill? They're digging foxholes right outside our cell. They've got machine guns set up all over the prison yard. They're digging the foxholes deep—real deep. I can't believe all the friggin' foxholes. First time I've seen the little bastards work up a sweat.

Then they cover all the cell windows, so we can't watch them. They're still afraid the helicopters are going to come—great big US helicopters loaded with great big US Green Berets.

Thanks again for trying to get us out. Escaping or being rescued by guys like you was always one of my dreams while there.

MIKE BENGE, A CIVILIAN POW 1967-1973

I was working for the US Agency for International Development when I was taken prisoner by the North Vietnamese. I arrived at Camp D-5, about 20 miles west of Hanoi on New Year's Eve in 1969. I was first put in one of the cells in a motel-style brick building of eight or so units. I was given a bowl of greens consommé which had a small piece of a chicken bone in it (more than likely by accident). Being malnourished and hungry as hell, as one might expect, I began trying to bite the bone into tiny pieces so I could swallow them, a small but precious bit of a needed mineral. The guard heard me, and reported it to one of the camp officers and they unlocked the door and began berating and accusing me of attempting to communicate with the other POWs using the Tap Code by clicking my teeth together. I was immediately taken from the cell and moved across the camp into one of three isolation "brick outhouses," separated so no two people could talk with each other.

There I remained until November 24th, 1970 when I was moved to the "Plantation" POW camp. After a while there, Lieutenant Steve Leopold was able to tell me that he and Warrant Officer Dave Sooter heard the raid during that night of November 21st, 1970. I actually may have heard the raid but, since the North Vietnamese had built a new MIG airfield near Camp D-5, I probably just thought it was just noises related to the airfield.

The benefits I received as a result of the Son Tay Raid were:

- I was no longer in isolation. After 11 months of solitary confinement, I had other POWs to talk with.

- The food in the Plantation was an improvement over that at D-5.

I wish to thank my brothers, the Son Tay Raiders, immensely! GBU (God Bless You)

US NAVY LT COMMANDER DOUG BURNS, POW 1966 - 1973

In early 1969 I was at the POW camp in downtown Hanoi that we called "The Zoo." We gave it that name because they used it to make propaganda films of certain POWs. I and a number of others were moved from one building we called "the Pig Sty" (where we had been kept since 1967) to another building we called "the Stable."

There we only 3 stanchion beds in the room I was put in and there were four of us POWs, so I slept on a bed board on the floor. We were the dish washers for both buildings and we quickly became the communications link to the building we called "the Pool Hall," using the deaf/mute hand code thru the slit in our upper wall.

The room next to us was a larger room and there were 8 POWs in it. The reason for that large of a group in one room that Earl Cobiel was in bad shape from torture. The Communists wanted more confessions and propaganda. Two Cuban interrogators were particularly bad to Earl. As a result, Earl was so despondent and hopeless that he wouldn't eat. He'd decided he'd rather die. The POWs weren't going to give up on him. His roommates force fed Earl. It took 6 guys to hold him down while he was force fed. It didn't work. Earl Cobiel continued wasting away and eventually died.

Jim Kasler was in the room at the other end of the building and he was also being interrogated by the Cubans.

Our room was on the outside wall of the camp and I wanted to see what would be required to get out and escape. I removed a few tiles from the roof and climbed up in. I found a way.

Jim Young and I were waiting for a stormy night when the lights went out. As it turned out, a stormy night did come, the lights did go out, and so Jim and I started into our plan. We were just climbing my bed board to get into the overhead area when the lights came back on.

The next day, May 11th, 1969, we found out that John Dramesi and Ed Attaberry had made their now-famous escape attempt in the night. We now know that they had escaped out the other side of the camp.

The North Vietnamese torture on Dramesi and Attaberry after the escape attempt:

The left side of John Dramesi's head was swollen "like a pumpkin." Dramesi could not speak for many months. Dramesi was put face down on a table, and while one guard held his head, two others beat him with a four foot length of rubber taken from an old automobile tire. This went on for days, in ninety-minute sessions.

For 30 days, they gave him only bread and water.

At other times during the next two weeks, Dramesi's arms were bound tightly together behind him and his wrists and ankles were clamped in heavy irons. A rope was looped around a two-inch-thick bar attached to his ankle irons, taken around his shoulders such that the rope forced his head literally between his knees. He was held in this position for 24 hours without sleep. His circulation impaired, the flesh on his ankles died, and he still bears the scars. After two weeks of this, the Vietnamese realized he might lose his feet, so they removed the irons and treated the wounds, but placed the irons back on his ankles. Dramesi wore those irons continuously for 6 months, removing them only once a week when allowed to wash.

Ed Atterbury did not survive the torture. His remains were returned in March of 1973.

Thank God we didn't go.

USAF 1ST LT JOE CRECCA, POW 1966-1973

On the night of November 21st, 1970 I was a POW in "Camp Faith," a camp just about 10 miles south of Son Tay and about the same distance west of Hanoi as Son Tay. This was during the bombing halt declared during LBJ's time which allowed the North Vietnamese Communists lots of time to improve their Soviet- and Chinese-supplied air defense network. And they did that in spades.

At Camp Faith there were four POW compounds. Two were located east of a center section occupied by our captors and two more west of that center section which were the VC living quarters. I was in the southwest rectangle of this arrangement in a cell of eight POWs.

It is important to note that, since October 1968, because of the unilateral bombing halt, none of the Americans held captive had heard any sirens, anti-aircraft gunfire, SAM launches or the invigorating sound of the afterburners of Phantoms or Thuds.

So, it was a real shock when we heard the unmistakable sounds of an air assault. The first sounds I remember were explosions in the distance. They were either the detonations of bombs being dropped or the report of anti-aircraft cannons, possibly a mixture of the two.

But then we witnessed a SAM launch.

What we saw in our 8-man cell was the orange glow of the SAM sustainer rocket motor displayed as the shadow of our barred window on the far wall as it progressed from the upper left corner to the lower right corner of our cell as the SAM climbed to its intended target.

In my spare time (of which I had plenty), I had derived an algebraic formula that would tell me how far away the SAM explosion was based on how many seconds it took to hear the blast. This one was about 10 miles away.

There was a considerable amount of AAA and bombs going off. Without a wristwatch or wall clock I could only guess at what time this was occurring. But we had bedded down not too long before, so I was guessing at about 0100.

Pretty soon the noise of gun fire, SAMs and explosions died away.

At what was probably 0200 hours, I could hear activity outside in the form of our guards entering our sector.

The next day was full of surprises. When we were unlocked and allowed to go outside, one of the POWs in my cell asked one of the English-speaking guards what had happened the previous night. The guard was very reticent to answer. What I did hear him say in response to the incessant badgering was, "Not for you to know."

Even though I would not have trusted any reply coming from the lips of a communist, nevertheless I asked my own question fully confident that I would get an answer: "How many airplanes did you shoot down last night?" The response was immediate. "One F-4 and one helicopter." I noticed the guard's countenance as he let this info slip. It was a look of, "Oh, I shouldn't have said that."

The other POW and I looked at each other in disbelief. I said to my cellmate, "Hear what he said? A helicopter! What the hell is a helicopter doing this far north? He's full of crap."

It didn't come out until a few days later about what had happened. Within 48 hours we were all packed up, placed onto 6x6 trucks and ferried into Hanoi. Sometime after that on our in-room hi-fi speaker the voice of Hanoi Hannah complained about "The White House clique's dangerous escalation by trying to rescue American prisoners." That's not word-for-word. We were usually referred to as, "American criminals captured in their piratical attacks against the peace-loving people of the Democratic Republic of Vietnam."

We found ourselves at Hoa Lo, the Hanoi Hilton. I was in Room 4 with 49 other POWs. In Room 3 there were Asian prisoners, presumably RVN soldiers and commandos. The South Vietnamese were climbing up on the bars separating our two rooms and tossing candy and cigarettes to us.

That night they tried to communicate with us. The johns of these two rooms had a common wall. By reaching outside, our RVN allies were able to slip us a note. The note was all in Vietnamese. I was asked to try to translate because, somehow, I was thought to be the most knowledgeable about the Vietnamese language. Their confidence in me soon faded when I said I couldn't decipher anything.

But the interesting part of their note showed a stick figure in a parachute, the number "250" and it was signed "CC31." There were all kinds of guesses as to the significance and meaning of these ciphers. We never did figure out what CC31 meant.

No sooner than we had arrived at our new lodgings near downtown "Bullseye" than we began to organize. Communications were set up very rapidly between all buildings at Hoa Lo between the head shed commanded by USAF Colonel John. P. Flynn, vice-commander of the 388th Tactical Fighter Wing from Korat AB, Thailand and "Charlie-Charlie" which term was used to refer to the rest of the POW population in the Hilton. Communications were a vital part of the survival of American and allied prisoners being held by the North Vietnamese communists.

But within each room another form of organizing was going on.

In Room 4 there were 50 POWs. Whereas before we had been held in much smaller groups – one, two, three, four, or even eight or ten - there were now 50 of us all together in a room of about 35 feet by 70 feet! New faces, new stories to tell and hear and putting faces of fellow Americans we only knew by name.

It wasn't very long before we began organizing our educational system. Chosen to be the "Dean" was a 6ft,4inch Navy A-4 pilot. Charlie took the bull by the horns and established a myriad of classes.

Language classes were taught in German, Spanish, and even Russian. Math classes were divided into three levels: appropriately enough X, Y and Z; X-Ray, Yankee and Zulu. We also had courses on history, sociology, politics, religion, wine selection (yes, we had a wine-tasting class), meat cutting and lumber selection. And I taught a course in physics, automotive theory & practice as well as one on classical music themes and composers.

I became a student of Zulu Math and was an instructor in X-ray Math. In X-Ray I had between six and eight students some of whom only had an associate degree. So we started out in high school algebra and worked our way up to and completed differential calculus the night before they moved 209 of us up to Dogpatch on the Chinese border. But that's a whole other tale….

I can only speak from my own experience here but each day I had to come up with a lesson plan and problems to be solved by the studs. Classes would begin when we got locked up at around noon. I called this "Happy Hour" because we almost never got interrupted by the VC for an interrogation. It was also "Happy" because of the 1330 RF-4C TOT and the ensuing 1530 air raid that would occur at this time replete with sounds like you cannot imagine unless you've sat through an air attack; SAM boosters and rocket motors, F-105s, F-4s, F-8s and A-4s roaring overhead and the incessant AAA of 37, 57, 85 100 and sometime 120 millimeter anti-aircraft artillery (AAA) blasting away. By comparison the firing of AK-47 and SKS 7.62x39 rounds being fired inside the camp sounded like a bunch of popcorn poppers.

It was the highlight of the day to hear our boys hammering the commies and one of the few times we could issue obscenities to Uncle Ho at the top of our lungs. Use your imagination...

We were still being held captive. But since the raid on the Son Tay prison camp by the incomparable Son Tay Raiders, life was so much better.

Hats off to all the raiders and those who supported the raid: Air Force, Navy, Marines and all those at their support bases, on land and at sea. Bravo!

USAF 1ST LT RICHARD BRENNEMAN, SON TAY POW CAMP (POW FROM 1967-1973)

I was in the Son Tay POW camp. Capt Dave Ford had a rotted tooth that was giving him much pain. One day, an entourage of high-ranking Vietnamese showed up that included a French-speaking doctor who held the NVA rank equivalent to a Colonel. Capt Bill Butler was fluent in French, so he explained to the doctor about Dave's need to have that tooth looked at. The V prison staff were upset that the doctor and the prisoner were talking in French, which they could not understand. (During the conversation, the doctor said that all this Communism stuff is just temporary. He said that, as a doctor, he was dedicated to helping people. He had been trained in France.) Before he departed, the doctor said he would have it taken care of and would even order Novocain.

The next day, a nurse showed up. The camp guards took Dave outside. They sat him in a chair. The nurse put some ugly looking pliers in his mouth and asked, "This one?" Dave said, "Yes." They yanked out the tooth…and THEN gave Dave the Novocain shot—in the arm!

Dave passed out. We brought him back to the room.

My theory on why we left Son Tay is that it flunked the inspection. With the Paris Peace Conference going on, the V tried to spruce up the camp. We made little walkways, planted some plants, the V added an addition and another new building, we got to write letters home, etc. On a few occasions, the V would have some high dignitary walk around the camp and then the next week we did more sprucing up.

We left Son Tay and only moved a few clicks down the road to Camp Faith.

On the night of the Raid, we stood looking out our cell windows at all the fireworks and knew something big was going down.

That next morning the camp "V" were really in a commotion and seemed confused and disorganized. An English speaker said a move was in our near future.

The move back to Hanoi now put us in large groups and we had a better interaction among our fellow POWs, many of whom had spent long times in solitary confinement. Much info was exchanged which helped morale. For one or two days, the guards had hand grenades with them and an English speaker said that if "they come for you here we will kill you." The grenades went away in a few days or less.

USAF CAPT LEON "LEE" ELLIS, SON TAY POW CAMP (POW FROM 1967-1973)

The night of Nov 20/21 at Camp Faith, we POWs were awakened in the middle of night, hearing explosions, aircraft, SAMs launching, and several minutes of chaos. We could not have guessed that our old camp at Son Tay just a few miles up the road was entertaining guests—uninvited guests for sure. The next morning, we saw fear in the eyes of our guards and turnkeys and within forty-eight hours, we were loaded up and moved back to Hanoi. For the first time ever, we were in large groups. We had 335 POWs in 7 large open area cells in one compound. Quickly we established communications and named this part of the Hanoi Hilton "Camp Unity." It was a compound that had formerly been occupied by Vietnamese prisoners. Our leaders formed the 4th Allied POW Wing and morale shot up as life completely changed. In my cell of 53 guys—most of whom had been at Son Tay—we used our varied talents to organize classes using the best qualified as teachers. We studied subjects like French, Spanish, German, Engineering, and even studied differential calculus using pieces of broken brick tiles as chalk to work problems on the concrete slab floor. Suddenly, life had changed as we set goals and went to work.

Though we were not rescued by the Raid in many ways our sanity and teamwork were saved by that event. We will always be indebted to The Raiders for what they did for us.

US NAVY LT JR GRADE PORTER HALYBURTON, POW 1965-1973

At Camp Faith on November 21st, we heard gunfire and jet noise from somewhere close by but had no idea what was happening. A few days later, without any warning, the guards came into our compound and told us to pack up—we were leaving. In a couple of hours, we were loaded into trucks bound for Hanoi and back to Hoa Lo, the Hanoi Hilton, where our misery had begun.

This time, however, we were packed into the large cells of about 60 to each cell. We still did not know what had happened, but in one of the cells were some South Vietnamese POWs. Some of them spoke French and some of us spoke French, so we learned from them what they had learned from the loudspeakers—that there had been a rescue attempt at the prison at Son Tay.

The elation that we felt, knowing that our government had tried to rescue us, was the most powerful morale booster imaginable. We were especially thankful to the guys (Son Tay Raiders) who had volunteered for this mission and risked their lives to try and rescue us.

US NAVY COMMANDER PAUL GALANTI, SON TAY POW CAMP (POW FROM 1966-1973)

How did you feel when you first found out about the Raid on Son Tay?

We actually heard small arms fire from the Raid from our camp. We weren't sure what it was. There was no active war going on near us and we had not heard an airplane for months. We heard the helicopters and small arms fire and suspected something big was happening. One of the South Vietnamese POWs slipped a note to us showing parachutes and American Flags. So we knew Uncle Sam was involved.

What impact did the Raid have on you and other POWs?
The Vietnamese seemed stunned. They really didn't know what to do. We were ecstatic because it forced them to put us into big rooms rather than solitary or a 6ft x 7ft cell. The fact that we were moved so fast and they didn't like it made us very happy even though we didn't know exactly what had happened.

What is your most memorable moment of the Son Tay Raid or time in captivity?
The Son Tay Raid itself was the most memorable moment of my captivity. We knew Uncle Sam wouldn't forget about us. The Son Tay Raid proved that.

What would you say to those men and all the support teams who helped on the Son Tay Raid?
Thank you, Thank you, Thank you times 1,000.

With deepest respect, Paul Galanti
POW 6/17/1966 - 2/12/1973
VA-216, Shot down on 17 Jun 1966 on my 97th combat mission in an A-4C near Qui Vinh, North Vietnam.

The following are the camps Paul Galanti was held in:

Boondocks	17 June 1966- 29 June 1966
Heartbreak	29 June 1966-July 1966
Zoo	July 1966- Aug 1966
Heartbreak	Sept 1966 - March 1967
Little Vegas	March 1967 - June 1967
Plantation	June 1967 - July 1967
Power Plant	July 1967 - July 1967
School	Aug 1967 - Oct 1967

Little Las Vegas	Oct 1967 - Dec 1969
Camp Hope (Son Tay)	Dec 1969 - Jul 1970
Camp Faith	Jul 1970 - Nov 70
Camp Unity	Nov 1970 - May 1972
Dog Patch	May 1972 - Jan 1973
Camp Unity	Jan 1973 - 12 Feb 1973

USAF 1ST LT MIKE BURNS, POW 1968-1973

We had recently been moved into a POW camp on the outskirts of Hanoi we called Camp Faith. The cell had a window with bars at ground level with a view of the courtyard.

It was after dark, I was falling asleep on the wooden bed when suddenly, there was a huge explosion that sounded like it was just outside our cell. It was so loud I jumped out of the bed and was wide awake. Immediately after this "BOOM," I heard what sounded like the roar of a huge rocket launching into the night. It must have been a SAM that was just outside the camp. I went to the window and could see bright tracers off in the distance and could hear the roar of anti-aircraft guns and the roar of jet engines. There was a lot of distant racket. Then I saw something burning in the sky. It looked huge and was falling out of the night sky in a slow spin. Before the burning thing hit the ground, it exploded with a light that lit up the night for a second or two. When that light went out, a Vietnamese guard stuck his AK-47 through the bars in my face and said, "Suleep! Suleep!" (sleep).

The next day, I saw three important-looking, older, civilian Vietnamese men walk quickly through the camp.

I believe it was on that very next night that they loaded every one of us into trucks and took us back into Hanoi to the "Hanoi Hilton" POW camp. This time, they put us in large cells, 40-60 men to a room. We had all been in that prison at one time or another. I saw heavily armed regular troops rushing around in the courtyard there this time. The Vietnamese put up machine gun emplacements on the corners of the prison walls.

They must have thought there was a real possibility that the next raid was going to be in downtown Hanoi.

We all were jubilant because, after so many years of waiting, something finally happened! Fighter pilots like to make things happen and are probably worse than most people at doing nothing.

US NAVY LT COMMANDER MIKE MCGRATH, POW 1967-1973
(Historian of the NAM-POW Association)

I was in Camp Faith, about 10 miles away, the night of the Raid. I remember the glow on the horizon. Action of some sort was going on, but we had no idea for many months what was going on just a few miles away.

There were four main sections of Camp Faith. I think—but not sure—that the Son Tay guys were in one of the sections. We had been moved to this new camp (Camp Faith), several miles outside of Hanoi, a few months earlier. Conditions were better and the V were making efforts to improve conditions every week or so. My section, having been moved from "the Zoo Annex," could not communicate with the other three sections at Camp Faith.

When the Raid started, our camp went black...all lights out. Guards came to our open windows and pointed guns at us. They told us to sit quietly on our bed boards and to keep silent. We did as told. I am now convinced that if the Raiders had jumped to a secondary target (our camp, only few miles away) that we all would have been shot immediately upon a US helicopter approaching the camp [since there would have been no element of surprise after the first assault.]

We were all moved to Camp Unity (a portion of the Hanoi Hilton) three days after the raid. I think we moved November 23rd, 1970. We moved into the Big Rooms (Rooms 1-7), 56 men to a room. It was great to be with new friends. Camp Unity was heavily defended: Men with guns on the roof tops.

The North Vietnamese military were acting paranoid, but paranoid of what? We had suspicions that something had happened, but we didn't know what. We first learned of a raid of some sort from South Vietnamese prisoners in Room 5. They passed notes and drawings of parachutes, helos, etc. Some event had taken place. They spoke only Vietnamese and could not explain the event in English, French or German, etc. We could only guess at what they were trying to tell us with the passed notes between cell blocks.

USAF MAJOR D.W. "WAYNE" WADDELL, POW 1967-1973

I was in the group of 57 taken from the POW camp called "the Zoo" on September 29th, 1970 to new camp we named "Camp Faith." On the night that you guys came to liberate the Son Tay POW camp, we were awakened by all the excitement. We heard airplanes and automatic weapons firing. We saw AAA exploding and what seemed like a 'local war.' One of the fellows speculated, "They are coming to get us!" But that was not fathomable.

A few days later, all of us at Camp Faith were moved to the Hoa Lo POW Camp, "the Hanoi Hilton." They put us in a large section where some ARVN (Army of the Republic of Vietnam—South Vietnam) prisoners were still in a few cell blocks. Using fractured French and pictures of paratroopers floating down over obviously Vietnamese buildings, they managed to get across the message that you guys had actually paid North Vietnam a clandestine visit. A notable feature of their pictures and statements was, "USA— Good Boy!!"

As you now know, you guys made the biggest positive change in our sojourn in North Vietnam and we can never repay you for taking that risk for us—THANKS!

USAF 1ST LT LARRY "LUCKY" CHESLEY, SON TAY POW CAMP (POW FROM 1966-1973)

I was captured in 1966 and spent the next 2,495 days, just short of seven years, as a POW.

I was at Son Tay. We had prayed for months that God would move us to a better camp. He did on July 14. I guess a person needs to be careful what he prays for—he might get it! We loaded in the trucks and went to a better camp, which fulfilled our prayers.

Then the Raid came. We were blessed once more when we moved to a better camp in Hanoi where we had big rooms--about 48 of us in a room. We now could teach each other such things as languages, choir, movies (we told movies) and had programs on each Sunday and also for Christmas, Easter, Fourth of July, Marine day, etc. When we got packages (and that was not very often) those who got packages shared them with those that received nothing. I never received any packages or letters for four years. Yes, for four years my wife and family did not know if I was dead or alive.

I am eternally grateful to the heroic things that the men of the Son Tay Raid did for our country and those incarcerated in Vietnam.

USAF 1ST LT LEROY STUTZ, SON TAY POW CAMP (POW FROM 1966-1973)

Some time before the 14th of July 1970, someone in the camp came up with the idea to put folded blankets out on a concrete slab to air them out. They were laid out to spell POW. Never did I hear anything about it from the intel officer I talked with upon return.

He was a LtCol and seemed to know a lot about the POW info…so maybe intel couldn't read!

On the 14th of July, I was out in the courtyard pouring piss on the plants. I guess they knew I was a farm guy and know how to raise plants. A Firebee reconnaissance drone came right over the camp and I waved at it. Years later after our release, I was talking with an intel officer and he told me that on the 14th of July they knew POWs were in the camp. He even told me he had seen my picture. A command decision was made to not put any more flights over the camp so as to not let the V know that the US knew something. I guess from that picture that day it put all the thinking, training, hard work, etc into being.

Here are my thoughts on why we were moved. The well inside the walls had gone dry.

We were moved to Camp Faith, a few miles away, built recently. As I remember, there were four sections to the Camp Faith and we from Son Tay filled just one quarter of the new camp. I believe the move had simply been a scheduled event—I don't believe the move was due to intel leaks. Just my thoughts on the entire thing.

On the night of the Raid, I was at Camp Faith, about 10 miles down the road from Son Tay. In my cell, I (and we all) thought it was a rescue attempt for someone who had been shot down. Within a few days, we were moved to the Hanoi Hilton. It was a big move: We were now in large cells! We found out from some South Vietnamese prisoners what you guys had done. I had really, really been down. I had been thinking, "No one gives a shit about us. Why not do SOMETHING and get it over with!!"

Your raid probably—when I think about it—is what kept me alive.

I know I want to thank all the Raiders for their efforts. The changes in treatment and getting into the large cells in Hanoi was a real blessing. I'm sad to say it, but until the Raid, I had just about given up hope as it seemed no one in the US gave a shit about us (i.e., the great leader from Texas [LBJ]).

The following is Son Tay POW Leroy Stutz's explanation of the buildings at the Son Tay POW camp (see photo below).

> I'm not absolutely certain of the cardinal directions, but assuming your photo is oriented to the north, then the POW building in the southeast corner of your photo was called the Cat House, I lived in cell #5 there.
>
> In the long POW building:
>
> The two large cells on west end was called the Beer Hall,
>
> In the middle were the Quiz Rooms
>
> The smaller cells on east end were called the Opium Den.
>
> The well was in the southwest corner of the camp in your photo.
>
> The bath house is the smaller building just west of the Cat House.

The concrete slab where we laid out the laundry was just to the north of the bath house.

The well was just an open pit with some water at the bottom. When it went dry they put some POWs down there digging and bringing the dirt up with a bucket and rope. You'd climb down on a ladder.

One time, they took my cell out to dig. The guard pointed for me to go down the ladder and dig. I refused (and may have tossed in a swear word or two). Anyhow, I was sent back to our cell in the Cat House and the door was slammed and locked. No sun and fresh air for me that day.

No one worked very hard on the well. As I remember (don't hold me to this) we didn't get to wash for several weeks before the move.

Image 58: Artist's rendering of the signals. This was created
with the help of Son Tay POW Leroy Stutz who sent the signals.

Image 59: An actual reconnaissance photo taken in 1970. Discovering that this was a POW camp was an amazing feat. The intelligence community deserves great credit, not the childish armchair quarterbacking they received from people with a political agenda.

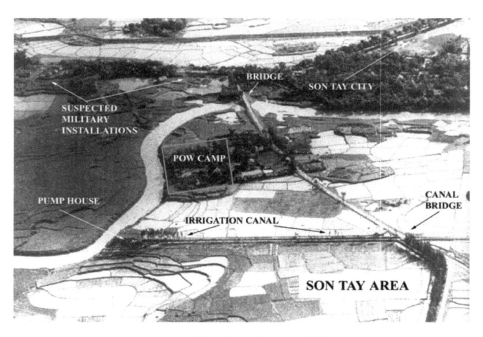

Image 60: Son Tay in 1970.

Image 61: Son Tay in 2020.

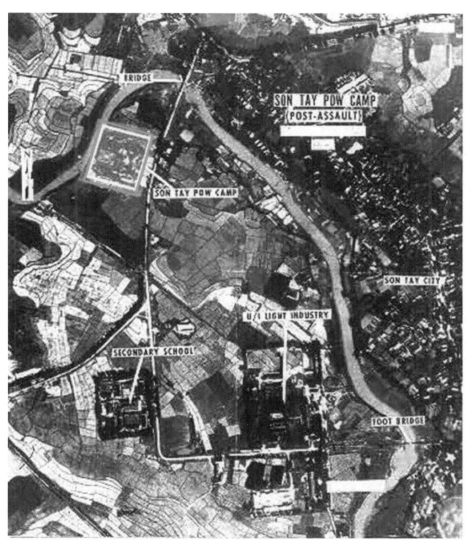

Image 62: Son Tay in 1970 (photo indicates
the Secondary School).

Image 63: Son Tay in 2020 (Secondary
School is still recognizable.)

Image 64: Location of the Son Tay POW camp.

Image 65: Location of the Son Tay POW camp. Image created by the author using Google Earth. The illustration is a Joint Contingency Task Group sketch adjusted by John Gargus.

Image 66: Location of the Son Tay POW camp. Image created by the author using Google Earth. Illustration from the National Museum of the USAF.

Image 67: The red arrow shows the angle
from which the photo was taken.

Image 68: The red arrow shows the angle
from which the photo was taken.

Image 69: The red arrow shows the angle
from which the photo was taken.

Image 70: *Cherry 1*, *Banana*, and *Apples 1 - Apple 5* in 1970 over the north end of Aux Field #3.

Image 71: The north end of Aux Field #3 (today named Duke Field) in 2020.

Image 72: *Apple 1* (tail number 68-10357) is on display
at the National Museum of the US Air Force at Wright-
Patterson AFB in Dayton OH. Flown by LtCol Warner A.
Britton and Major Alfred C. Montrem, it carried Greenleaf,
the command element for the raid. Built at Stratford CT
as a HH-53C Super Jolly Green Giant, it was continuously
upgraded over its service life, to MH-53E, MH-53J and
finally MH-53M. It flew its last mission in 2008 in Iraq after
38 years of continuous front-line service. (U.S. Air Force)
The window outlined in red is where one of the three
"miniguns" was positioned (see the USAF photo below).

Image 73: A minigun in the left side window of an HH-53. For a helicopter, the best defense is a good offense.

USAF MAJOR JAY STRAYER, APPLE 2

My Most Memorable Moment, as the co-pilot of *Apple 2* carrying Redwine Group, was watching with shock as our lead HH-53 *Apple 1*, carrying Greenleaf Group, mistakenly landed far short of the POW camp and unloaded his force in the wrong place (at 0220). At that point we went to Plan Green. To give *Apple 1* their due, they quickly returned (0228), loaded up Greenleaf, and the brought them to the POW camp (at 0229). What a night and memory (among others).

Image 74: Crews with an HH-53 (near) and an HH-3.
Back Row:
___, TSgt Leroy Wright (*Banana*), Price (support), ___,
TSgt Larry Wellington (*Apple 4*), Capt Tom Waldron (*Apple 3*),
LtCol John Allison (*Apple 2*), LtCol Warner Britton (*Apple 1*).
Front Row:
SSgt Daniel Galde (*Apple 5*), SSgt James Rogers (*Apple 3*),
TSgt William Lester (*Apple 2*), SSgt Aaron Hodges (*Apple 3*),
Major Fred Donohue (*Apple 3*).

USAF CAPT TOM WALDRON, APPLE 3

<<**Make sure also to read Tom Waldron's book** *I Flew with Heroes*>>
<u>Memorable Moment</u>: When we *Apple* crews first were told about Son Tay and saw its location, we kind of took a really deep breath and wondered if they had the wrong target!!

When we first met "Barbara" and saw the camp's location relative to the river bend and the trees inside the compound, we proposed that the approach path of the HH-3, *Banana*, should be a 45 degree angle off the west wall of the camp. The guard towers were at the north and south ends of that wall. Colonel Simons did not like that angle. He worried that it would make the gun towers hard to hit with the HH-3's miniguns.

Major Marty Donohue then spoke up, "Sir, I have a solution to your problem." Col Simons asked, " Now who are you?" "Sir, I'm Donohue, pilot of one of the *Apple* HH-53 helicopters. During the final approach, our HH-53 could drop down and speed ahead to cross the wall of the POW camp first. We'd be at 20 feet and 50 knots. My door/window gunners can take the towers out with our miniguns. We have another gun in the rear." Col Simons was open to the idea and decided he wanted to see how Air Force guys shoot guns.

So, we set up a mission at one of Eglin's gunnery ranges. The staff had set up sheets to simulate where our "items" would be located—no holes would be allowed there. Colonel Simons went along on the flight. After an hour's flying, we were done.

At the debriefing, the major who was in charge of the range explained to Colonel Simons, "Sir, I did not find any bullet holes in the sheets." Colonel Simons said, "Do it." So, now our Flight Engineer Staff Sgt Aaron Hodges would be on the crew entry gun (left side), PJ Staff Sgt Jim Rogers on crew window (right side) and PJ Staff Sgt Angus Sowell would be on the rear. That is how *Apple 3* became the mission gunship.

Memorable Moment: At our mission brief on the night of the launch, Colonel Simons had the large map of the Hanoi area. He told his soldiers, "We'll bring them home for Thanksgiving." The whole briefing room exploded, with all of the Army Green Berets on their feet cheering. Just across the room were the USAF helicopter crews. The Green Berets would be on three of them: *Banana*, *Apple 1*, and *Apple 2* during the assault. There had been so little direct interaction between the Green Berets and the aircrews. Each had their job to do and there had been VERY little opportunity to talk. At that moment in the Theater, I felt—and today I continue to feel—deep respect for the Army Special Forces as we all stood together, unified in mission. What a country we have.

As people study this mission, the question sometimes arises: Why were Air Force helicopters used, rather than Army helicopters? The answer is a function of distance and payload: Most helicopters could not carry that load that distance. USAF had the capability of air refueling. These Aerospace Rescue and Recovery Service choppers could air refuel behind HC-130Ps. During the mission, we air refueled, making it as if we were starting over fresh, fully fueled up. I knew the 130 pilot—he and I had been rooming in the BOQ (Bachelor Officer's Quarters) leading up to the mission.

When we heard over the radios that the Green Berets on the ground inside the POW camp said, "Negative ITEMS," I think my belly reached the floor. "What?" I looked at Marty and said, "This plan worked. We would've gotten them all out—where the hell are they??"

After landing at Udorn RTAFB and shutting down our engines, I remember seeing two medevac C-141 jets that would no longer be needed...

It was an amazing experience. The training was excellent. There were no losses for our team. BGen Manor came around and thanked each crewmember for their efforts.

Image 75: An HH-53 is positioning its refueling probe
to capture the HC-130P's refueling drogue.

USAF MAJOR RYLAND "ROY" DREIBELBIS, APPLE 4

I was stationed at the 37th Aerospace Rescue and Recovery Squadron at Da Nang Air Base when Major Royal Brown and I were ordered to come back from Vietnam to Eglin AFB for the mission. Of course, we did not know the real purpose, only that we were going to Eglin to receive some additional operations training that could be implemented in Vietnam.

We arrived at Eglin on Labor Day weekend and were told to attend a meeting on base. As soon as I walked in the room, I realized that this was not going to be a normal training program. Several of the attendees were HH-53 instructors stationed at Eglin who had checked us out in the HH-53. It made sense that they would be at the meeting as I assumed they would probably be our flight instructors. But then, one of the officers on the stage told us that this was going to be a classified program and that a classified mission may (or may not) be flown at the end of a preparation effort. The officer added that the mission may involve considerable risk and if there is anyone in the room that does not want to participate, please leave the room immediately. No one left the room. Those of us who came from outside the local area were told to obtain off base accommodations and to limit coming to the base except for meetings and scheduled preparation flights.

Our operational training began immediately. We started with familiarization flights that included flight line familiarization and a look at the local flying area where most of our future flights would take place. The flights were with instructor pilots that were part of the training staff at Eglin. We soon realized that some of them were going to participate in the mission we were preparing to conduct.

The first preparation flights included some basic flying maneuvers, a look at the area where we would be conducting the most of our flying, some instrument flying including approaches to Eglin and formation flying with one or two HH-53s and an HC-130 tanker, The HH-53s would take turns connecting to the refueling drogue and taking on fuel. All us had done this many times but this gave us a chance to improve our individual refueling skills. Crew coordination was emphasized. More and more of our flights were conducted at night including refueling.

One of my first formation flights included a UH-1 Bell Huey! What? I was totally surprised. A Huey flying formation with a HC-130 tanker and HH-53s. The Huey could not conduct air refueling, so why was it flying with a tanker and HH-53s? If the mission could be done with a Huey then why involve an HC-130 tanker and HH-53s? Proof-of-Concept? One or two flights ended Huey participation. A twin-engine Sikorski HH-3 replaced the Huey. It could be air refueled and it could carry a larger payload. An HH-3, its crew and passengers, played a key role in the Son Tay Raid. It was going to be landed inside Son Tay POW camp walls.

Sometime in this time period, the aircraft crew members were told that we were preparing to rescue US airmen imprisoned at the Son Tay POW camp located near Hanoi, North Vietnam. Our efforts took on a new light. We were preparing to bring home our fellow airmen that were in the hands of our enemy, some for years! Our incentive grew to new highs. We had to do this right the first time!

The number of aircraft flying in our formation had grown to seven: One MC-130 with six helicopters. Three helicopters flew behind the left wing. One of them was the HH-3 that was going to land inside the prison walls carrying Green Berets that were going release the POWs from their prison cells and two HH-53s. They would land in a safe area near the prison and stand by for potential rescue needs and pick up POWs as they were released at the prison. Three HH-53s flew behind right wing on the MC-130. Two would carry the ground assault teams and the third was assigned the responsibility of suppressing ground fire (the Gunship, Apple 3).

One night, we were told to fly two HH-53s to Aux Field #3 just north of Eglin, pick up passengers, and then fly a planned mission. We were not told specifically who we were to pick up. We were told to park in a line on the ramp facing the woods with engines running. As soon as we parked two lines of men appeared out of the woods. Amazing! Two lines of men suddenly appeared out of the dark woods! One line walked directly to my helicopter and passed directly under my side window of the cockpit. They were boarding our helicopter. I could see that they carried variety of weapons and their faces were blackened. I thought to myself that I would not like to meet any of them at night on a dark street. These were the kind of war troops you would want on your side. I will never forget this event. I was so impressed with that part of the mission that I can't remember specifically what we did after loading the troops. We must have flown them to the range where they performed a practice assault on the simulated prison.

I distinctly remember one refueling flight over the Gulf of Mexico at night. I was at the controls and always took pride in my refueling capability – trying to be smooth on the controls and make a connection with the refueling basket deployed from the HC-130 always on the first try. This night tested my refueling skills. It was a totally dark night and we were far enough from shore that shoreline lights could not be seen. Instrument flying was the only option. It seemed like the HC-130P tanker and my HH-53 were in a dark hole, suspended in space. I could not recognize movement except by looking at the flight instruments and the C-130 ahead of me. It turned out to be an uneventful refueling operation, but one that I will never forget.

I was fortunate to have my family nearby in Tallahassee during the preparation effort. I was able to drive over and spend time with my family when I was not scheduled to fly. It so happened that I was there when I received a telephone call saying that I had to return to Eglin as soon as possible. I and Brown were scheduled to depart Eglin in a few hours. It sounded like the mission was a go. I called the airport to find out if there was a flight to Fort Walton. There was one departing at 10pm (as I recall) and I could make that flight. My family and I immediately went to the airport and after arrival learned that the flight was not going to land because the airport was below minimums. The only option – rent a car and drive to Ft Walton. I could make the flight departure from Eglin if all goes well. Two airline passengers at the airport also wanted to go to Ft Walton. I said okay and they joined me for the drive. I said goodbye to my family. It was not easy. I didn't know when I would see them again. I joined up with Brown at the motel where we had been staying since arrival from Vietnam. We packed and headed for the flight line to board the C-141.

In short, we made the departure on the Air Force C-141 and we were off to the far east (Thailand). Brown and I discovered that we were the only Raiders on the flight. We did not know how, or when the other Raiders were going to join us. The flight was long and uneventful. I know that we landed at Travis AFB in California for refueling. There may have been a C-141 crew change. No airline seats on C-141s! We ended up at Takhli RTAFB in Thailand. We spent two or three days there and were joined by other Raiders. We were briefed on the steps that would put in motion at Udorn RTAFB, the jumping off point for the Raid. Mission details were reviewed.

On the night of the raid, November 20th, 1970, the briefings included the Green Berets. When they were told the mission objective, they all cheered.

We aircrew members of the helicopters were airlifted to Udorn by C-130, as were the Green Berets. We off loaded and went directly to our assigned helicopters. Each crew had been told in advance where their assigned helicopter would be parked. We boarded our helicopter and started the engines at the predetermined time. We did not communicate with the anyone including the tower. One of the mission planners had gone to the tower and told the tower operators that aircraft would be departing and not try to contact them. Everything was done with no radio calls – radio silent. At a planned time, we took off in trail and joined the C-130s *Lime 1* and *Lime 2* that arrived overhead at the planned time to assume lead of our six helicopters in formation. Our formation was on the way to Son Tay.

The flight was proceeding as planned when we flew into a cloud deck. Visual contact between aircraft was lost. Fortunately, the possibility of this happening had been included in our preparation plans. The H-3, *Banana*, stayed in its position directly behind the left wing of *Lime 1*. I turned left by 30 degrees and then turned right to resume the heading we were all flying before flying into the cloud, *Apple 5*, which was flying formation on my left side, turned 60 degrees left and then resumed the original heading. The H-53s on the right wing performed the same procedure. Separation between aircraft was achieved. We soon emerged from the cloud and the original formation was reestablished.

Our next thing we had to do on the way to Son Tay was air refuel. Refueling baskets (drogues) are available behind both wings of the C-130s. Two helicopters can be refueled simultaneously one on the left drogue and one on the right drogue. Crossovers were not required.

This refueling for us was a bit more complicated. Helicopters *Apple 4* (me) and *Apple 5*, flying behind the left wing, could not use the left drogue because the H-3, *Banana*, could not leave its position behind the left-wing drogue because of power limitations. Therefore *Apple 4* (me) and *Apple 5* had to fly over to the right wing to refuel off the right-wing drogue, a crossover. We did this one at a time. *Apples 1, 2*, and *3* had to move to the right so that the drogue would be available to us for refueling. Full of gas, at last! Now, back to the left-wing position and on to Son Tay!

Another change was required in order for us to reach the objective. The change gave us a new leader, another C-130, *Cherry 1*. This was an MC-130 that had advanced capabilities that could lead us at low level through the mountains west of Hanoi. It was also going to take us the rest of the way to the POW camp at low altitude (as I recall, it was 500 feet) so that the chance of being detected would be minimized. Our change of lead was accomplished at a predetermined time. Our lead, *Lime 1*, pulled away and below us was *Cherry 1*. All we had to do was descend in formation to establish formation with our new leader.

The plan called for us to arrive at the prison at 2:20 AM. That time would provide the optimal light for blackout formation flying and for the ground troop action inside the prison.

I and the other helicopters followed *Cherry 1* to the POW camp at 500 feet. *Apple 1* (with Greenleaf Group aboard) and *Apple 2* (with Redwine Group) delivered their troops to the POW camp. *Apple 3* flew at low level over the prison walls and used their miniguns to destroy the guard towers at two corners of the prison wall.

Apple 1 mistakenly flew to a facility that looks similar to the Son Tay POW camp, just a few hundred meters to the south. They landed and the troops disembarked. They met some resistance which they immediately neutralized. The mistake was soon realized, they landed again, the troops reloaded, and were immediately taken to the POW camp.

While this was going on, we climbed to approximately 1500 feet and prepared to drop flares over the prison. We were backup to this action if the proceeding aircraft flares failed to ignite. Their flares worked and I got my first look at the real thing. I flew to what was called the lake area just northwest of the prison and landed. We were told to wait there to avoid ground fire which might damage our helicopters and impair our primary mission—loading POWs at the prison after they were released and flying them to Udorn. While on the ground, I witnessed the light flashes/reflection of action taking place at the prison. I also witnessed SAMs being launched at our fighter aircraft that were overhead protecting all of us while we were on the ground. I think I saw 15 or so SAMs fired at our protectors. I saw one explode close enough to one of our fighter aircraft that it was momentarily visible, like a camera flash bulb. I found out later that two of our fighter aircraft had been damaged enough to leave the area and one bad enough that the crew had to eject over Laos. That became an important part of our mission that night. *Apple 5* also participated in that rescue later that night.

After waiting approximately 30 minutes or so, we heard bad news. One of the troops on the ground at the prison announced that there were no "Items" at the Son Tay prison! I will never forget that radio transmission. What?! No POWs to remove from isolation and away from home for so many years. I couldn't believe it. We were going to take them to safety. Instead we would be going to Udorn empty. How could this happen. They could have gone home to see and be with their families, their loved ones.

After that "No Items" radio message soaked in, our focus was on getting back to Udorn safely. We didn't know what we might encounter. The North Vietnam military would be onto us now.

As planned, all the helicopters would return to Udorn on their own. There would be no formations. We all knew the heading back to Udorn so we were on our way. Not far out of the Son Tay area and just into the mountains, someone called, "MiG, MiG, MiG!" Someone thought they had seen a MiG on a path to attack us. The mountain valleys had filled with fog and the half-moon shining on the fog made our silhouettes easy for a MiG to see. I immediately made a descending steep turn toward a mountaintop that was visible above the fog layer. I wanted to hide there, using the dark mountain as a background. Once there, I flew slowly along the mountain ridge. We would have been difficult to see especially from a fast flying jet. We soon realized that the call was wrong, so we resumed our flight to Udorn.

Not long after that, we learned that the crew of one of the damaged F-105 fighters, *Firebird 5*, had to eject on the way to their home base. *Apple 4* and *Apple 5* now had a rescue mission on our hands. It was our job to locate and recover them.

Both of us had already been refueled, so that was not a problem. But the darkness very much complicated the rescue effort. *Apple 5* located one of the crew members and we located the other. Hoist pickups could not be made until sun-up. I made radio contact with *Firebird 5* "bravo," Capt Ted Lowry.

> *[Read Capt Ted Lowry's telling of this story from his point of view in another section of this Appendix below.]*

I flew over him, so we generally knew his location. We had to wait until first light to safely recover him. The same situation existed with *Apple 5*'s recovery effort. There was a village in the valley off to our left, so there was some concern that we might receive some ground fire. At daybreak, we spotted Ted and we made a hoist pickup. We did have to perform another refueling on the way back to Udorn. *Apple 5* made their recovery of the other F-105 crewmember, Major Don Kilgus, and arrived at Udorn just ahead of us. That rescue took a little the sting out of not bringing home the POWs.

We attended a short debrief. We were informed that those of us who, prior to the months of training at Eglin, had been stationed at Da Nang and Udorn would simply return now to our previous duties at those bases. I felt a little left out and deflated. All the other Raid participants were already on a C-141and were on their way back to Eglin. The Raid team had dissolved. We were instructed to not talk about the Raid with personnel when we returned our home bases. Brown and I boarded a C-130 and were flown back to Da Nang. That was it. Duty called.

Brown and I were given 30 days of leave, so we did get to return stateside to see our families and I really appreciated that. We both missed an awards ceremony at Fort Bragg where participants in the Raid received medals for Raid participation. We both were awarded Silver Star medals by the Commander of Military Airlift Command at Scott AFB. This was after I completed my Vietnam tour and was assigned duty at Rescue Headquarters at Scott. My wife and my two daughters were able to attend the ceremony. I really appreciate the award and the opportunity to participate in the Raid. I got to work with some of the greatest men in the US military. The POWs expressed their appreciation when they came home in 1973.

I am proud to have been a Son Tay Raider. En route during the mission, I had to convince myself that this was the real thing—and I'd been flying helicopters since 1955! I am truly thankful for the opportunity. That's what rescue is all about.

Cherry 01

This Lockheed MC-130E-LM Combat Talon, serial number 64-0523, was CHERRY 01, leading the assault helicopters during the Son Tay Raid. After 47 years of service, 64-0523 made its last flight, 22 June 2012. It is shown at Duke Field, Florida, on its final flight. It is on static display at Cannon AFB, New Mexico.

Image 76: *Cherry* 1 is on display at Cannon AFB, NM.

USAF MAJOR IRL FRANKLIN, CHERRY 1

For me, the Raid began in August 1970. As a member of the 7th Special Operations Squadron, I was deployed to Greenham Common, England, for our annual Western Europe exercise with numerous NATO and other friendly countries. Our squadron commander received a message from Headquarters USAF requesting Capt Tom Stiles and myself along with a MC-130 Combat Talon crew be sent to Eglin AFB for an undetermined time. Since I was Chief of the Standardization & Evaluation program for all squadron aircraft (which included the C-47s, UH-1Ns and MC-130 Combat Talon Birds), I did not have a crew that I was assigned to. Since our squadron was on a crew system, we always tried to not break up crews. So our commander, LtCol Rich Reeder, started firing messages back and forth between the squadron, USAFE (US Air Forces in Europe Command), and HQ USAF objecting to the by-name requests instead of complete crews. If I remember right, he even tried to object through EUCOM (European Command) as we were deployed under that Unified Command—but, no luck!

I was not sure why we were requested by name except for the fact that we were among the original six Combat Talon crews and were responsible for developing a lot of the tactics and techniques used by the three Combat Talon units worldwide. Later, I was to learn LtCol Ben Kraljev (whom I had served with in C-123 units at Pope AFB and in Southeast Asia) was the AF Chief Operations Officer for the Son Tay Raid. He also knew that we had deployed to Na Trang Air Base, South Vietnam, so I assume that he and BGen Manor knew that we were well versed in Combat Talon tactics and techniques. In addition, we were familiar with the Southeast Asia countryside. It was ultimately determined that Tom Stiles and I, along with members of one of our squadron's crews, would be sent to Florida.

After arriving at Eglin and getting bedded down, we were ush-ered into the briefing room at Special Operations Forces (SOF) Headquarters. Much to my surprise, we walked into a group of 200 people. I noticed Special Forces, other Army personnel (UH-1 pilots), Air Force personnel including A-1 crews, HH-53 crews, HH-3 crews and LtCol Albert "Friday" Blosch's Combat Talon crew from Pope AFB. Then, focusing upon the front of the room, I noticed BGen Leroy Manor, Colonel Bull Simons, and some HQ USAF Staff. We were told, "You are here to work on a joint exer-cise that could develop into a dangerous mission. If anyone in the room wishes to be excused, you may leave now, and no questions will be asked." A silence fell over those gathered. People looked around the room and at the front of the room and did not move. A period went by with no one moving or speaking, then BGen Manor said, "Excellent. I am glad you are all with us because you have all been chosen for your unique experience and abilities which will make the mission a success." Administrative details were covered and we were dismissed to go to our quarters to ponder the next actions.

The next day, Combat Talon aircraft commanders along with one navigator and one electronic warfare officer (EWO) from each crew met with the chiefs of the A-1 group, the helicopter group, and the Special Forces group in the SOF briefing room. This time we were briefed on the mission and the training that we would undergo. We were told of the mission objective, the deployment bases, and were asked to develop the routes and methods of getting to Son Tay.

Thus, began numerous days of flight planning! The remaining crew members and participants were to be kept in the dark as to the mission we were training for (KITD-FOHS: Kept In The Dark—Fed Only Horse Shit).

We had aerial photos of the routes, the POW camp, and other items of interest (such as SAM sites). We had our own photo interpreter and intelligence people available.

We planned in the day and flew at night. Tactics were developed for the Talons to fly in formation with the UH-1s, HH-3s, HH-53s and the A-1s. The idea was for the C-130s to provide navigational and electronic assistance to the aircraft within the formation at low level. Both Talon Crews flew formations with the helicopters and the A-1s. After a few flights, it was determined the HH-3 (rather than the UH-1) would be the better aircraft for the inside-the-compound portion of the mission due to its capability to air-refuel. Upon a few more nights of flying, it was determined that my crew would become lead crew *"Cherry 1"* and would lead helicopters into the objective area.

Two interesting side stories that arose during the flight planning and practice:

1. The purchase of and raising of a rooster. Someone (I think Capt Tom Eckhart) knew the story of Maynard and went out and purchased a baby chick. The chick was kept in the Bachelor Officers Quarters (BOQ) by the crew. As the maid complained and the billeting officer snooped, the chick was passed from room to room. The chick grew to fryer size by the time we were to deploy from Eglin. You may ask, did the chicken deploy as did Maynard? No, the last time I saw him he was sitting in the cockpit of the B-25 in the little park in Valparaiso, CA.

2. As I stated earlier, the crew members were kept in the dark about the mission and their first idea was that we were there to fly a mission to rescue the people from an airliner hijacked by terrorists in the Middle East. Time passed, the airliners were blown-up, and the people were released, and we were still practicing! Next, an American embassy in South America (Chile, I believe) was under siege and we were going to rescue those in the embassy. I don't remember what happened to this situation – I guess they negotiated out. We continued training! The final theory the crews developed was the Russians were building submarine bases in Cuba. Since we were so close, we could launch from and recover to Eglin. We were going to invade Cuba and Special Forces were going to destroy the bases. This theory lasted until we deployed.

We were ready to deploy in October but were held because, we were told, a typhoon was developing in the South China Sea. In my mind, it seemed completely political (as much of the actions in Southeast Asia were). Elections were coming up in November and the results of the mission could have been a big factor if we had met with disaster.

Finally, it was time to deploy from Eglin! The Talon crews were told we were headed to Okinawa Japan. The Green Berets and the support personnel were told that we were headed to Norton AFB for practice in more mountainous terrain. The ground personnel were loaded onto C-141s and headed toward (they were told) Southern California. Although I didn't hear it myself, I was told the folks got a little suspicious when they landed at Elemendorf AFB and saw snow. By the time we arrived at Kadena AB, the Talon crews were beginning to form the idea that we were headed to Southeast Asia. So the EWO on my crew, Major Tom Mosley hit upon an idea for our crew patch and that is when the phrase "KITD-FOHS" was conceived.

Image 77: This is one of the original 30 patches made. Bloodshot eyes, treated like a mushroom. It was designed by Tom Mosley (EWO), Tom Eckhart (Navigator) and Bill Guenon (Pilot) of Cherrry 1 on the back of a napkin for the patch-maker in Kadena City, who could only commit to make 30 overnight, since they were leaving Kadena at 10am the next day. *Cherry* 1 was en route from Eglin to Takhli RTAFB, Thailand.

After we arrived at Takhli RTAFB around the 15th of November, we were again called together and this time all were told what the mission was and when it was going to happen. I really can't remember too much except for the last-minute flight planning and the readying of the aircraft and equipment.

The night of the Raid, my crew was all at their stations. I punched the starter button for number three engine and…no rotation. Maintenance came out and opened the cowling and messed with it for a few minutes and worried that it couldn't be fixed in time. We were then asked by BGen Manor if we could fly on three engines. I told him that we could, but not safely at the slow speed of 108 knots, the max speed of the helicopters. So the decision came down that the aircraft roles would have to be switched. We would lead the A-1s at higher speed and Friday's crew would now lead the helicopters. I advised the general that we would try a windmill taxi start on takeoff.

In the meantime, I remembered from simulator training the idea of pushing both three and four starter buttons at the same time would open bleeder valves, causing both engines to rotate and start at the same time. After maintenance was done with their work and the cowling was closed, I tried it and it worked beautifully!! We had all four engines running, but by this time we were 20 to 25 minutes late. We notified BGen Manor that we could make up the lost time and rendezvous with the helicopters on schedule. He said, "Have at it".

We had planned on flying a low-level route to the rendezvous to check out everything to ensure proper operation—we bypassed this and flew direct to the rendezvous point instead. As we passed Udorn, the tower started broadcasting on Guard frequency that we were headed into unfriendly territory and to turn around. The tower was supposed to have had a trusted agent to eliminate that possibility. However, since we were late, I suppose that he had left the tower.

We continued the route to the rendezvous point – arriving exactly on schedule. The helicopters were just finishing refueling. They smoothly descended away from the HC-130 tankers into their drafting position behind us and we headed toward Son Tay.

As we approached Son Tay, we had a great piece of luck! The Vietnamese lit up the road which led to the prison camp. The road that was paralleling our inbound track had a truck convoy on it leading us in. We had studied the approach so much that we really didn't need maps.

We arrived over the prison camp right on time (0218) and lit the camp with our flares. However, when the helicopters left us, they went to the wrong place.

As we turned to head outbound, we were to drop two large BLU-27s (long-burning, ground markers that use napalm as the fuel) and a series of smaller players to light up the exit route for the A-1s and helicopters. As luck would have it the plywood pallet under one of the BLU-27s was warped and got caught in the skate wheel roller – all I could think of was, "Damn, that thing is armed! What if it goes off in the aircraft?!" I sent everyone I could spare back to help free it. Then I got to worrying, when it was freed and out, would it light up the wrong path for the exiting aircraft? The Lord was with us – when the guys freed the BLU-27, we were over a lake. I think it went into the lake and didn't go off – or if it did, it apparently had no effect on the exiting aircraft.

As we exited the target area (0225), we set up orbit points and transmitted signals to the helicopters and A-1s so that they could home in on us with their ADFs to remain oriented. Friday's crew, *Cherry 2*, and ours played leapfrog, orbiting so the exiting aircraft could easily fall in behind us. I recall, as we orbited, receiving the word that no POWs had been rescued. I think that is as close to crying as I had ever been since reaching adulthood.

At 0235, SAMs were beginning to be fired. At our low altitude, it appeared that they were headed towards us – but they weren't. They were after our cover aircraft – the F-105s and F-4s.

We recovered at Udorn. To top it all off, they made us park way out in the boonies at Udorn. After such a draining mission, we were all tired. And then we find that we could not get transportation to the debriefing room. After several radio calls to the tower with no luck, we walked. As we walked, we got madder and madder; but by the time we got to the debriefing room we had cooled off and decided to just get the thing over with so that we could rest.

Most of the procedures and tactics used, parties involved, and official results are fairly accurately portrayed in Benjamin Schemmer's book *The Raid*, John Gargus's book *The Son Tay Raid: American POWs in Vietnam Were Not Forgotten* and Bill Guenon's book *Secret and Dangerous*. This is mostly my story as I remember it. Maybe some of your readers will enjoy my thoughts.

Image 78: *Cherry 1 (Photo provided by Bill Guenon)*
Standing (l-r):
Sgt Robert Renner (support), TSgt William Kennedy,
TSgt James Shepard, MSgt Leslie Tolman,
TSgt Kenneth Lightle, SSgt Earl Parks.
Front:
Major Thomas Mosley, Capt James McKenzie,
Capt Thomas Stiles, Capt Thomas Eckhart,
Capt William Guenon, Capt Randall Custard, Major Irl Franklin

USAF CAPT BILL GUENON, CHERRY 1

<<Make sure also to read Bill Guenon's book *Secret and Dangerous*>>

During our defiant night moves while romping in Uncle Ho's backyard, this vision clearly stands out. It happened on *Cherry 1*, the MC-130E(I) pathfinder leading the helicopters, crawling along the final run-in leg approaching Son Tay from out of the west. We were maintaining 105 knots in order for 1.) us to stay in the sky, and for 2.) *Banana* (the HH-3 stuffed with 14 heavily armed, Blueboy Assault Group Green Berets) to keep up in formation behind our left wing.

Glancing up from the instrument panel of dimly lit, round dials and gauges, I looked outside for a quick how-goes-it peek in the moonlight. That's when I eyeballed the milky lights rising up from the enemy's capital, Hanoi, right off our nose. Certainly, no mistaking that checkpoint! It was much like one would see on a night approach into hazy Los Angeles.

That's when it hit me like a swift baseball bat. After four months of mission planning, flying, and tweaking, the raid was really on, actually real, very up-close and most personal. At that point I recall thinking to myself, "Hey, we're here. It's show time!" Funny stuff a button-down mind spews out in tense situations. Then it was eyes back inside the flight deck for another airspeed nudge with both hands—two throttles in each—for precise energy management.

Now, fast-forward to the days after our Raid. The crew of *Cherry 1* had just returned to the states island-hopping our way back across the Pacific. We were standing alone with our bags on a bare ramp on the Monday before Thanksgiving at Norton AFB, CA. In the smoggy distance we could see *Cherry 1* gracefully lifting off the runway with another crew at her controls, flying her over to Ontario airport for some aircraft de-modifications. Having spent four trusting months under her faithful wing, she certainly had been good to us. Indeed, on the edge of a stall, she had taken us into the lion's den and safely back home. Her takeoff that afternoon sparked a spontaneous "Pass in Review" feeling in that moment while we mentally saluted her as she quietly slipped into the mist.

Today, that ancient bird, tail number 64-0523 (64 is the year of manufacture), is sporting her earned name, "Godfather." She was honorably retired in 2012 and flown west from Duke Field, FL, and placed on permanent display at Cannon AFB, NM, home to

Air Force's Special Operations flight training. On her last flight, the intrepid Irl Leon Franklin, *Cherry 1*'s Aircraft Commander, was on hand, leaning over from the Flight Engineer's seat, to ceremoniously shut down her engines at Cannon for the last time.

Assault Formation: MC-130E (Cherry One) with HH-3 (Banana) and HH-53(Apples).

Image 79: *Cherry 1* Assault Formation.

USAF MAJOR JOHN GARGUS, CHERRY 2

<<**Make sure also to read John Gargus' book** *The Son Tay Raid: America's POWs Were Not Forgotten*>>

I flew in the Raid on *Cherry 2* as the radar navigator. I was behind the curtain all the time ensuring that my console lights did not hamper the night vision of the other crew members. We orbited in a mountain valley within sight of Son Tay where we monitored and recorded six radio frequencies used in the Raid.

As we approached the target area, our ECM (electronic countermeasures) signals indicated that we had not been detected and that we were not tracked on our inbound heading.

Even though I anticipated the "Alpha! Alpha! Alpha!" call from *Cherry 1* upon release of the flares (at 0218), I remember being startled by the reality that the freeing of our POWs was now at hand. The crew in the cockpit confirmed seeing four good flares.

The next startling radio call (at 0220) was, "We lost Axle." That shocked me because Axle was the code name for Bull Simons. I knew this from our planning sessions, but some crew members asked who Axle was. We all thought that *Apple 1* with 22 Greenleaf Group Green Berets was gone.

When we heard the next transmission from *Apple 2*, "You let them out at the wrong place!" I rejoiced. I realized immediately that the "wrong place" was the Secondary School, which looked similar to the Son Tay POW camp 400 yards to the north. I had assured Bull Simons that our helicopter pilots would make sure not to mistake it for the POW camp. *Apple 1* with its 22 Greenleaf troops was not downed! We presently heard that *Apple 1* was correcting the mistake.

Apple 1 was calling for a flare to point out the Greenleaf exfiltration point, when at 0229, we all heard the incredible transmission from Capt Dick Meadows, commander of Blueboy Assault Group inside the camp, "Negative Items, Negative Items." There were no POWs at Son Tay. That was the biggest shock of all transmissions. We explained the meaning of this to all crew members. No one wanted to believe it. Then we heard the troops being told to search again. We hoped. We wanted them to be there! Then came the second report telling all that there were Negative Items. Even after that, we failed to grasp the reality because when Capt Jim McClam began reporting the total numbers of all exfiltrated personnel (Assault Force plus any POWs rescued), our crew members were not clear on how many of those were rescued POWs. Basically, we were all in total disbelief.

Our mood changed only when we learned en route home that two crew members had bailed out over Laos from their missile-damaged F-105, *Firebird 5*. After we confirmed that all the departing aircraft had crossed the Black River on the way home, we set a course for the *Firebird 5* rescue location. We were comforted to hear that they were both OK and were rescued.

Strike Formation: MC-130E (Cherry Two) with A-1E (Peaches).

Image 80: *Cherry 2* Strike Formation.

USAF SGT BOB CLEELAND, CREW CHIEF FOR CHERRY 1 AND CHERRY 2

My most memorable moment was at Takhli RTAFB when, during engine start on the night of the Raid, *Cherry 1*'s engine #3 failed to rotate. Every specialist rushed out from the launch trucks and troubleshot the problem. We found a malfunctioning bleed air valve under engine #3's horse collar. The valve was replaced, engine #3 rotated, and the mission was on! A little tense moment but it all worked out.

Image 81: *Cherry 2, (Photo provided by John Gargus)*
Standing:
SSgt William J. Brown, TSgt Jimmie O. Riggs,
Sgt Failus Potts, TSgt Billy J. Elliston,
TSgt Dallas T. Criner, Major Harry L. Pannill,
Capt William D. Stripling, and
SSgt Melvin B. D. Gibson
Front Row:
Major John Gargus, Capt Norman C. Mazurek,
TSgt Paul.E. Stierwalt,
Capt Ronald L. Jones, Capt Gerald. M. Carroll,
LtCol Albert P. "Friday" Blosch, and
Capt John M. Connaughton.

USAF MAJOR JOHN WARESH, PEACH 1

On the Friday night, November 20th, 1970, a C-130 picked us up from Takhli RTAFB, where we had been housed in the CIA compound since deploying from Eglin AFB. The NKP (Nakhon Phanom RTAFB) flight line was blacked out when we landed— even the air traffic control tower people had been relieved of their stations for secrecy. The C-130 landed without any lights on the aircraft or on the runway. It taxied to the parking ramp. With the rear ramp open, and taxiing very slowly, but without stopping, the C-130 crew let us ten A-1 pilots hop out the back, two pilots for each of the five A-1s. The C-130 continued taxing, pulling up the ramp, out to the runway and took off. They had other people to deliver to other locations.

It was about 10pm. The only people on the flightline were the crew chiefs and us. The wing commander came out to us. As we were walking to get our flight gear at life support, he was asking question after question, none of which I was I authorized to answer. He got rather pissed.

We went straight to the birds, cranked up and taxied out. No aircraft lights. No radio calls. No taxiway lights or runway lights. Total silence. (The radio was not to be used until we were over the POW camp.)

Major Jerry Rhein and I were in the lead aircraft. Taking off at the exact second, we did a 360 over the base to join up. A specially equipped MC-130 "Combat Talon" was to rendezvous with us there and lead us onto our target.

For this mission, timing was everything. Our MC-130 wasn't there. We did two more 360s and couldn't wait any longer. The "backup plan" was to navigate ourselves to Son Tay, following the planned route and arriving at the appointed time, 0200 local Saturday, November 21st. No way Jose! We had agreed among ourselves earlier that this was not was not a viable plan. We would, however, fly the course until we got lost (which we knew we would) and then head straight for Hanoi. We'd just hold south of the IP, which was at a point along the Black River, due west of the camp. When the TOT (Time Over Target) came, we'd hop in and do our thing.

The route was NKP direct to Vientiane, Laos. Then, we were to head due north and drop to low-level. The plan was to weave through the karst and valleys all the rest of the way to Son Tay. Impossible at night for A-1s.

The first backup plan was to rendezvous with the Talon over Vientiane at the appointed minute, but because we had made an extra 360 over NKP we could not make that time. We hit Vientiane a little late—maybe five minutes late. There was no Talon.

We turned north and pressed on. After Vientiane, there were no ground lights. The ground was ink black. And then, our worst nightmare loomed in front of us: a cloud bank. Being lead, I wasn't worried about my wingmen colliding with me. But the rest of the flight broke out in every direction, like a covey of quail, everyone in God-only-knows-what direction. Pushing it up, I climbed straight ahead and soon popped out on top. Not an A-1 in sight. Hopeless to rejoin without lights or radio, we were all on our own.

After a short time, Jerry Rhein and I noticed a speck of light far ahead. A star? After watching it a while, we were sure it was below the horizon. It had to be something else. Heading straight for it, it took some time to catch. A fully loaded A-1 is no speed demon. Sure enough, there was our Talon with a teeny-weeny white light on the top of the fuselage and a dim bluish glow coming from the open ramp in the rear. You really couldn't see the bluish glow until you were only a few meters from it. There were already two A-1s there, one on each wing.

We moved up. The left one moved outside and let us take our assigned place on the left wingtip. A few minutes later, our other two A-1s slowly pulled up. Once we were all in place, the little white light went out and the bluish glow went out. The Talon then led us down into the terrain-hugging. From there on in, it was 'hold on tight' as it bobbed and weaved through the hills and valleys.

The Talon driver was top notch. His power applications during climbs and descents and gentle banking allowed our heavy A-1s to hang right in there. The three day "moon window" we had for this operation provided good night visibility. But several valleys we drove through were so deep that the mountains sometimes blocked the moonlight. When that happened it, was like diving into an ink-well. You could make out only a few feet of wing tip and that was only because of our own exhaust flame. When turns or ups & downs occurred at those times it was tough.

As we emerged from the mountains and were out over the Red River Valley, it was almost like being over Iowa with Omaha and Council Bluffs up ahead, lights everywhere…but this was Hanoi. Soon thereafter, the Talon started climbing and we knew the IP (Initial Point from which we will approach the POW camp) was coming up.

We had an assigned altitude to be at over the IP. The choppers, with their own Talon, were going to be under us coming in from a different direction. They should have been slightly ahead of us, but you couldn't be sure everyone was on time. The planned time of each of the various flight elements involved in the mission was based upon everyone's overhead time at the Son Tay POW camp itself. The IP times were calculated for the different speeds of all of the different raid aircraft.

At the IP, then the Talon transmitted the first word of anything we heard on the radio all night. The transmission was to be picked up by a high orbiting EC-121 and relayed back to the ground command post. It let them know we had crossed the IP. (We were two seconds off. The best we had ever done during practice without the Talons leading us was ten minutes!) The Talon then accelerated out ahead and up and disappeared in the night.

The heading the Talon announced was 091. Trying to reset our high-technology Directional Gyro by a wiggly 'whiskey compass' was an exercise in futility. Good thing all the towns, cities and roads were lit up. With all the target study we had done, it was like we were in our own back yard.

Peach 5 'peeled' off to the right. He was backup, just in case anyone was shot down. His assigned orbit was a large hill just south of our course. As it turned out, the hill was a North Vietnamese Army artillery practice range and it wasn't long before they started taking a few rounds. They moved off to somewhere else, probably closer to the camp.

Then *Peach 3* and *Peach 4* peeled off to the left to hold just short of the camp until called in. The plan was to call them in when we and *Peach 2* had expended 50% of our ordnance. Then they would do the same with us, each time expending 50% of what you had left. That way, if someone went down, there would always be aircraft in the air that had some ordnance left to support.

Then *Peach 2* dropped back so we could set up a two-aircraft 'daisy chain' around the POW camp. It was like a precision ballet.

At 3,000 feet, rolling into a bank alongside the POW camp, I saw, down below me, two flares pop right over it, having been released from one of the Talons at 1500 feet. *Apple 3*, an HH-53 Super Jolly Green Giant helicopter, opened up with mini-guns on the guard towers and the guard quarters. The towers either blew apart or caught fire. At this time, our job was to make sure no one approached the camp.

No one did. We could see the sparkles from a Firefight Simulator dropped by one of the Talons on the other side of town as a distraction. Soon after, we could see a large explosion and fire where another Talon dropped napalm on an infantry base armory a few klicks to the South.

Then we heard Gearbox (the ground command team) transmit, "We've lost Axle." 'Axle' was Colonel Bull Simons' call sign.

One *Apple*, carrying half the assault force and Bull Simons, had landed the in the wrong place. They had drifted slightly off coming in from the IP, placing them a few hundred meters south of the camp.

The FM and VHF radios were almost impossible to read, let alone get anything in of your own. (The UHF was kept for AF use to call the MIG Cap or Weasels if needed or to talk among ourselves.) The *Apple* that had dumped the guys did a 180 and went back to pick them up.

Bull Simons and the rest of the assault force made it back to the camp without a casualty. The whole incident only lasted a few minutes. As soon as Simons got on the radio, he asked Blue Boy for a status report. The answer was "Negative Items, so far. Still searching." ('Item' was the code word for a prisoner.)

Simons then told us to take out the foot bridge to the Citadel. We called a group of buildings surrounded by a small moat 'the Citadel.' It was a few hundred meters southeast of the POW camp and had a small foot bridge on the side nearest the POW camp. Intel had told us it was a military cadet training facility and probably had a small armory. We didn't want anyone coming across that bridge armed and get within rifle range of the camp. Jerry and I put two WP (white phosphorus) bombs on it and when my wingman came in, he saw the bridge was wiped out and dropped short to get anyone that might have already come across. WP does a real number on wooden structures. The fire storm was not small.

Image 82: An A-1E drops a 100 lb M-47
White Phosphorus bomb.

Then the first SAM took off.

You cannot miss a SAM launch at night. It's like a miniature Space Shuttle launch—it lights up an area for miles in all directions. The first few were called: "SAM, SAM! DIVE! DIVE!" But that soon became silly. There were so many launches that you couldn't call them all. There seemed to be about four launch sites within a few miles of the camp on the west side of Hanoi. The rest were further east, and we didn't think of them as a threat to us. Most of the SAMs went high, aimed at the F-4s (the MiGCAP— Combat Air Patrol defending against MiGs), and at the Weasels, and at the Navy's 100-aircraft diversionary raid on the east side of Hanoi. The idea was to make the NVA think there was a major raid on Hai Phong harbor and not bother with a few planes on the west side of Hanoi. It worked.

From signals intercepts, the NSA told us later that the North Vietnamese Air Defense Commander screamed, "FIRE AT WILL," then shut down his air defense early warning radars and his command net and went off the air.

We were at our briefed 3,000 feet until the SAMs started coming our way. We all hit the deck and kept an eye on the launch sites closest to us. The site just a few miles to the northeast launched one that never got higher than the horizon. (This was a bad sign for us.) I watched it rise and almost immediately it leveled off… then the thing stopped moving on the windscreen. You know what that means: It's coming right at us. We dove into the Red River and turned west. Jerry was flying and I was turned around keeping an eye on the damn thing as it charged toward us over my right shoulder. I kept bumping the stick forward saying, "Lower, Lower." Jerry kept bumping the stick back saying, "We're going to hit the water!" When the rocket plume on the thing seemed as big as our aircraft, I yelled, "Break left!" We went up and over the riverbank, about 50 feet, leveling off just a little above the phone poles, heading straight south. We never saw the thing again. It either hadn't had time to arm, or buried itself in the water and mud so deep that the flash of the detonation was masked.

That's another thing you can't miss at night: The detonation of a SAM. It's a large lightning flash. They were going off over us constantly and when you got used to them, you didn't even bother to look up. For about a 30-minute period, there were no less than three SAMs airborne at any given time. At times, there were so many you couldn't count them. All the SAMs that missed their target would self-detonate, either at a pre-set altitude or at motor burn out.

Then there was a different type of light. The flash was yellow-ish instead of bright white. Looking up, there was a large fire ball with flaming debris falling from it. "Damn, someone got nailed." Then the flame was like a dashed line across the sky, heading southwest. Another flash and then another. Three dashes were all I saw; I couldn't spend any more time looking up. Later, we learned that a SAM had detonated close to a Weasel and filled his bird with holes. Fuel was streaming out and his fuel was igniting it in dashes across the sky. They got to Laos before bailing out.

About this time, Blueboy calls Axle and says, "Search complete, negative Items." Silence, then Simons asks for a repeat. "Search complete, negative Items. I repeat: Negative Items." More silence. I don't know what anyone else was thinking then but for me it was, "Setup. Ambush!" "But hell, we'd already been there 20 minutes—they'd have sprung it by now." So, then it turned to, "What the hell are we doing here?" and, "How the hell are we go-ing to get our asses out of here intact." Simons must have been thinking the same thing. He called for the perimeter teams to pull back and the *Apples* to come in for pickup.

Then he told us to take out the Big Bridge.

All sounds very simple but it sure wasn't. First of all, we had no hard ordnance and couldn't take out the Big Bridge. We had no more WP bombs and that was the only thing that would have dam-aged this wooden bridge. A little poop about the Big Bridge. The bridge was a few hundred meters northeast of the POW camp on the road that ran in front of the camp. It was about 100 feet long, heavy duty construction, and could carry any vehicle up to a tank, we were told.

This was now our second turn. (Earlier, because we had expended 50% of our ordnance, we had called in *Peach 3* and *Peach 4* for their first turn. Now they had done the same and called us back in.) We dumped our Rockeyes on the bridge. The Rockeye is a Navy fast-mover ordnance. At Eglin, we had to certify the A-1 to carry Rockeyes. It's a multi-munitions thing with gobs of little shaped charges to take out vehicles, even tanks I guess—but they're not very good for bridges. We put a lot of holes in it though. After that, we laid down continuous strafe until everyone was in the *Apple* helicopters and on their way. I might add we, ourselves, never saw any vehicles or people moving anywhere near the camp. There was a lot of traffic on the east-west road along the Red River, about a klick north, going into and out of Hanoi, but no one turned south toward the POW camp.

About this time, the SAM launches were slowing down, but the MIG calls were increasing. Roughly 20 minutes of our 40 minutes on-station, we started picking up MiG calls. Intel told us they had no night-qualified pilots so we should have no serious threat with MiGs. There was one call of an air-to-air missile firing. They said it zoomed right past their plane. I don't know who it was and never saw any myself. That was the only call of an air-to-air missile I remember hearing. But the MiG warning calls from College Eye or whoever makes those calls were coming regularly.

Once the choppers were off the ground, we putted along, above and behind them, guessing where they were since it was hard to see them, looking down on the darkness. Everyone was to call the IP outbound. One by one we heard the calls, thank God. Then we hear this voice, "Is everybody out?" It was the last *Apple*. "Where are you?" we asked. "I'm back at the ground holding point waiting to be sure everyone got out okay." By this time, we had nearly reached the IP ourselves. Jerry and I looked at each other and said,

"We don't have a choice." With possible MiGs around, a lonely Super Jolly Green Giant all by himself makes for a pretty good target. We turned around, climbed to a nice tempting MiG target altitude (3,000 – 4,000 feet), and went Christmas Tree—we turned on every light we had and we putted back toward Hanoi. With MiG calls coming every few minutes I was sweating profusely. Don't know if it was hot, or if it was just that I was scared, but I was soaked. It seemed an eternity, but just as the POW camp was scrolling under our nose, we heard the "IP Outbound" call.

Lights Out.

Split-S. (A 180-degree turn in the vertical.)

We beat feet west for the IP on the deck. Getting away from the river valley and into the dark countryside, we climbed to a safe altitude to clear the mountains en route to Udorn.

Then we started to take care of some pilot stuff. We had used up the fuel in the left stub tank getting there and most of the right. We were on the internal tanks over the target and we were using the centerline while holding. Time to clean up this messy fuel situation. The right stub ran out almost right about then—just a couple minutes were left in it, so we needed to jettison that one.

That's when the longest two seconds of my life occurred. I hit the button, but instead of falling away, it pitched up and slammed back against the leading edge of the right wing! The empty fuel tank was in a 'V' shape and came bashing along the leading edge of the wing toward the fuselage. I can see it to this day, making four bashes and then falling away, under the wing. It all happened in one or two seconds. I sometimes wonder what would have happened to the right horizontal stabilizer if it had decided to break off, up and over the wing instead of under. I don't dwell on it though, too scary.

Image 83: The right wing fuel tank (white) protrudes far ahead of the leading edge (some configurations protrude even farther than this example). You can see how, when the releasing bolt malfunctioned on *Peach* 1, the nose of the fuel tank rose above the leading edge, slammed into the wing, and 'clamped' onto the right wing for a few seconds.

The five Jollies, three carrying the assault force and two empty because of no prisoners, were all together having had to hit a tanker in order to make it back. The five A-1s were spread out who-knows-where but were still in radio contact. As we crossed the Plaine des Jarres (an area of Laos), we picked up the beeper of the downed Weasel crew. They were both all right.

Then we made contact with four Sandys (fellow A-1Es) launched out of NKP in answer to the Weasels' May Day. They didn't know who we were because of the call signs. It took a while to convince them that '*Peach*' and '*Apple*' really meant 'Sandy' and 'Jolly.'

It was decided that *Apple 4* and *Apple 5* would hang around with the four Sandys and make a first light pick up.

[Read Capt Ted Lowry's telling of this story from his point of view in another section of this Appendix below.]

Landing at Udorn we were all rushed to debriefing, a building right on the flight line. As I walked in, I was met by a group of Intel people with wide smiles across their faces. They asked, "How many prisoners?" I said "None, the camp was empty." The smiles disappeared and their faces turned pale. "What?" I don't remember ever being debriefed and don't think anyone ever was.

Colonel Simons, Major Jerry Rhein, Captain Dick Meadows and others were whisked off to meet with BGen Leroy Manor at Monkey Mountain, the command post at Da Nang Air Base.

The sun was coming up by then and we all wandered out onto the ramp. We sat down on the cement, in circles of about ten, we in our reeking sweat-soaked flight suits and the Green Berets with their blackened faces, guns, grenades and what-have-you hanging off of them. To me, they looked like they were bleeding from every square inch of exposed skin from dozens of cuts, scrapes and bruises. We were all just sat, mumbling to each other. No stories were being told—we had all just done it, seen it, and heard it. Someone came out and handed a bottle to each of the circles. Everyone took a sip and passed it around and around and around, till it was empty, all of us still just mumbling to ourselves and each other.

I can't attest to what was going on at the other circles, but there wasn't a dry eye at ours—a tear running down every cheek.

A gallant effort with nothing to show.

To hell and back for naught.

(Authors' Note: This was excerpted from John Waresh's article in *The Southern California Sentinel: Newsletter of the Quiet*

Professionals, Special Forces Association Chapter 78, February 2017, www.specialforces78.com. Used with permission.)

USAF CAPT TED LOWRY, FIREBIRD 5
THE F-105 SHOT DOWN PROTECTING THE RAID

My most memorable moment was reading about the mission the next day in the Stars & Stripes newspaper. That's when I learned the objective of the mission that I had been supporting that night. Our F-105 had been shot down by a SAM from the Son Tay area during the Raid, flew as long as we could toward a safe area, ejected, and were rescued by *Apple 4* and *Apple 5*.

But a really memorable event for me was 25 years later at the Ft Walton Beach Son Tay Raiders Association reunion when Russ Wright came up to me and told me he had been waiting 25 years to meet me. He had been in the F-4, call sign *Falcon 5*, who followed us out of North Vietnam acting as chase plane and spotter as we limped home in an effort to make it back to our base.

Here's the story of our shoot-down and ejection. Five F-105 Wild Weasel aircraft participated in the mission in an air defense suppression role intended to shield all other aircraft in the area from North Vietnamese surface to air missiles, which intelligence sources had indicated included five separate sites in the immediate target area. There was nothing different in this mission than the hundreds of missions the five Weasel aircrews had flown prior to 21 November other than the fact that we were not privy to the mission objective, and due to the 1968 cessation of bombing none of us had ever been to the Hanoi area. So, we were not accustomed to the heavy concentration of air defenses that we would encounter. Aside from that the Raid was a "perfectly normal" mission for all 10 Weasels.

On 19 November we were offered an opportunity to volunteer for a special mission so highly classified that none of us were permitted to discuss it even among ourselves. We were given no details except that we were not on the schedule to fly normal missions pending this one. About noon on 20 November our Squadron Commander informed us that we would be briefing at 1930 hours that evening in a location separate from our normal mission planning and briefing facility. The building was heavily guarded and when we entered the briefing room, we were all required to provide identification. When the briefing was set to begin the room was secured so no one could enter or leave.

Our Squadron Intelligence Officer handed us our SAR cards and told us to be sure we knew what they said, particularly the answers to questions we had provided when we arrived in theater; that we would "need them." We also received completed mission planning packages complete with charts, routes and times for each leg and target area details. Only then did we learn that our mission was to support a ground operation near Hanoi, and that a lot of other American aircraft would be in the area with us. The briefing was extremely detailed and included the most recent intelligence information with regard to enemy air defenses. This was a very unusual amount of detail in that most missions we flew were preceded by pretty generalized information with respect to threats we might encounter. The briefing also included locations we could attempt to reach should we be forced to eject from our aircraft for any reason. Our instructions were to remain in the area until all friendly forces had safely left the area. That meant a very long time over target and the need to manage fuel consumption very carefully. As events played out there was a certain amount of irony in that requirement. We still did not know the objective.

We were given the callsigns *Firebird 1* through *Firebird 5*, which I'm told was borrowed from the Navy. Lt Colonel Bob Kronebusch and Major John Forrester were *"Firebird 1"* and were the two aircrew who planned the mission tactics and prepared our mission packages along with General Manor's planning team and our squadron intelligence officer whose last name I can't remember even though I remember her first name was Nina. *"Firebird 2"* were Major Bob Reisenwitz and Major Ray MacAdoo, *"Firebird 3"* were Major Bill Starkey and Major Everett Fansler, *"Firebird 4"* were Major Murray Denton and Captain Russ Ober, and *"Firebird 5"* were Major Don Kilgus and me, Captain Ted Lowry. From here this narrative will be predominately in first person because each of the ten of us would remember their own role independently and differently. Of the ten who flew to Son Tay, I'm aware of only two who remain.

From a personal standpoint, participation in the Raid was a watershed event in that it forever shaped my views and what I believe is worth worrying about. As *Firebird 5*, Major Kilgus and I were the on-scene airborne spare whose task it was to "replace the first weasel who was shot down." We took off from Korat Royal Thai AFB at ten minutes to 1:00 am and headed toward our first refueling stop in far Northeast Thailand. We were loaded with a full internal fuel load, 1500 gallons of fuel in our three external fuel tanks, and we carried two AGM-45 Shrike anti-radiation missiles for self-defense. Aside from those two missiles we had to rely on our ability to evade any missiles that were fired at us.

Coming off the tanker, we could see off our right wing a huge array of navigation lights going in the same general direction we were flying. We realized that was the strike force and commented on how many aircraft were involved. We left them behind as we followed our planned flight path to the target area. We had an uneventful ingress, just doing our normal prestrike preparations, with the difference that we programmed the preplanned emergency North Vietnam ejection point into our doppler navigation computer. It was a mountain southwest of the objective area that was about 3500 feet high and would afford some degree of protection due to its rough terrain and that it was pretty much devoid of people. In case we did have to leave the aircraft, we wanted to be in the most isolated area possible.

Image 84: An F-105 Thunderchief SAM suppression aircraft takes off from Korat RTAFB in 1971 — identical to the ones used in the Son Tay Raid.

When our flight arrived in the objective area ahead of the ground force according to plan, we were able to operate with little to no opposition from the North Vietnamese air defenses initially. They were totally unprepared for an attack just after midnight Friday/Saturday, so they took several minutes to get their defense systems operating. But when they did engage us, we were in a pretty desperate fight.

Several minutes after we arrived in the objective area an SA-2 missile exploded near *Firebird 3* causing a massive fireball that looked like it completely surrounded *Firebird 3*. Looking on from our position we were sure they had sustained a lethal hit, but in seconds Major Starkey radioed, after his initial Mayday call, that they were all right and their aircraft was still working. The F-105 was a remarkable machine that could absorb really major damage and continue to operate. Three's engine was vibrating so he left the area to return to our emergency base, Udorn Royal Thai AFB. On his way out, one of the *Falcon* MiG suppression flight offered to chase him back but the last thing anyone on our frequency heard was *Firebird 3* telling the *Falcon* that "I'm in burner." I don't think the F-4 ever caught them. Now, *Firebird 1* directed us to take Three's place. By this time, we were seeing massive anti-aircraft artillery fire directed at the American armada, but it was never a serious threat to any of our aircraft. SAMs were a different story.

After the mission, estimates were that the North Vietnamese fired between 16 and 20 SAMs from the sites around Hanoi, so the Weasels and everyone else in that small amount of airspace were all over trying to avoid being hit. We don't know how many aircraft were actually targeted although we believe our Weasel flight received the majority of fire. It's easy to tell if you are the target when a SAM is fired; at night you see a reddish orange fireball that oscillates as it flies. If the fireball does not move in your canopy except to get larger you are its intended target. In our case, we almost immediately engaged a firing site with our first Shrike as almost the same time it fired on us. My front seater may have been the only member of *Firebird* flight who had seen a SAM live because he had served several tours in F-100 Super Sabres and had been fired on before. Within seconds of entering the fight we lined up on one of a number of SAM sites that were beginning to become very active. As we lined up for a shot from more than 13 miles out the Shrike acquired the target emitter as we climbed at about 25 degrees nose high and less than 350 knots. As we fired the Shrike the first SAM to target us fired almost simultaneously. Kilgus waited until the SAM was well into its flight. We saw it was aimed at us, and he began to evade. He dove and, as we knew it would, the SAM dove with us. He timed our flight and, as the SAM got to a point it could not turn well, Kilgus pulled up in a 4g pull. The SAM could not make that turn. By this time the second SAM was airborne so with less speed and lower maneuverability Kilgus evaded the second SAM. A third SAM was fired at us somewhere in the fight, and we avoided it as well. In the meantime, our other flight members were all dodging SAMS and probably other American aircraft as well. Near the end of the time on target a fourth SAM was fired at us.

This time we were not able to evade it, and it exploded probably 100 meters or so from us, its warhead's shrapnel hit our fuselage area aft of the rear cockpit primarily. It exploded near our aircraft causing what at the time we believed to be manageable damage. Apparently, most of the shrapnel struck our fuselage where the P2 hydraulic system is and where our fuselage fuel tanks were housed. Since our stability augmentation system was no longer functioning, I said, "We're hit. Do we need to leave." Kilgus said, "The airplane is still flyable, and we have people down there. We need to stay." We knew we still had Americans on the ground, and Kilgus would not leave until we knew that they were safely away. We had only used one of our Shrikes, so we still had a small level of defensive capability. In that short time, we engaged a final SAM site with our remaining Shrike although we did not have to do any other evasive maneuvers. This whole incident lasted less than 15 minutes probably – I did not keep track of time.

About that time *Firebird 1* directed our flight to egress the area. Kilgus then told me that we had apparently been hit in our fuel tanks because we no longer had enough fuel to make it back to Thailand. The truth here is that we had stuck around simply because Americans were still in the area and our job was to protect them. There were no radio calls about being hit until about 15 minutes after the hit. The call from *Firebird* lead was for the *Firebird*s to simply egress the area—there was no rejoin into flight formation. By this time, it starts to become apparent that we were hurting for gas, so Kilgus made this call, *"Firebird 5* is hit. We're losing fuel and need a tanker to head this way."

That's all there was, nothing dramatic. His words to me were, "Ted we don't have enough gas to get home. Put the SAFE areas in the doppler and we'll head there." He then cruise climbed to 32,000 ft because that's all we could get, and he knew we would need as much altitude as possible to get maximum distance in a glide. All this time, he's talking to the Ground Control on guard frequency. After leaving North Vietnamese airspace we turned toward another designated SAFE (Selected Area for Evasion) area to minimize the chance of jumping into hostiles.

He called the emergency and asked that a tanker be sent to try to reach us before we were out of gas. The ground controller at Udorn immediately relayed our request, and a KC-135 tanker started north into Laos to try to get to us. As we waited for the aircraft to flame out, we turned to the west to find the best area where we might eject without landing in a gathering of unfriendly forces. All the while, our friend at Udorn was working as hard as he could to get us to the tanker and to get the tanker close enough that we could refuel and get home.

We flamed out only a few minutes before the tanker arrived near our position. There was no way we'd be able to get to him.

The conversation between Kilgus and Udorn was interesting and showed both men's professionalism. Udorn continued to call tanker position relative to us, and Kilgus would respond that "even if we could get up to him, we don't have enough hydraulic pressure to open the refueling door." And finally, Kilgus said after hearing we were 8000 feet below the tanker "ask him to open his side door and maybe these seats will get us up there to him." At the time I don't think either of us saw much humor in that.

As we approached 12,000 MSL (about 4000 feet above ground level) Kilgus said, "Ted it's time for you to go." I pulled my ejection handles. He ejected several seconds later although I did not see his seat. Kilgus would have ejected somewhere around 11,000 feet.

An ejection is a really traumatic event and one that will live with you your longest days. As I started up the rail watching the canopy blow off, I was almost immediately unconscious and woke up in my parachute. I could see lights below me and knew I did not want to land there but also knew that I would land wherever the chute and wind took me. I landed on a hillside and immediately sat down on my survival pack and drank a bottle of water as we had been taught in survival schools. I then turned on my survival radio and heard American aircraft in the area. They relayed that Kilgus had landed safely and was asking about me. I assured them that I was fine; then they started talking about a rescue.

When I landed I tried to follow the instruction that if you were in a mountainous area you need to find the "military crest" or upper third of a hill because that would afford you the most cover from the horizon. I did that, and when I settled in, I could hear dogs barking below and to my right. I had found my way to a place withing hearing distance from a populated area of some sort. Because we did not have good intelligence with respect to which side controlled that part of Laos this could have been a real problem had I been there very long after daylight. So, the idea of an imminent rescue really appealed to me.

Unfortunately for me, the rescue helicopter overflew my location after I had lit a flare (I swear I heard them tell me to do it although the *Apple 4* pilot says he did not). I have no idea where that came from, but I did hear a question about whether I had flares, and then was sure they said to light it when they said to. This is one of a number of questions we have no answers to 50 years after the event.

[If they had been successful, it would have been the first night rescue of the war.]

After losing my first radio, either to its failure or my inability to operate it correctly, and getting a second radio out, the rescue force commander told me that "we know where you are, and we'll be back in the morning." Right then I went from being scared absolutely witless to a feeling of total peace and safety. I knew nothing would hurt me, so I lay down and went to sleep.

I was awake at sunrise and turned on my radio and heard *Apple 4* call me and ask if I was still there. We had a short conversation about fog that was moving up the mountain and the pilot asked if I wanted them to pick me up before they got my front seater. Given my experience the previous night and my proximity to unknown people I asked them to get me first. Next question was they asked me to "FAC" (forward air control) them in (direct them in verbally on the radio). I looked over my shoulder, saw the helicopter, and told them I was at their 11 o'clock. He responded that he had me in sight and would be there shortly. They hovered some 50-100 feet above my location, so I had to move to the jungle penetrator. They asked if I needed assistance and I told them I was fine and could get on, and when I was secure on the device, they hoisted me into the helicopter.

We then followed *Apple 5* to where they picked up Major Kilgus then we flew on to Udorn Royal Thai AFB.

There we went through a round of x-rays and medical exams before they released us. A C-130, waiting for us to finish the medical stuff, flew us back to Korat. A second round of medical checks followed and then we were released to enjoy the celebration with our squadron mates and other *Firebird*s that Saturday night.

The next day, we learned that the Raid had been an effort to rescue American Prisoners of War but that no prisoners were there. Years later we learned that the prisoners had been moved out of Son Tay in July 1970. Politicians in 1970 such as Senator William Fulbright and others made a large outcry over the "failed" mission, and even Senator John McCain, himself a POW, called the mission a failure as late as 2018. In spite of these assessments many former prisoners called the Raid a real success in that it helped get them consolidated into a single place where they could communicate with each other and conduct themselves as a cohesive American military unit. A former POW Senior Ranking Officer at Son Tay told me the Vietnamese guards were more afraid of the POWs than the reverse. That was, he said, because the Vietnamese saw that the prisoners had a country that was willing to go to those lengths for them, that they had such great faith in their country, their values, and God that nothing the Vietnamese could do to them would break their will for more than a very short period of time.

The aftermath was Silver Stars for all *Firebird*s and Purple Hearts for *Firebird 5*. Kilgus and I rotated back to the United States on 8 December 1970 and subsequently were assigned to the 561st Tactical Fighter Squadron in the 23rd Tac Fighter Wing at McConnell AFB, KS.

Don Kilgus, a true American hero, survived multiple tours in Vietnam, was promoted to Colonel and retired as a member of the Air Force Inspector General's staff. After surviving all of those combat missions, Don Kilgus was killed by a drunk driver in 1988. He made an enormous impact on all of us who knew him. I could not have asked for a better man to spend 300+ hours 3 feet behind him in harm's way.

USAF CAPT MIKE GOLAS, FALCON 4

I was stationed at Udorn in the 555 Tactical Fighter Squadron on my second tour flying F-4s in Southeast Asia. I checked the schedule board for my next day's activities and saw a note directing a list of crew members, including my name, to get some crew rest and come back for a briefing very early the next morning, soon after midnight. No other info on what was going on.

I went to my quarters, got a bit of sleep, and came for the briefing, which was in the auditorium, which was not common. As we lined up to enter the auditorium, we had to walk up to a desk at the door with a civilian sitting there and another civilian standing at each side of him. He looked at each one of us and authorized us to enter the room. Very strange.

The briefing said we were to provide MIGCAP (meaning Combat Airborne Patrol to be available to engage any enemy fighters—typically MiGs—that may come up) for an unspecified mission over North Vietnam. We were each assigned an orbit point and info on which radio frequencies to contact, etc.

I launched at 0118. I arrived at my orbit, which was a bit south of the Hanoi area, at 0210.

That night I saw one SAM launch (hard to miss at night with its flaming propulsion). Also saw a low-level, bright object heading west, which I found out after the mission was an on-fire Wild

Weasel aircraft that was trying to get into friendly Thai airspace before bailing out.

No MiGs came near me so when our time was up, we left our orbit and went back to Udorn.

In our post-mission debrief we were finally told that the mission was to rescue POWs from the Hanoi region. That was the most exuberant feeling I have ever felt in a debrief as most POWs were fellow pilots and we were all rooting for them to get home somehow. As I was feeling so happy and proud, we were then told that no POWs were at the site, so none were rescued. That was the biggest drop I have ever experienced, from a super happy moment to a very disappointed feeling.

Ever since then, I have had the utmost respect for the personnel who risked their lives to attempt this rescue. I am sure we all share this disappointment, but we can take pride in knowing that the POWs were treated better after the Raid and made the North Vietnamese aware of the capabilities we had.

USAF CAPT RUSS WRIGHT, FALCON 5

Two events burned into my memory:

Memorable Moment One: On egress as the last F-4 out from the high CAP (Combat Airborne Patrol), I heard a "MiGs" call. My WSO (Weapons Systems Officer) Major James Malaney identified the source and determined that the transmission came from someone behind us. We then heard from *Firebird 5* (Maj Don Kilgus/ Capt Ted Lowry) that they had been hit by a SAM and were losing fuel. I did a 180 and headed back toward Hanoi. We picked up three targets on radar. Figured out which one was *Firebird 5* and joined up with them. Approaching the PDJ (Plain des Jarres, Laos), Kilgus advised that they were not going to make the tanker.

We watched *Firebird 5* Bravo, Capt Ted Lowry, eject. *Firebird 5* Alpha, Maj Don Kilgus, said, "If I don't make it, tell everyone I didn't screw up...it was a SAM." We watched him eject and we set up a SAR (search and rescue).

Memorable Moment Two: Since we stayed on scene until *Firebird* 5A & B were picked up, when we recovered to Udorn, the rest of our F-4 formation had already debriefed and left HQ/Intel. As I walked across the ramp, there was a large number of ambulances and medical personnel. When I asked someone, he said he heard that a Papa site in Laos had been overrun and there were mass casualties inbound. Outside HQ/Intel was a group of the meanest looking SOBs armed to the teeth and not looking happy. As I came out of the intel debrief, a LtCol asked me if I was with the F-4 MIGCAP. He said I should get into the debrief BGen Manor was receiving. So, this low man on the totem pole got to hear firsthand, at same time as the Mission Commander, the initial debriefs of the ground forces. I could not help but look at Colonel Simons. He turned, caught me looking at him and stared me down... scared the shit out of me. I thought he just might come over and lop my head off. It was the Most Scary Moment of the Raid for me. He was an intimidating force.

USAF CAPT KEN GARDNER, FALCON 1

Ken Gardner's stream of consciousness:

The mission has the blessing of those at the top - things are starting to approach reality. Now, to brief our individual parts for this gigantic play. I can't believe it, but the countdown is about complete. The final word comes through: the mission is go. Tensions mount as never before. My inner feelings are beyond description standing there briefing my flights at Udorn RTAFB, for in the background is a beautiful sound - the sound of the choppers that are moving with a fine piece of cargo - the Army types who carry the keys to that nasty little prison up there. The hardware they possess fits various descriptions, but tonight it all serves as keys. I just wonder, though, could it be? No way, never—never—no possibility.

Time for my own act now, so let's do it. Properly, though, more properly than I ever did my thing before because it's worth more tonight, more than it has ever been worth before.

The burners are running and the gear shows up and locked so the machine looks good, and I'm thankful for that. This is no time for equipment drop-outs. Now, if we find that guy in the dark for some extra gas we'll be on our way. With that complete, it's time to serious up; the final heading checks and our times are straight, point of ingress—Hello, North Vietnam. (My goodness, it's peaceful tonight.) Point of orbit now. The Low Force should be along any minute now, but I wonder altitude?

Yeah, yeah, just let me see those Mk-24 flares out there and I'll become a believer. Should be any minute now if they've made it this far. Damn, there they are! Right on schedule. I do believe we are in business, folks. Maybe we're doing okay. Here comes that first missile of the evening. Why did they have to do that? We just want to get a few people out of jail. And so it's maneuver, dodge, play the decoy role, look for MiGs.

My EWO, Roger Henry tells me it's egress time now, the Army types should be back in the choppers and ready to move on out. Play it careful, you guys; you have those special items with you now. I can't imagine what they're thinking or feeling to see some friendly faces drop in for a chat and extend an invitation to dine out. But this is that chance - could it be? ("No way, never—never—no possibility.")

The rest of this flight is fairly routine; one crew downed in Laos, but I hear their pick-up under way. Can't wait to land and get the results of this ballgame. I can hear the landing clearances for the chopper force, so they must have made it back in good fashion. Time to wind this thing up now; it's been a long evening. Gear is down and locked, if I can just get a turn at the runway—lots of traffic all of a sudden.

There, good drag chute. It's all over but the drinking. I can see the medical buses on the flight line as I taxi in—seems funny though, not much activity in that direction. They should be hauling the rescued to the hospital according to the plan.

Engines are shut down; let's go debrief. I'm anxious to get the news. Hey, there are the Special Forces troops on a smoke break. What? They said there were no POWs in the prison camp. There must be some mistake. It must be a stock answer they're supposed to give as continued cover for the real results. Let's go inside.

Hell, the word's the same in there. I don't understand it; I don't understand it. A chance gone, forever. A chance to realize and feel one small act of man's humanity towards man amidst the inhumanities of war.

But then again, could it ever really have been? No. Never. Never—no possibility.

USAF CAPT BRUCE HOST, LIME 2

There are a number of memorable moments. I was the navigator on the HC-130P with the call sign *Lime 2*. We were at Udorn pulling our normal TDY (temporary duty) from Cam Rahn Air Base, South Vietnam.

Our wartime mission was to fly orbits in the area where aerial strikes were taking place, listen to the radios – all frequencies – and follow the battles. If an aircraft was shot down, we pinpointed the aircrew, called in covering support, and directed the recovery of the downed airmen. And, as required, would provide an aerial refueling platform for the "Jolly Green" helicopters that did the pickup.

First: My Squadron Commander LtCol Syd Spilseth woke me up at "0-Dark-Thirty" at Udorn RTAFB. I was told to grab a bag of clothing for a couple of days. The obvious questions, "Where am I going and what am I going for?" were not answered. Our crew members were loaded onto a C-47 and flown to Takhli RTAFB, arriving at nighttime. We were loaded onto a bus which had the windows covered (all very strange) and driven inside a hanger. We were then assigned BOQs (Bachelor Officer Quarters) and told to meet at the Theater that afternoon. We still did not know why we were there.

Second: My memory of seeing Colonel Bull Simons in his Army brown tee shirt, fatigues and combat boots, on stage at the Takhli Theater, was one I'll never forget. He was square jawed, and crew cut, in his gravel voice he explained that we were going to raid a North Vietnamese POW camp. It was an unbelievable experience to hear the cheers from the soldiers who were listening to their leader explain for the first time what was about to happen. We were all very excited to be part of this rescue mission.

Third: Working in the crew room of our assigned building at Takhli with Capt Chuck McNeff, the navigator on *Lime 1*. We designed the route of flight from Udorn to Son Tay to include level off, join-up with the helicopters, refueling locations with the helicopters, rendezvous location with the MC-130s (*Cherry 1 & Cherry 2*) for the turn-over of the helicopters to take them from the Laos/N.Vietnam border to Son Tay.

Fourth: Inflight from Udorn to Son Tay. The night was cloudy with partial moonlight. We were flying in loose formation with

Lime 1 who was drafting the HH-3 helicopter (call sign *Banana*) inside his left wing and the HH-53s (call sign *Apple*). The only light was from *Lime 1*'s dim formation lights on his wings and from his open rear door. There was no radar in use and no communication. (As an aside, who would ever come up with names for combat mission aircraft as fruit salad?)

Fifth: After refueling the helicopters and handing them over to *Cherry 1*, *Lime 1* retuned to Udorn to refuel while *Lime 2* took up orbit on the Laos/N.Vietnam border. Shortly after started the most exciting fireworks display one has ever seen. Flares which were being dropped by the MC-130 *Cherry 1*, the anti-aircraft fire, and SAMs. It was like the Fourth of July. An amazing view from 20,000 feet. At the same time, we were listening to the radio chatter and trying to figure out how many POWs had been freed. We could not make sense of it.

Sixth: During the return to Udorn, *Lime 2* refueled the HH-53s *Apples 4 & 5* over Laos and picked up *Firebird 5*'s mayday call. (This was an Air Force F-105 that was hit by a SAM and both crew members had to bail out. Both were picked up.) *Lime 1* now arrived, having refueled at Udorn. They were assigned to change their call sign to King 21 and assume on-scene command of the rescue pickup. That was much to our disappointment—we wanted to command that rescue of *Firebird 5*.

Seventh: Upon landing at Udorn, we went to base operations for a debriefing which never happened. We walked past a number of Green Berets who were very sad-faced. That was our confirmation that we had gotten no POWs at Son Tay. It was a very sad and disappointing time.

Image 85: *Lime* 2 is on display at Cannon AFB, NM.

Image 86: *Lime 2* is on display at Cannon AFB, NM. On the plaque are Capt Clyde "Neal" Westbrook, Capt John Pletcher, Capt Bruce Host, MSgt Billy Gartman, MSgt Lawrence Durbin, TSgt Richard Klasser, SSgt Luther Hollums. Operation Kingpin was the execution phase of the Son Tay Raid (Thailand/Vietnam) Operation Ivory Coast was the training phase (Florida) Operation Polar Circle was the proposal planning phase (The Pentagon)

USAF MAJOR JOHN PUGH, C-130 TRANSPORT FROM TAKHLI TO UDORN

I was the Aircraft Commander of one of the two C-130s that flew the Raiders from Takhli RTAFB to Udorn RTAFB the night of the Raid. I had been briefed only that I was supporting a Top Secret operation and I was given no other details. I flew my aircraft from Utapao RTAFB to Takhli not knowing what to expect. I deplaned at Takhli and went into the Base Operations Building to file my Udorn flight plan. When I returned to my plane, I saw about 25 to 30 very stern-faced Special Forces troops in full face camouflage aboard my aircraft. I could tell no one wanted to talk to me so I said nothing to them. After landing at Udorn I was told to reconfigure my cargo compartment for possible aeromedical evacuations and that nothing would happen for a few hours. Then I went to a cot in a nearby hanger to try to get some sleep. Eight hours later, I was told my plane was no longer needed so I flew back to Clark Air Base, Philippines. I will never forget the expressions on those men's faces that night of the Raid as they were heading toward combat.

USAF MASTER SGT JIM CHEVRIER, FROG ONE

I was called to a meeting in our office at 7pm. This was very strange and I had no idea what it could be about. Beside Colonel Mulherron, there were about 15 or so who had been involved with the SEAOR-62 program. The Southeast Asia Operational Requirement 62 was an upgrade happening in the summer of 1970 to the EC-121 College Eye (in the civilian world, it the "Constellation") command and control aircraft that made encrypted code communication standardized among Air Force and Navy so that the ground commanders could see in real-time what the airborne radars see.

Also present was LtCol Homer Willett from the Air Staff in the Pentagon. He told us we had been selected to participate in a super-secret mission. They wanted only volunteers who were willing to go to some undisclosed place to do some undisclosed mission, which would involve a degree of danger. We were sworn to secrecy (even though we didn't know anything about anything except that it could be dangerous). The only thing we knew was that we would be leaving by 3 November.

Image 87: EC-121T "College Eye."

I went home and started to get my things together and my wife Inge said something like, "Now what?!" Of course, I could only tell her I was leaving on Tuesday, 3 November, and I didn't even know where I was going or when I would be home.

The next day Colonel Mulherron took me out onto the flight line, behind our office, away from everyone and told me we were going on a mission to support an attempt to rescue POWs in North Vietnam. He said we were taking two EC-121Ts and two full crews. He told me to pick the radar crews because I knew who had attended SEAOR-62 training and flown the test missions. He also told me to be sure that everyone I picked knew it was on a voluntary basis. He said, "How in the hell am I going to tell Colonel Timmerman, the Wing Commander, that we were taking two T models (and also one G model) and can't tell him anything more?!" I told him I felt Colonel Timmerman would be unhappy but would probably live with it if he knew it was an important mission we were going on.

I don't recall where Captain DiCarlo was, but I know he wasn't available at the time. Some of the radar operators that had attended training or flown the test missions were not available for one reason or another. I managed to get together two crews who were willing volunteers and who could leave on very short notice to an unknown location to do something undisclosed.

I was very busy for the next few days getting people together and preparing to depart McClellan. I would be the Radar Crew Chief on the primary airplane. Senior MSgt Darrel Crossman was the Radio Operator.

We departed McClellan on 3 November for Hickam AFB in Honolulu. I was on one of the T models with Colonel Mulherron, Darrel Crossman and Chief MSgt Forrest Wright. Forrest was a Radar Technician and oversaw maintenance. Colonel Mulherron was the Task Force Commander. We stayed overnight at Hickam and since we had classified equipment and materials onboard, we could not leave the airplane unguarded. I stayed with the plane most of the night.

The next day we flew to Wake Island and lost a day crossing the International Date Line. We stayed overnight at Wake. I don't recall for sure, but I think the base provided security guards for our airplanes. Besides that, Wake Island is in the middle of the Pacific and no one except military and civilian employees are on the island. Wake Island barely has enough room for a runway and a few buildings.

We stopped the next day at Clark Air Base in the Philippines to refuel, then on to Anderson AFB, Guam, to spend the night.

On 8 November we reached Tinian Island, where we would wait until we were told to proceed and where we would go. By this time most everyone knew we were probably going to Korat RTAFB but that had not been established yet.

Because they didn't have any room for us at Tinian, they had to put us in one of the hotels in town. It was not far from the NCO Club. We had no duties to perform and so we just sat and waited. I was in my hotel bathroom sitting on the toilet when we experienced an earthquake! My room was on about the 10th floor and as I sat on the toilet, I could feel the building sway. I thought about getting out of there, but I quickly gave up that idea: I decided that if I was going to die, I would just as soon not be full of crap when I did. Things settled down after a few seconds and all was well. Darrel came to my room a few minutes later and asked if I had felt the earthquake. So, I told him where I had spent the time during the shaking.

We arrived at Korat on Thursday, 12 November. We planned to start flying two missions a day, in order to get the operators and maintenance people some training on the equipment. During the training months ago (in Greeneville TX at LTV ElectroSystems Corporation) there was no actual equipment available to train on and the equipment was still being modified, so all of the learning was in a classroom without any equipment. Darrel Crossman (Radio Operator), Technical Sgt Gary Walker (Radar Tech) and I would fly both the morning and afternoon missions with different crews to help in the training. We planned to start the flying regimen on Saturday, 14 November.

Both Darrel and I had picked up a cold and didn't feel all that good. We both went to the Korat hospital and saw a flight surgeon. He determined we each had an upper respiratory infection with sore throats, earaches, and cold symptoms and immediately ordered us grounded ("DNIF"—Duties Not Involving Flying) and gave us medication to take. When we got back to our building, Colonel Mulherron was in his office. Darrel and I put all our medications on a desk and we agreed to not tell Colonel Mulherron that we had been grounded. It turns out that he was standing nearby and could hear everything we were saying. Darrel asked me what I was going to do. I said that I am just going to keep on flying. We really felt there was no other choice. I had an infection in my right ear and Darrel's was in his left ear, so Colonel Mulherron joked that we must have been sitting next to each other while we were under the desk hiding from Col Mulherron!

After our crews had arrived at Korat and gotten a little rest, we started our two-a-day flights on Sunday, 15 November. It was a hard-enough schedule to be on without being sick but both Darrel and I did it without missing a beat (or a flight). Our day ran from about 5am to 6pm. We were quartered in a large open bay with double bunks and probably 60 in the bay. The College Eye task force was too big to put us in hooches where the aircrews normally stayed. There were mostly ground maintenance people in the bay and they were all working different shifts so sleep was difficult at best.

We had operated EC-121s from Korat months ago. Our cover story for our return to Korat with two T models was, "We are doing additional testing on these two T models." In August we had used only one airplane. So, it seemed reasonable to everyone that we were there to do additional testing. No one paid much attention to us and everyone went about their business as usual. The College

Eye Task Force Commander Colonel Milton McEwen knew we were there for some special reason, but he didn't know what it was. In fact, most of the people who were on our crews with us didn't have a clue what we were up to either.

There were a couple of EC-121T models already at Korat, but they were being flown as D models since they were still in the process of being modified. So, we sometimes used those airplanes—reconfigured as T models—in our training flights. When we started our two-a-day flights Colonel Mulherron told me to pick the two airplanes with the best radar to use on the mission. Too bad he didn't tell me to pick one that wouldn't have a mechanical failure. You can see why I liked Colonel Mulherron and have proclaimed him the best boss I have ever had. He trusted my judgment and gave me a lot of responsibility seemingly without reservation.

We settled into our rigorous flying schedule, morning and afternoon. Darrel Crossman, Gary Walker and I flew every mission even though Darrel and I were not supposed to be flying. It was painful at times and I know I felt lousy as I am sure Darrel did.

Colonel Mulherron, Captain Edney (one of the Air Weapons Controllers with us) and Captain Bomhoff left Korat on Thursday 19 November along with LtCol Willett (from the Air Staff) to go to Takhli RTAFB for a meeting. It was the final briefing for the mission. Both BGen Leroy Manor and Colonel Arthur "Bull" Simons were there and gave the briefing.

Meanwhile back at Korat we stood down from flying our two-a-days because we knew we were getting close to doing what we had come to do. The rest of our crew still didn't know what we were there for. They knew it was an important mission, yet to be identified. This was the first day not flying since the 14th, so Darrel and I took the time to visit the Flight Surgeon and convince him we were cured. He returned us to flying status that morning.

When we returned to the College Eye operations building, Colonel Willett called from Takhli and asked to speak with me. When I got on the phone Colonel Willett said, "Sergeant Chevrier, I am paraphrasing: Jakes hunting party is on for tonight. Do you understand?" I said, "Yes sir. I understand." We had not made any previous arrangement about notification that the mission was on, but I knew exactly what Colonel Willett meant. I told Forrest and Darrel that we needed to put both crews on crew rest because we were going that night. I also picked the two airplanes we would take and told Colonel McEwen of Maintenance that we needed those two planes ready to go. Colonel Willett had called because Colonel Mulherron with Captains Edney and Bomhoff were on their way back to Korat.

We went back to the barracks and tried to get some rest but because of maintenance people coming and going there wasn't much chance of that.

I don't know how they figured out the call signs we used that night but the C-130s and helicopters all had fruit call signs, i.e. *Cherry 1*, *Cherry 2*, *Banana*, *Lime 1*, *Lime 2*, etc. Our call signs for the mission were Frog 1 and Frog 2. I was on Frog 1 and we departed Korat at 2200 hours. Frog 2 was airborne just ten minutes later as we headed for the Gulf of Tonkin with an orbit just beyond SAM range northeast of Hai Phong North Vietnam.

Shortly after we were in the air on our way, Colonel Mulherron got onto the airplane's public address system and announced to everyone that we were going to provide air support to a group of Special Forces who were going to attempt to rescue American POWs being held at Son Tay, North Vietnam just 23 west of Hanoi. Everyone immediately recognized the importance of this mission and was excited to have the chance to participate. We had all volunteered not knowing what it was we were going to do. With a couple of exceptions, no one had any idea. Now that they knew this was probably the most important mission that most of us would ever be involved with.

It took us two and half hours to reach our orbit. Immediately after we assumed station and had notified the command center at Monkey Mountain, we had to shut down one engine. In John Gargus' book, *The Son Tay Raid: American POWs in Vietnam Were Not Forgotten* page 284 he wrote that, at 0035, Frog 1 aborted due to a broken fuel line and recovered at Da Nang AB. I personally don't recall what was the problem with the engine, but I do know we had to shut it down. The Aircraft Commander, LtCol Barwick decided to abort the mission and land at the nearest US airbase, which was Da Nang.

I know that all of us on the crew were disappointed that we were aborting such an important mission. When you consider that we routinely flew from Station One, two hundred miles west of Seattle, to McClellan on three engines, a four-hour flight orbiting over the Gulf of Tonkin didn't seem that risky. Da Nang was less than an hour away. But LtCol Barwick was responsible for the airplane and the crew and, although the US Navy pretty much owned the Gulf, there were many North Vietnamese "fishing boats" in the area. The reason we had Frog 2 was to take our place in just such an event. So Frog 2 took over and we headed to Da Nang. It's too bad Colonel Mulherron didn't tell me to pick the airplane with the best radar AND in the best mechanical shape. He only relied on me to know which airplane would have the best radar. Beyond that, I didn't have the expertise to determine which airplane was in the best mechanical condition.

We spent the night sitting on the ramp parked in front of the Base Operations building at Da Nang. We listened to our radio to see if we could discover how many POWs the raid would retrieve.

Since we had the operations order and knew all of the code words and call signs of everyone involved, we wanted to follow what was happening. Meanwhile the maintenance people were attempting to repair the engine.

We were parked next to the T-39 that had brought BGen Manor, the overall commander of the raid, to Da Nang. BGen Manor had gone up to Monkey Mountain to observe the information the EC-121T would provide. As the raid progressed, we heard mixed messages and, at one point, thought that all the POWs at Son Tay had been rescued. Then we heard that none had been found.

Around 0530, BGen Manor came out of Base Operations. We all saluted and said, "Good morning General." He replied, got in his T-39, and flew away.

We were one of the first airplanes to take off in support of the mission. I think only Combat Apple, an RC-135M who was already on station over the Gulf before we got there, took off before us. We returned the next morning, arriving at Korat after 0830.

Darrel Crossman and I made it back to our open bay barracks around 0900, dead tired. Just after that, one of the maintenance people who lived in that open bay came in all excited about the news on Armed Forces Radio Network. They had announced that a daring raid had been attempted, during the night to rescue POWs from North Vietnam. He asked if we had heard about it. Since no one had told us differently, we were still sworn to secrecy. We told him that we hadn't heard and acted all surprised.

Image 88: BGen Manor monitored the raid at the command post set up at the Tactical Air Control Center at the top of Monkey Mountain.

USAF 1ˢᵀ LT MICKEY BATSELL, GENERAL'S AIDE

I first met Leroy Manor in June of 1969 when he became the commander of the 835th Air Division at McConnell AFB, KS. I was a young 1st Lt and he was a Colonel. We got to know each other through my monthly briefings in my role as a Management Analyst for the comptroller of the 23rd Tactical Fighter Wing, The Flying Tigers.

Shortly after he was selected for promotion to Brigadier General, he asked me to be his aide-de-camp. I warned him that I had never been a general's aide before. He responded that he had never been a General before. That set the tone for what became a unique and rewarding relationship. At his promotion ceremony some weeks later, his wife Dee pinned the star on one shoulder, and I had the honor of pinning the other.

In each Friday morning weekly review, the first topic was the activities of the past week. Next, we would discuss the activities on the calendar for the coming week. In February of 1970, one particular Friday morning session had a different tone to it.

BGen Manor began with the question, "Have you ever been to Florida?" He explained that we would be flying to Eglin AFB on Sunday. My response was intended to help me with my packing and preparations for the trip, "How long will we be gone?" His answer was not what I expected: "It is a PCS (permanent change of station). I have been selected as the new Commander of USAF Special Operations Forces." My reply: "I'm in."

Arriving at the billeting office at Eglin that Sunday, we learned that BGen Manor's quarters were ready and in good order, but billeting was not aware he was bringing his aide-de-camp. Because of the extremely heavy TDY traffic and foreign pilot training taking place at Eglin during that time, there were no quarters available for me. Manor asked about his accommodations. The desk clerk described his quarters as being spacious, having a screened patio, outdoor grill, nice kitchen, living room, a fully stocked bar, and two bedrooms. "Then put Lt Batsell in the other bedroom," he said.

That was the beginning of almost two months of the intense equivalent of a post graduate degree in leadership development, decision-making, and communication skills. During our workday I was invited into most of the meetings and conferences he held. Many times, after a meeting was completed, he would ask me my opinion as to what action he should take and my reasoning. He would then critique my answer. Often, he would tell me that my answer was correct, but the reasoning was incorrect. Then at the end of the day when we were back in our quarters, we would review all of the day's activities and the rationale involved for the decisions he made, and the actions taken.

After we each were able to establish our permanent on-base quarters and get our families relocated, we settled into a routine. The staff car would pick me up every morning and we would go by BGen Manor's quarters to get him and then head to the office.

There was a significant amount of turnover of personnel at USAF SOF HQ at the time. BGen Manor had a "First Day" policy for newly assigned personnel. On the first day that an officer, NCO, airman or civilian began their new assignment with SOF I would accompany him to the workstation of the newcomer. He would introduce himself, welcome them to the unit and ask them if they encountered any problems getting themselves and their families settled. If they needed any assistance, he told them not to hesitate to reach out to Lt Batsell for help.

As planning and preparations for the Son Tay rescue mission began in May and June of 1970, the daily routine changed. It was important to continue as much as possible all appearances of "everything as usual." Normal duty hours continued from 7:30am to 4:30pm. Head home for dinner as normal. But then it was back to the office around 8pm until the early hours of the morning.

Security was of utmost concern. We made several trips to Andrews AFB and the Pentagon. I was charged with carrying a briefcase containing a number of classified documents.

One night back at SOF HQ around 2am, BGen Manor asked me to round up Colonel Bull Simons to come to a meeting in his office. I promptly went to Colonel Simons quarters to extend the invitation. When I arrived, one of Colonel Simons' NCOs was sitting outside the front door. I explained to the NCO that BGen Manor would like Colonel Simons to come to a meeting. The sergeant told me that Colonel Simons was asleep. I asked the sergeant to wake him up. His reply: "With all due respect, lieutenant, you can wake him up." I was a bit stunned by that and started to take a step through the door. "You might want to think twice about that sir, because the Colonel sleeps with a loaded 45 under his pillow." I heeded the sergeant's advice and paused to consider my options. After a few pensive moments, I said, "Sarge, when he wakes up, would you tell him that BGen Manor needs to see him?" The good sergeant replied, "Yes sir," and I went on my way.

The days and weeks after the Son Tay Raid, with BGen Manor back at Eglin, were a hectic time. I became a buffer between the general and the press and others that wanted access to him. I was also given the assignment to assist in compiling all of the costs associated with the mission.

In February of 1971, General Manor was promoted and assigned to the Pentagon. After learning of his assignment, he explained to me that he was not going to be in a command position in his new job so was not entitled to have an aide-de-camp. He asked me where I would like to be assigned. I told him that my family and I enjoyed being at Eglin and would like to stay. I was assigned to the HQ SOF Comptroller's office. Almost six months later I got a phone call. As it turned out, I was one of two USAF Captains selected to become briefing officers for Secretary of Defense Melvin Laird. Someone had suggested my name for this special assignment.

I think I know who that someone was.

Image 89: General Manor retired in June
1978 as a Lieutenant General.

USAF SGT KEN RUUD, SPECIAL OPERATIONS SUPPORT

I was in Detachment 2 of the 1st Special Operations Wing at Pope
AFB when I was assigned to deliver "Barbara" to Eglin AFB from
Pope. I was an E-4, so when I bumped a Colonel from his flight,
I knew I was a courier for something very special, but I had no
idea what was in that box! (Sgt Ruud arrived at Aux Field #3 with
"Barbara" at 11am on Tuesday September 8th, 1970.)

Image 90: Barbara (with Major John Gargus)

Image 91: Two statues of Son Tay Raiders at the Special Forces
Museum at Fort Bragg: Bull Simons and Dick Meadows

APPENDIX 5

A Compilation of the Life Lessons from this Book

LIFE LESSON 1: Add Humor. It really helps when things are getting tough. Sometimes it's not easy to find it within you, but even the POWs somehow found a way to pass some slivers of humor through the cracks in the prison walls. The soul needs it. Make sure you contribute some for the benefit of the people around you.

LIFE LESSON 2: Your Life is Significant, so be Excellent in Everything you do. No matter how insignificant you think your job is, it could turn out to be a life-changing position. One of the reasons Capt Dan selected me to be paired with him was that, during all the time I spent pulling guard duty and training, I never complained, but always did what was asked of me. I credit my dad for instilling this attitude in my brothers and me. He always told us, "If you're going to do anything, do your best."

LIFE LESSON 3: In your Work, always be Training and Improving. During the first month of our training, there were several changes made as to how we approached our positions. I learned a very important lesson: Invest the time in training—it pays off. Just like a football team trains for the big game, we were training for our big game. The major difference: our life depended on how well we performed. Training sometimes gets boring, but when the bullets start flying in both directions, you're sure glad that you know what is expected of you and your team members.

LIFE LESSON 4: Have Patience and Aggressiveness and Contentment. Guarding the TOC, we were not allowed to know the "Why." As I saw my opportunity slipping away. I was aggressive, hungry to be in the middle of the action. That's OK—it's not a fault to be aggressive. It's a virtue—if you can choose in your heart and in your mind to be at peace and to be thankful, trusting God with the outcome.

LIFE LESSON 5: Be Prepared for Death. Don't worry about it. You can't completely control it. Make sure that the day you meet your Maker is not the first time you've been introduced. If you are prepared at all times, you're free to live life fearless.

LIFE LESSON 6: Don't be "Indispensable." Always be training a backup person for your job and always be learning to be a backup for your teammates. This applies to any job in life. The graveyards are full of "indispensable men."

LIFE LESSON 7: Don't be a Complainer. The world is moving on and needs people to solve problems. Evaluate your situation, make a decision, and execute any new plan without complaining and feeling sorry for yourself. You can't saw down a concrete telephone pole with a chainsaw! So, we improvised a new plan.

LIFE LESSON 8: Veterans, we all have a Mission: Listen to your fellow Veterans. My hope is that the contributions you read in Appendix 4 help to achieve this. It's important for the veteran, but it's also important for the listener. It's important for America. Good stories and bad, they need to be told. Please take my request to heart and talk with a veteran.

LIFE LESSON 9: Sacrificial Living. That scene as we arrived at Pope AFB back in November of 1970 really made an impression on me: It's not only the soldiers but also their wives who are heroes. These families are the type of people our world needs—people who know this life is not just about their convenience. I am thankful for what these families (which include those of first responders in civilian life) do for our country and for freedom around the world.

★ ★ ★

Image 92: The Son Tay Raider Patch.

APPENDIX 6

A Top Secret list of the Son Tay Raiders and certain Support Personnel

ON WEDNESDAY, NOVEMBER 11TH, 1970, BGen Manor provided the following Top Secret list to Chairman of the Joint Chiefs of Staff Admiral Thomas Moorer. This list helps to place names with their location during the Raid. It is not comprehensive. BGen Manor's primary purpose in this list is to identify those resources that would be deploying from Eglin AFB with him. The personnel already in-country are not on this listing.

So many others were involved in the Raid—literally hundreds. This includes Army, Navy, Air Force, Marines, and even civilian contractors. We hope in this book to have given honor to so many, named and unnamed, that deserve America's appreciation

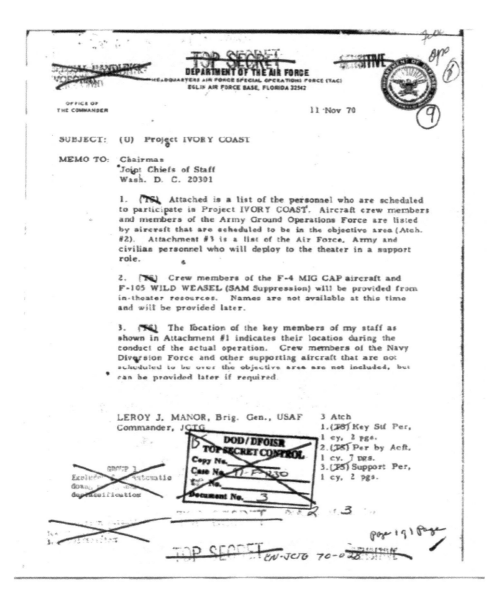

Image 93: Top Secret list of personnel.

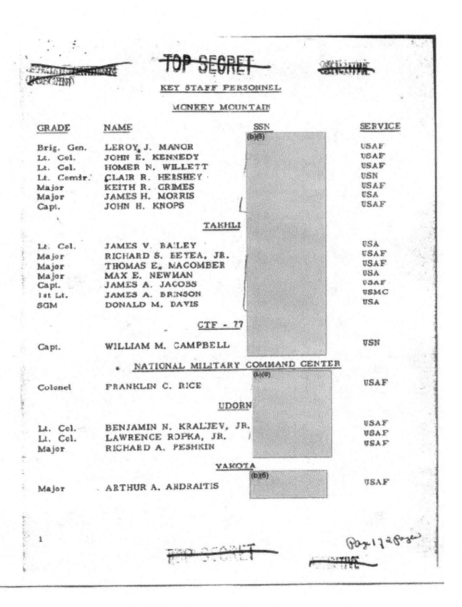

Image 94: Top Secret list of personnel

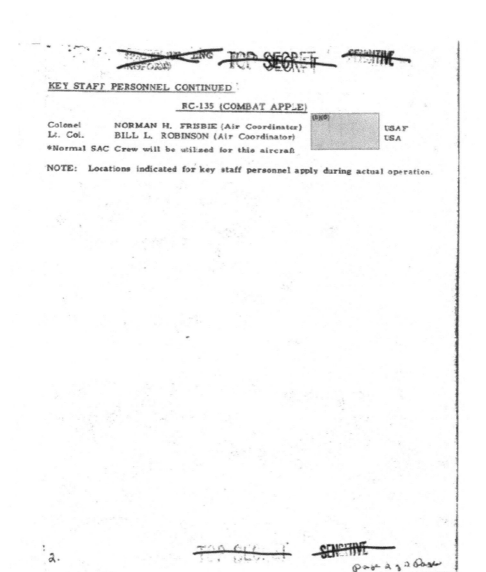

~~TOP SECRET~~   ~~SENSITIVE~~

KEY STAFF PERSONNEL CONTINUED

RC-135 (COMBAT APPLE)

| Colonel | NORMAN H. FRISBIE (Air Coordinator) | | USAF |
| Lt. Col. | BILL L. ROBINSON (Air Coordinator) | | USA |

*Normal SAC Crew will be utilized for this aircraft

NOTE: Locations indicated for key staff personnel apply during actual operation.

Image 95: Top Secret list of personnel

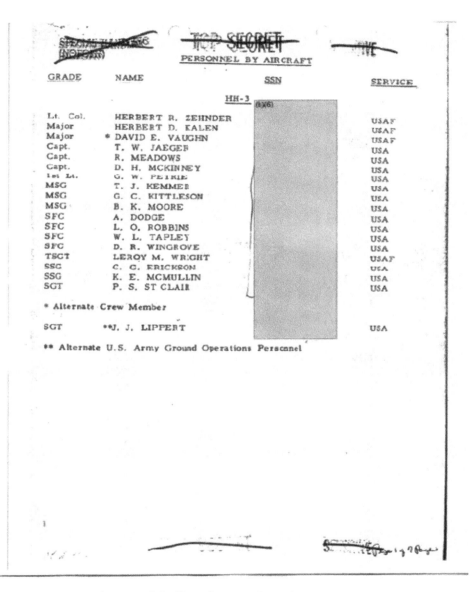

TOP SECRET

PERSONNEL BY AIRCRAFT

GRADE	NAME	SSN	SERVICE

HH-3 (b)(6)

Lt. Col.	HERBERT R. ZEHNDER		USAF
Major	HERBERT D. KALEN		USAF
Major	* DAVID E. VAUGHN		USAF
Capt.	T. W. JAEGER		USA
Capt.	R. MEADOWS		USA
Capt.	D. H. MCKINNEY		USA
1st Lt.	G. W. PETRIE		USA
MSG	T. J. KEMMER		USA
MSG	G. C. KITTLESON		USA
MSG	B. K. MOORE		USA
SFC	A. DODGE		USA
SFC	L. O. ROBBINS		USA
SFC	W. L. TAPLEY		USA
SFC	D. R. WINGROVE		USA
TSGT	LEROY M. WRIGHT		USAF
SSG	C. C. ERICKSON		USA
SSG	K. E. MCMULLIN		USA
SGT	P. S. ST CLAIR		USA

* Alternate Crew Member

| SGT | **J. J. LIPPERT | | USA |

** Alternate U.S. Army Ground Operations Personnel

Image 96: Top Secret list of personnel

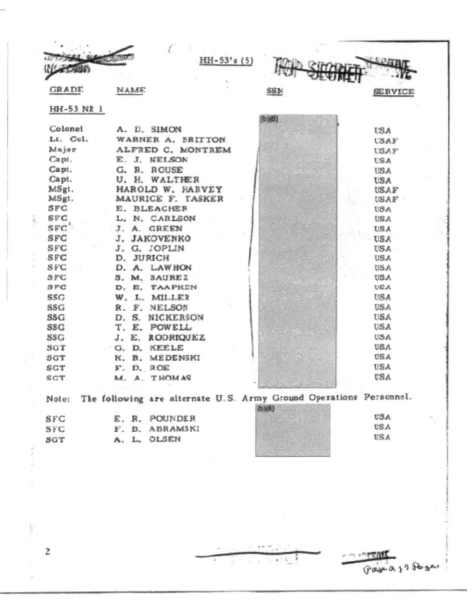

HH-53's (5)   ~~TOP SECRET~~

GRADE	NAME	SSN	SERVICE

HH-53 NR 1

GRADE	NAME	SERVICE
Colonel	A. D. SIMON	USA
Lt. Col.	WARNER A. BRITTON	USAF
Major	ALFRED C. MONTREM	USAF
Capt.	E. J. NELSON	USA
Capt.	G. R. ROUSE	USA
Capt.	U. H. WALTHER	USA
MSgt.	HAROLD W. HARVEY	USAF
MSgt.	MAURICE F. TASKER	USAF
SFC	E. BLEACHER	USA
SFC	L. N. CARLSON	USA
SFC	J. A. GREEN	USA
SFC	J. JAKOVENKO	USA
SFC	J. G. JOPLIN	USA
SFC	D. JURICH	USA
SFC	D. A. LAWHON	USA
SFC	S. M. SAUREZ	USA
SFC	D. E. TAAPKEN	USA
SSG	W. L. MILLER	USA
SSG	R. F. NELSON	USA
SSG	D. S. NICKERSON	USA
SSG	T. E. POWELL	USA
SSG	J. E. RODRIQUEZ	USA
SGT	G. D. KEELE	USA
SGT	K. R. MEDENSKI	USA
SGT	F. D. ROE	USA
SGT	M. A. THOMAS	USA

Note: The following are alternate U.S. Army Ground Operations Personnel.

GRADE	NAME	SERVICE
SFC	E. R. POUNDER	USA
SFC	F. B. ABRAMSKI	USA
SGT	A. L. OLSEN	USA

2

Image 97: Top Secret list of personnel

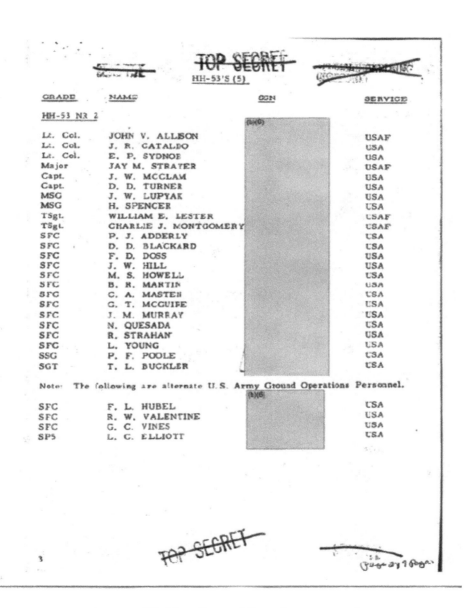

TOP SECRET

HH-53'S (5)

GRADE	NAME	SSN	SERVICE
HH-53 NR 2			
Lt. Col.	JOHN V. ALLISON		USAF
Lt. Col.	J. R. CATALDO		USA
Lt. Col.	E. P. SYDNOR		USA
Major	JAY M. STRAYER		USAF
Capt.	J. W. MCCLAM		USA
Capt.	D. D. TURNER		USA
MSG	J. W. LUPYAK		USA
MSG	H. SPENCER		USA
TSgt.	WILLIAM E. LESTER		USAF
TSgt.	CHARLIE J. MONTGOMERY		USAF
SFC	P. J. ADDERLY		USA
SFC	D. D. BLACKARD		USA
SFC	F. D. DOSS		USA
SFC	J. W. HILL		USA
SFC	M. S. HOWELL		USA
SFC	B. R. MARTIN		USA
SFC	C. A. MASTEN		USA
SFC	G. T. MCGUIRE		USA
SFC	J. M. MURRAY		USA
SFC	N. QUESADA		USA
SFC	R. STRAHAN		USA
SFC	L. YOUNG		USA
SSG	P. F. POOLE		USA
SGT	T. L. BUCKLER		USA

Note: The following are alternate U.S. Army Ground Operations Personnel.

SFC	F. L. HUBEL		USA
SFC	R. W. VALENTINE		USA
SFC	G. C. VINES		USA
SP5	L. G. ELLIOTT		USA

TOP SECRET

3

Image 98: Top Secret list of personnel

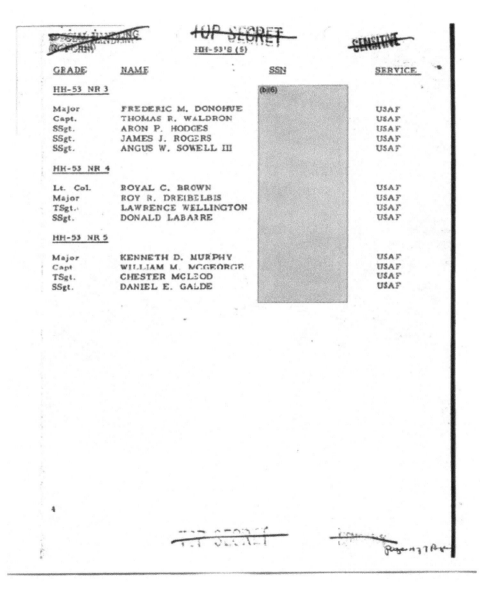

~~SPECIAL HANDLING~~
~~(NOFORN)~~
~~TOP SECRET~~
~~SENSITIVE~~

HH-53'S (5)

GRADE	NAME	SSN	SERVICE
HH-53 NR 3		(b)(6)	
Major	FREDERIC M. DONOHUE		USAF
Capt.	THOMAS R. WALDRON		USAF
SSgt.	ARON P. HODGES		USAF
SSgt.	JAMES J. ROGERS		USAF
SSgt.	ANGUS W. SOWELL III		USAF
HH-53 NR 4			
Lt. Col.	ROYAL C. BROWN		USAF
Major	ROY R. DREIBELBIS		USAF
TSgt.	LAWRENCE WELLINGTON		USAF
SSgt.	DONALD LABARRE		USAF
HH-53 NR 5			
Major	KENNETH D. MURPHY		USAF
Capt	WILLIAM M. MCGEORGE		USAF
TSgt.	CHESTER MCLEOD		USAF
SSgt.	DANIEL E. GALDE		USAF

4

~~TOP SECRET~~

Image 99: Top Secret list of personnel

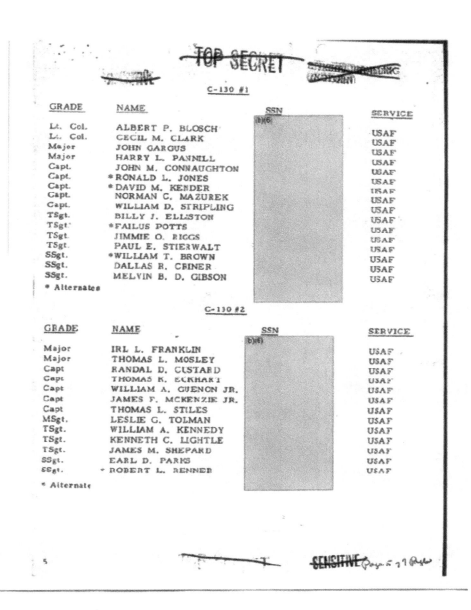

TOP SECRET

C-130 #1

GRADE	NAME	SSN	SERVICE
Lt. Col.	ALBERT P. BLOSCH	(b)(6)	USAF
Lt. Col.	CECIL M. CLARK		USAF
Major	JOHN GARGUS		USAF
Major	HARRY L. PANNILL		USAF
Capt.	JOHN M. CONNAUGHTON		USAF
Capt.	*RONALD L. JONES		USAF
Capt.	*DAVID M. KENDER		USAF
Capt.	NORMAN C. MAZUREK		USAF
Capt.	WILLIAM D. STRIPLING		USAF
TSgt.	BILLY J. ELLISTON		USAF
TSgt.	*FAILUS POTTS		USAF
TSgt.	JIMMIE O. RIGGS		USAF
TSgt.	PAUL E. STIERWALT		USAF
SSgt.	*WILLIAM T. BROWN		USAF
SSgt.	DALLAS R. CRINER		USAF
SSgt.	MELVIN B. D. GIBSON		USAF

* Alternates

C-130 #2

GRADE	NAME	SSN	SERVICE
Major	IRL L. FRANKLIN	(b)(6)	USAF
Major	THOMAS L. MOSLEY		USAF
Capt	RANDAL D. CUSTARD		USAF
Capt	THOMAS K. ECKHART		USAF
Capt	WILLIAM A. GUENON JR.		USAF
Capt	JAMES F. MCKENZIE JR.		USAF
Capt	THOMAS L. STILES		USAF
MSgt.	LESLIE G. TOLMAN		USAF
TSgt.	WILLIAM A. KENNEDY		USAF
TSgt.	KENNETH C. LIGHTLE		USAF
TSgt.	JAMES M. SHEPARD		USAF
SSgt.	EARL D. PARKS		USAF
SSgt.	*ROBERT L. RENNER		USAF

* Alternate

SENSITIVE

5

Image 100: Top Secret list of personnel

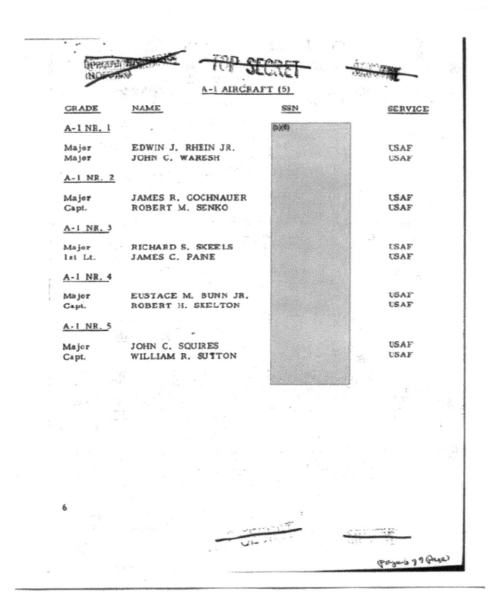

TOP SECRET

A-1 AIRCRAFT (5)

GRADE	NAME	SSN	SERVICE
A-1 NR. 1		(b)(6)	
Major	EDWIN J. RHEIN JR.		USAF
Major	JOHN C. WARESH		USAF
A-1 NR. 2			
Major	JAMES R. GOCHNAUER		USAF
Capt.	ROBERT M. SENKO		USAF
A-1 NR. 3			
Major	RICHARD S. SKEELS		USAF
1st Lt.	JAMES C. PANE		USAF
A-1 NR. 4			
Major	EUSTACE M. BUNN JR.		USAF
Capt.	ROBERT H. SKELTON		USAF
A-1 NR. 5			
Major	JOHN C. SQUIRES		USAF
Capt.	WILLIAM R. SUTTON		USAF

6

Image 101: Top Secret list of personnel

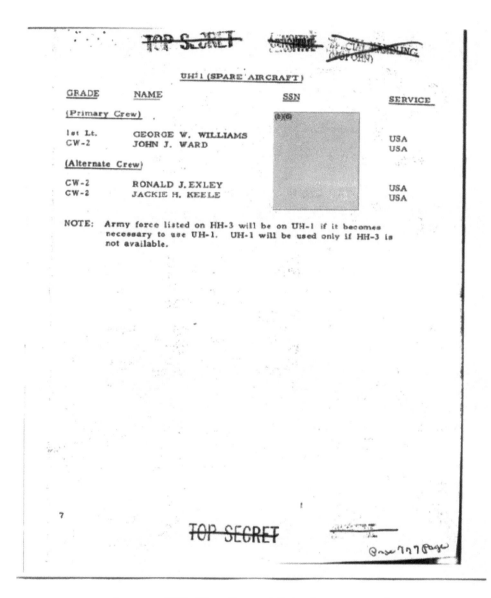

UH-1 (SPARE AIRCRAFT)

GRADE	NAME	SSN	SERVICE
(Primary Crew)		(b)(6)	
1st Lt.	GEORGE W. WILLIAMS		USA
CW-2	JOHN J. WARD		USA
(Alternate Crew)			
CW-2	RONALD J. EXLEY		USA
CW-2	JACKIE H. KEELE		USA

NOTE: Army force listed on HH-3 will be on UH-1 if it becomes necessary to use UH-1. UH-1 will be used only if HH-3 is not available.

7

TOP SECRET

Image 102: Top Secret list of personnel

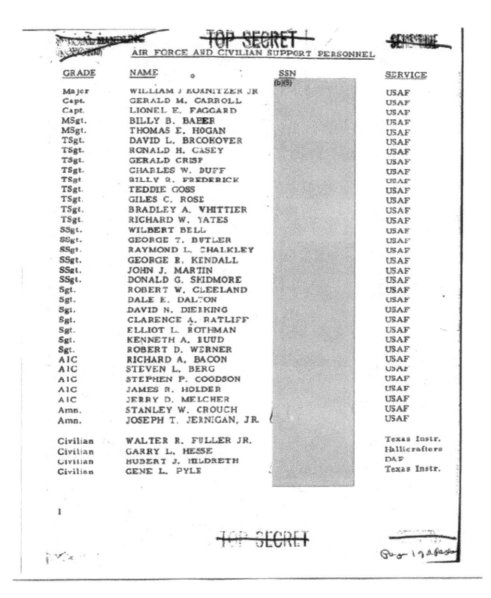

TOP SECRET

AIR FORCE AND CIVILIAN SUPPORT PERSONNEL

GRADE	NAME	SSN	SERVICE
Major	WILLIAM J KOXNITZER JR	(b)(6)	USAF
Capt.	GERALD M. CARROLL		USAF
Capt.	LIONEL E. FAGGARD		USAF
MSgt.	BILLY B. BABER		USAF
MSgt.	THOMAS E. HOGAN		USAF
TSgt.	DAVID L. BROOKOVER		USAF
TSgt.	RONALD H. CASEY		USAF
TSgt.	GERALD CRISP		USAF
TSgt.	CHARLES W. DUFF		USAF
TSgt	BILLY R. FREDERICK		USAF
TSgt.	TEDDIE GOSS		USAF
TSgt.	GILES C. ROSE		USAF
TSgt.	BRADLEY A. WHITTIER		USAF
TSgt.	RICHARD W. YATES		USAF
SSgt.	WILBERT BELL		USAF
SSgt.	GEORGE T. BUTLER		USAF
SSgt.	RAYMOND L. CHALKLEY		USAF
SSgt.	GEORGE R. KENDALL		USAF
SSgt.	JOHN J. MARTIN		USAF
SSgt.	DONALD G. SKIDMORE		USAF
Sgt.	ROBERT W. CLEELAND		USAF
Sgt.	DALE E. DALTON		USAF
Sgt.	DAVID N. DIERKING		USAF
Sgt.	CLARENCE A. RATLIFF		USAF
Sgt.	ELLIOT L. ROTHMAN		USAF
Sgt.	KENNETH A. BUUD		USAF
Sgt.	ROBERT D. WERNER		USAF
AIC	RICHARD A. BACON		USAF
AIC	STEVEN L. BERG		USAF
AIC	STEPHEN P. GOODSON		USAF
AIC	JAMES R. HOLDER		USAF
AIC	JERRY D. MELCHER		USAF
Amn.	STANLEY W. CROUCH		USAF
Amn.	JOSEPH T. JERNIGAN, JR.		USAF
Civilian	WALTER R. FULLER JR.		Texas Instr.
Civilian	GARRY L. HESSE		Hallicrafters
Civilian	HUBERT J. HILDRETH		DAP
Civilian	GENE L. PYLE		Texas Instr.

1

TOP SECRET

Image 103: Top Secret list of personnel

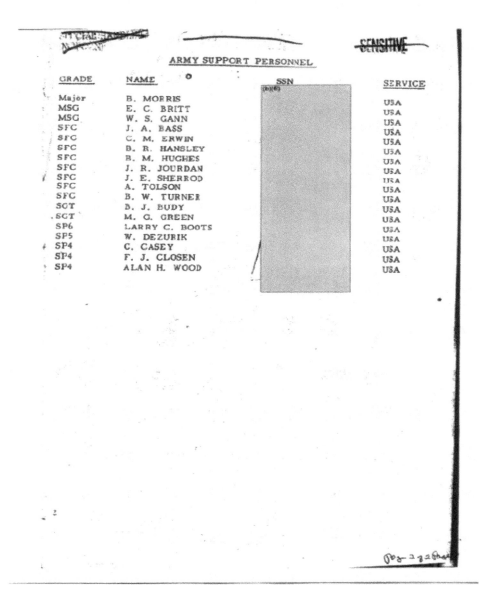

ARMY SUPPORT PERSONNEL

GRADE	NAME	SSN	SERVICE
Major	B. MORRIS		USA
MSG	E. C. BRITT		USA
MSG	W. S. GANN		USA
SFC	J. A. BASS		USA
SFC	C. M. ERWIN		USA
SFC	B. R. HANSLEY		USA
SFC	B. M. HUGHES		USA
SFC	J. R. JOURDAN		USA
SFC	J. E. SHERROD		USA
SFC	A. TOLSON		USA
SFC	B. W. TURNER		USA
SGT	B. J. BUDY		USA
SGT	M. G. GREEN		USA
SP6	LARRY C. BOOTS		USA
SP5	W. DEZURIK		USA
SP4	C. CASEY		USA
SP4	F. J. CLOSEN		USA
SP4	ALAN H. WOOD		USA

Image 104: Top Secret list of personnel

BIBLIOGRAPHY

Gargus, John, Col USAF, ret. *The Son Tay Raid: American POWs in Vietnam Were Not Forgotten*. College Station: Texas A&M University Press, 2010

Schemmer, Benjamin F. *The Raid*. New York: Harper & Row, 1976 (Updated 1986)

Waldron, Thomas R., LtCol USAF, ret. *I Flew With Heroes*. Lexington KY, 2019

Guenon, William A., Jr., Maj USAF, ret. *Secret and Dangerous: Night of the son Tay POW Raid*. East Lowell MA: King Printing Company, Inc., 2002

Harris, Carlyle S. "Smitty", Col USAF, ret. *Tap Code*. Grand Rapids MI: Zondervan, 2019

McRaven, William H., Adm USN, ret. *SPEC OPS: Case Studies in Special Operations Warfare: Theory and Practice*. New York: Ballentine Books, 1995

Nasmyth, Spike. *2,355 Days: A POW Story.* New York: Crown Publishers, Inc., 1991

Cordier, Ken, & Snidow, Chris. *Guardian Eagle: A Fighter Pilot's Tale.* Middletown DE, 2018

Rutledge, Howard and Phyllis. *In the Presence of Mine Enemies.* Grand Rapids: Baker Publishing, 1973

David, Heather. *Operation: Rescue.* New York: Pinnacle Books, 1971

Holy Bible, New International Version. Biblica, 2011.

1972, January 26. Youngest Man on POW Raid Attending MJC. *Moberly Monitor-Index*, p. 12. Retrieved from www.newspapers.com

IMAGE SOURCES

Cover photos of Blueboy, Greenleaf, Redwine are Joint Contingency Task Group photos provided by LtCol Sydnor, renovated by John Gargus.

1	Model of the Son Tay POW camp,	DOD
2	The Minigun	Public Domain
3	.30 Caliber Machine Gun	Public Domain
4	BGen Donald Blackburn	Public Domain
5	Duke Field and Range C-2	Google Earth, renovated by the author.
6	The Mockup, with Maj Macomber and chains	USAF photo
7	The Mockup, broad view (top) and soldiers (bottom).	USAF photo
8	The Mockup, Lupyak, Wingrove, Macomber, Paine	USAF photo
9	The Mockup, Kemmer, Lawhon	USAF photo
10	Reconnaissance photo of Range C-2	Provided by J Gargus
11	Night time training at the Mockup	USAF photo

12	CAR-15 with Sight	Dr. E. Burress, O. Lincoln, A. Kim. Photo by Colin Blount.
13	ArmaLite Singlepoint Sight	https://www.ar15.com/forums/ar-15/Single_Point_sight_article__ArmaLite_AR_18_/123-624446/?page=1&anc=bottom#bottom
14	Master Sgt Moore with CAR-15 with Sight	USAF photo
14A	Record of Events (Log)	USArmy Joint Contingency Task Group (Joint Chiefs of Staff)
15	Col Bull Simons	Public Domain
16	The Minigun	Public Domain
17	DoD/JCS After Action Report	Public Domain
18	Raiders at Pope AFB	Public Domain
19	Raiders at Pope AFB	Provided by George G. Petrie, son of Raider George W. Petrie
20	Raiders at Pope AFB	Provided by George G. Petrie, son of Raider George W. Petrie
21	Raiders at Pope AFB	Provided by George G. Petrie, son of Raider George W. Petrie
22	Raiders at Pope AFB	Provided by George G. Petrie, son of Raider George W. Petrie
23	Awards at Ft Bragg	Provided by John Gargus
24	Awards at Ft Bragg	Provided by John Gargus
25	Awards ceremony bulletin	Provided by Gary Perkowski
26	Awards ceremony bulletin	Provided by Gary Perkowski
27	Awards ceremony bulletin	Provided by Gary Perkowski
28	Awards ceremony bulletin	Provided by Gary Perkowski

29	Awards ceremony bulletin	Provided by Gary Perkowski
30	Hana	Photo by Dan Turner
31	Geographical overview of Southeast Asia	Created by Cliff Westbrook using Google Earth
32	Takhli RTAFB	Google Earth
33	Udorn RTAFB	DisabledVeteransThailand.wordpress.com
34	Summary of the Adm McRaven's book Spec Ops	Created by Cliff Westbrook
35	President Nixon memo	From Bill Guenon's book Secret and Dangerous
36	Oval Office meeting	USAF photo
37	Congressional Resolutions	Image of excerpts created by Cliff Westbrook
38	Reunion in 1973	Photos provided by Ross Perot's personal staff
39	Reunion in 1973	Photos provided by Ross Perot's personal staff
40	San Francisco Examiner front page	Photo provided by Tom Waldron
41	Duke Field photo location of Blueboy	Created by Cliff Westbrook using Google Earth
42	Blueboy	JCTG photos provided by LtCol Sydnor, renovated by J Gargus.
43	Blueboy in HH-3	USAF photo
44	Capt Dick Meadows	USAF photo
45	CSM Pat St.Clair and Apple 1	CSM Pat St.Clair photo
46	An HH-3	USAF photo by Ken LaRock

47	Painting of Blueboy	"Surprise at Son Tay" by Ronald Wong
48	Painting of Blueboy	"The Raid, Blueboy Element" by Michael Nikiporenko
49	Duke Field photo location of Greenleaf	Created by Cliff Westbrook using Google Earth
50	Greenleaf	JCTG photos provided by LtCol Sydnor, renovated by J Gargus.
51	Meadows Simons Sydnor	JCTG photos provided by LtCol Sydnor, renovated by J Gargus.
52	Duke Field photo location of Redwine	Created by Cliff Westbrook using Google Earth
53	Redwine	JCTG photos provided by LtCol Sydnor, renovated by J Gargus.
54	Grimes and Sydnor	JCTG photos provided by LtCol Sydnor, renovated by J Gargus.
55	Nixon and Raiders	Wally McNamee/CORBIS/ Corbis/Getty
56	Nixon and Raiders	www.nixonfoundation.org
57	List of POWs	Provided by Navy Capt Mike McGrath, NAM-POWs historian
58	POW signal at Son Tay POW camp	Created by Cliff Westbrook, USAF photo renovated by J Gargus.
59	Reconnaissance photo	USAF/National Archives

60	Reconnaissance photo	USAF/National Archives
61	Geographical overview of Son Tay POW camp	Created by Cliff Westbrook using Google Earth
62	Reconnaissance photo	Public Domain
63	Geographical overview of Son Tay POW camp	Created by Cliff Westbrook using Google Earth
64	Geographical overview of Son Tay POW camp	Created by Cliff Westbrook using Google Earth
65	Geographical overview of Son Tay POW camp	Westbrook/Google Earth/ JCTG/J Gargus
66	Geographical overview of Son Tay POW camp	Westbrook/Google Earth/Natl Museum of the USAF
67	Barbara w recent photos	Created by Cliff Westbrook, USAF/Gargus/vnafmamn.com
68	Barbara w recent photos	Created by Cliff Westbrook, USAF/Gargus/vnafmamn.com
69	Barbara w recent photos	Created by Cliff Westbrook, USAF/Gargus/vnafmamn.com
70	Cherry 1 Assault Formation at Aux Field #3	USAF photo adjusted by William Guenon
71	Aux Field #3 north end today	Created by Cliff Westbrook using Google Earth
72	Apple 1	USAF photo
73	A left window minigun	USAF photo
74	Helicopter crew members	USAF photo
75	Air refueling helicopters	USAF/National Archives
76	Cherry 1 in 2012	USAF photo
77	KITD patch	William Guenon photo
78	Cherry 1 crew	Provided by J Gargus
79	Cherry 1 Assault Formation	Provided by J Gargus

80	Cherry 2 Strike Formation	Provided by J Gargus
81	Cherry 2 crew	Provided by J Gargus
82	A-1E White Phosphorus bomb	Public Domain
83	A-1E with external fuel tanks	Public Domain
84	Korat RTAFB F-105G	National Museum of the USAF
85	Lime 2 on display at Cannon AFB	USAF photo
86	Lime 2 plaque at Cannon AFB	USAF photo
87	EC-121 College Eye	National Museum of the USAF
88	Monkey Mountain at Da Nang Air Base	Created by Cliff Westbrook using Public Domain photo
89	BGen Manor	Public Domain
90	Barbara plus one	USAF photo
91	Ft Bragg statues of Bull Simons and Dick Meadows	Public Domain
92	Son Tay Raider patch	Public Domain

 TERRY BUCKLER WAS THE youngest Son Tay Raider, a "buck sergeant" and Green Beret at twenty years old. Among his peers and his leaders, he proved himself every step along the way by his character—and by topping off Basic Training with a rare perfect score on the Army's Physical Fitness Test. In the 1970s, Ross Perot helped him secure a job at EDS, launching his business career. Years later, Buckler founded his own document imaging business, Delta Systems, based in Kansas City. Buckler is President of the Colonel Arthur D. "Bull" Simons Chapter XXIX of the Special Forces Association.

"Buck" has been instrumental in the Son Tay Raid Association which coordinates the Raiders to offer students of military history the perspectives of the Raiders themselves. A highlight was his leadership arranging a grand reunion in 2014 that included a televised ceremony at Kansas Speedway honoring the Raid and the Raiders at the start of the NASCAR race seen by millions. Contact him to speak at your event. Email: tbuckler@delta-kc.com

 CLIFF WESTBROOK, A 1988 graduate of the US Air Force Academy and a pilot of the B-1 bomber, is the son of Clyde "Neal" Westbrook, the Aircraft Commander of *Lime 2* during the Son Tay Raid. An active member of the Son Tay Raid Association, Cliff has interviewed numerous Raiders and helped gather the historical behind-the-scenes facts. He partners with veterans to tell their stories for the benefit of future generations. Contact him to help capture your veteran's story. Email: cliffwestbrook88@gmail.com

INDEX

T

Taapken 120, 125, 179, 312
Takhli 11, 79, 113, 150, 235, 245, 246, 253, 255, 282, 286, 291
Tapley 120, 126, 167, 311
Tasker 127, 312
Thomas 4, 120, 126, 179, 312
Tolman 249, 315
Tolson 319
Turner, B.W. 319
Turner, Dan x, xiv, 4, 32, 60, 63, 119, 125, 141, 148, 184, 313

U

Udorn 87, 89, 90, 112, 113, 150, 153, 191, 230, 235, 237, 238, 239, 246, 248, 264, 266, 271, 273, 274, 276, 277, 278, 279, 281, 282, 283, 286

V

Valentine 120, 126, 179, 313
Vaughn 311
Vines 313

W

Waddell 209
Waldron 127, 228, 314, 321
Walther 119, 125, 179, 182, 312
Ward 127, 317
Waresh 128, 255, 266, 316
Waters 128
Wellington 127, 228, 314
Werner 318
Westbrook 285

Printed in the USA
CPSIA information can be obtained
at www.ICGtesting.com
LVHW061510210224
772038LV00027B/171/J